The Heartbreak Diet

A story of family, fidelity, and starting over

By THORINA ROSE

CHRONICLE BOOKS
San Francisco

Library of Congress Cataloging-in-Publication
Data Available.

isbn 978-0-8118-6057-4

Manufactured in Canada.
Layout assistance : Janis Reed

10 9 8 7 6 5 4 3 2 1

Chronicle Books LLC
680 Second Street
San Francisco, California 94107
www.chroniclebooks.com

Dedicated to my two beautiful boys!

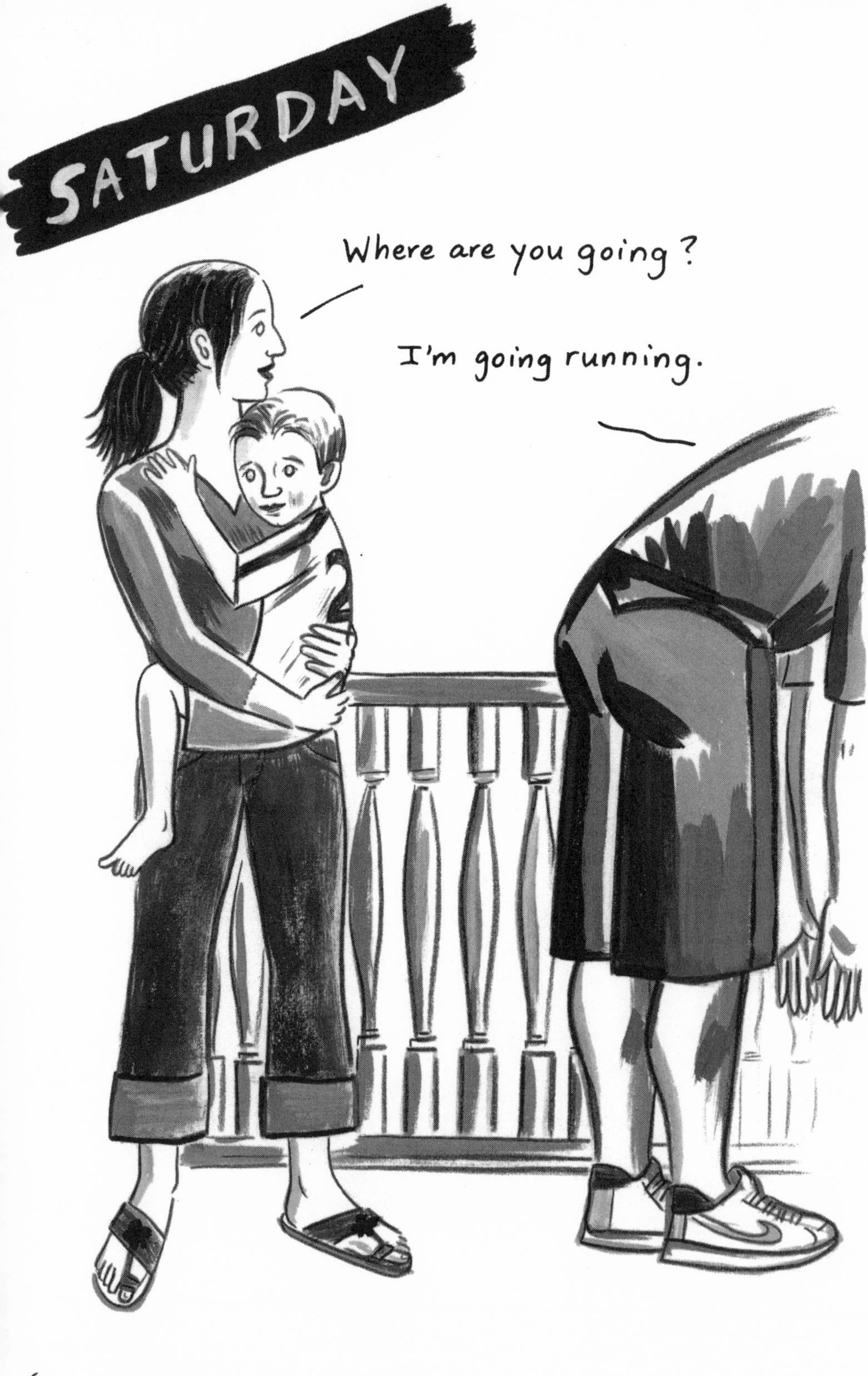
SATURDAY
Where are you going?
I'm going running.

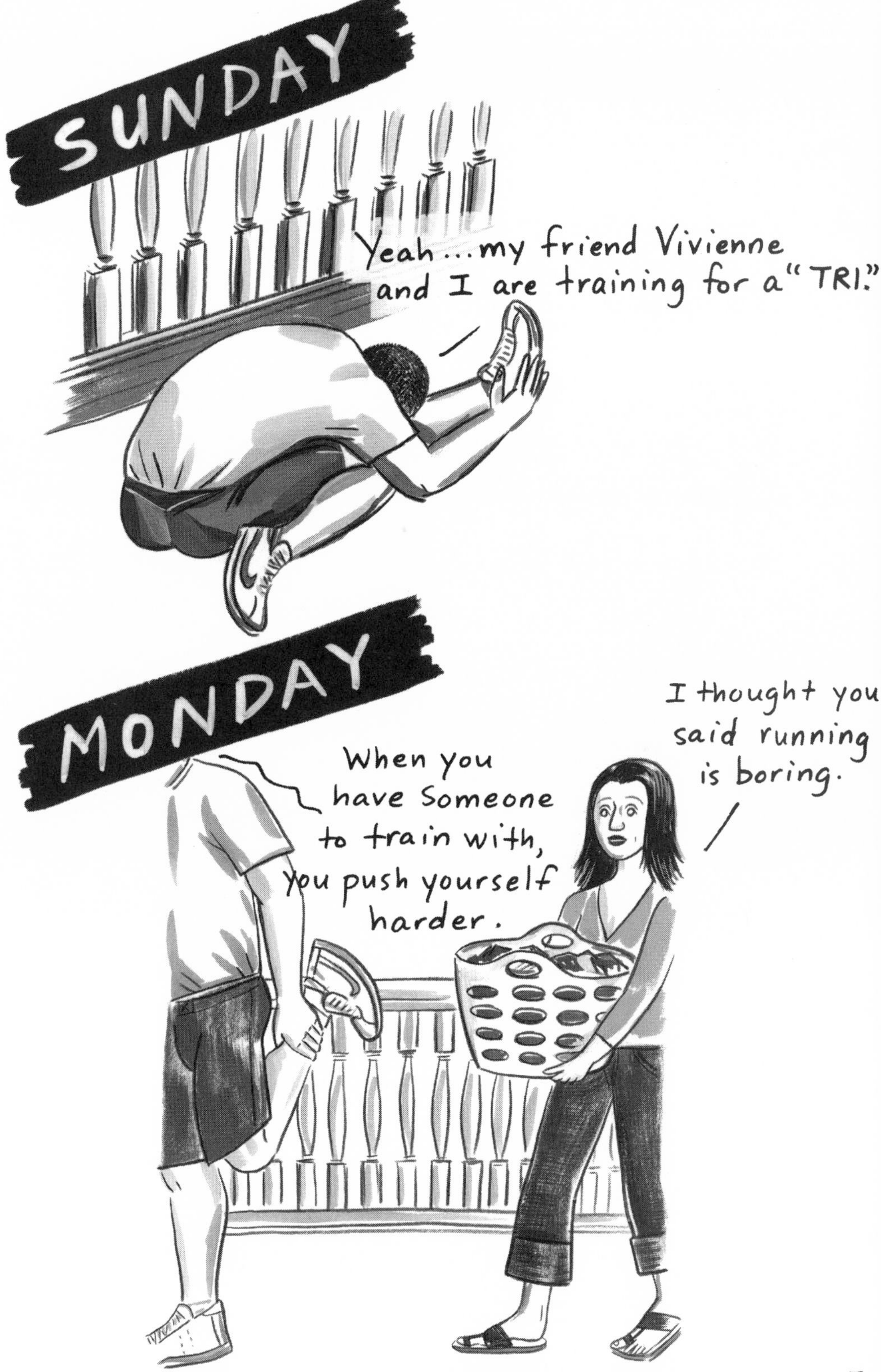
SUNDAY
Yeah...my friend Vivienne and I are training for a "TRI."
MONDAY
When you have Someone to train with, you push yourself harder.
I thought you said running is boring.

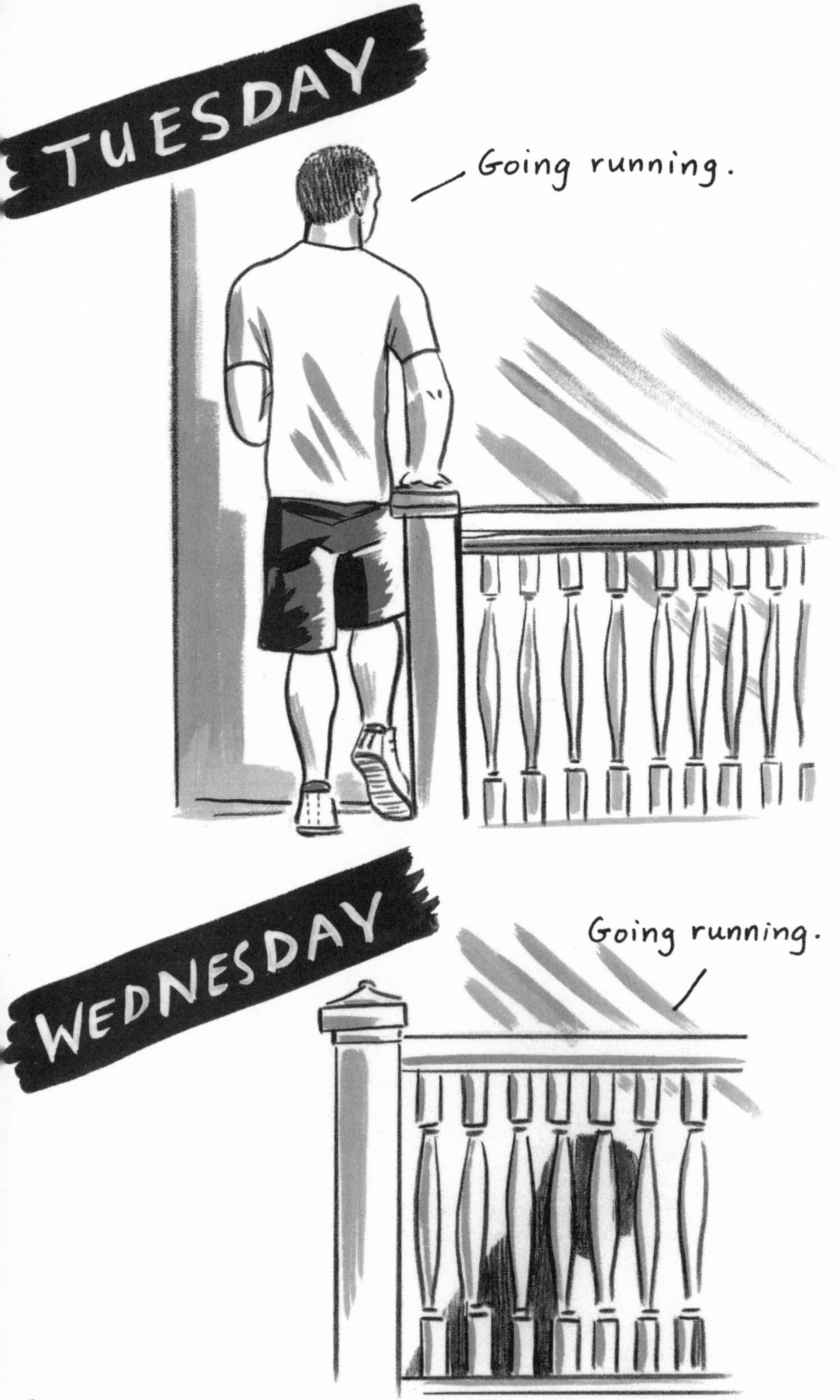
TUESDAY
Going running.
WEDNESDAY
Going running.

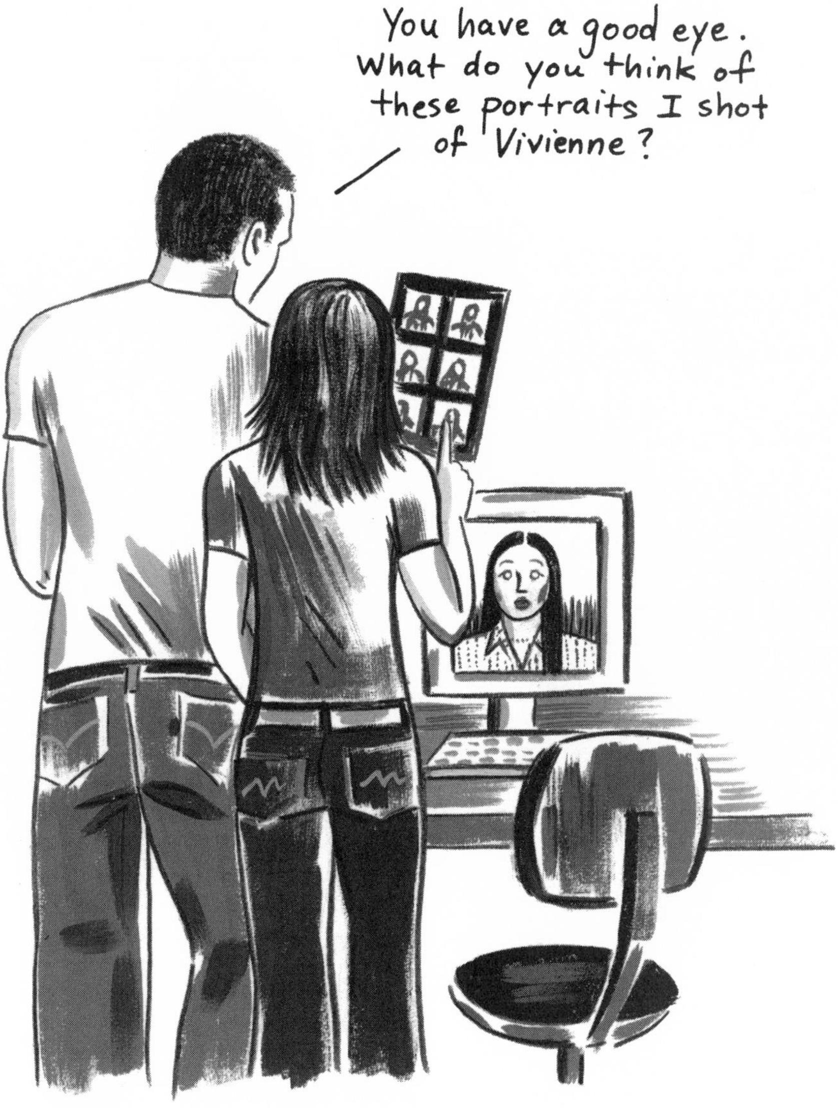
You have a good eye. What do you think of these portraits I shot of Vivienne?

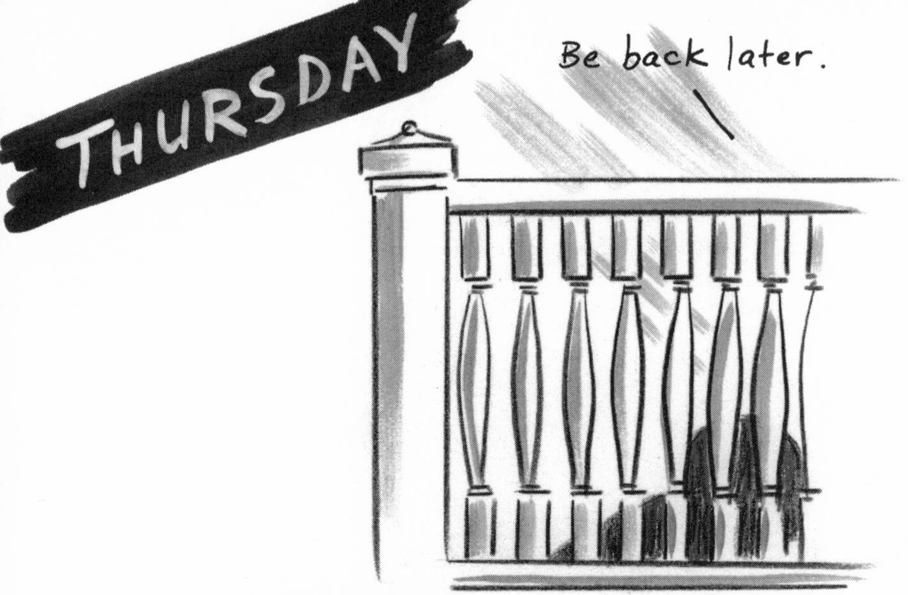
THURSDAY
Be back later.

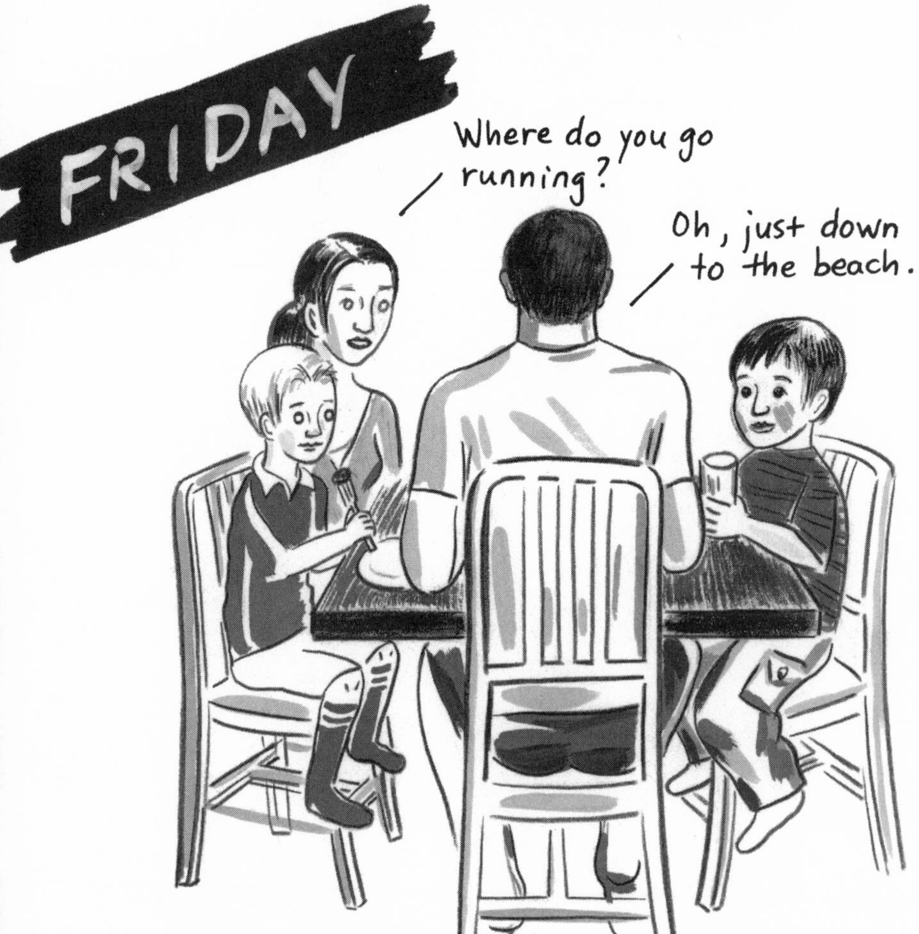
FRIDAY
Where do you go running?
Oh, just down to the beach.

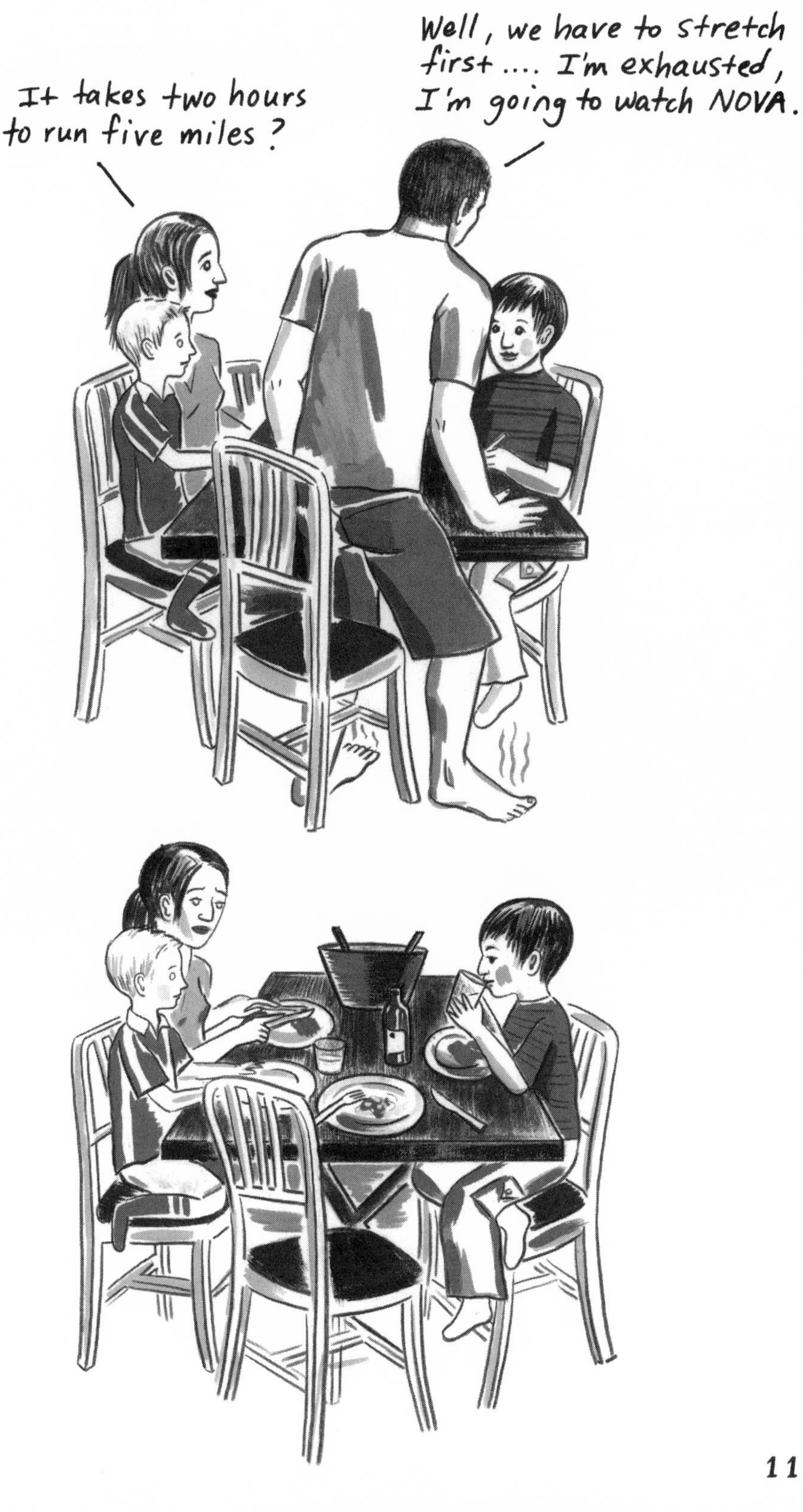
It takes two hours to run five miles?
Well, we have to stretch first.... I'm exhausted, I'm going to watch NOVA.

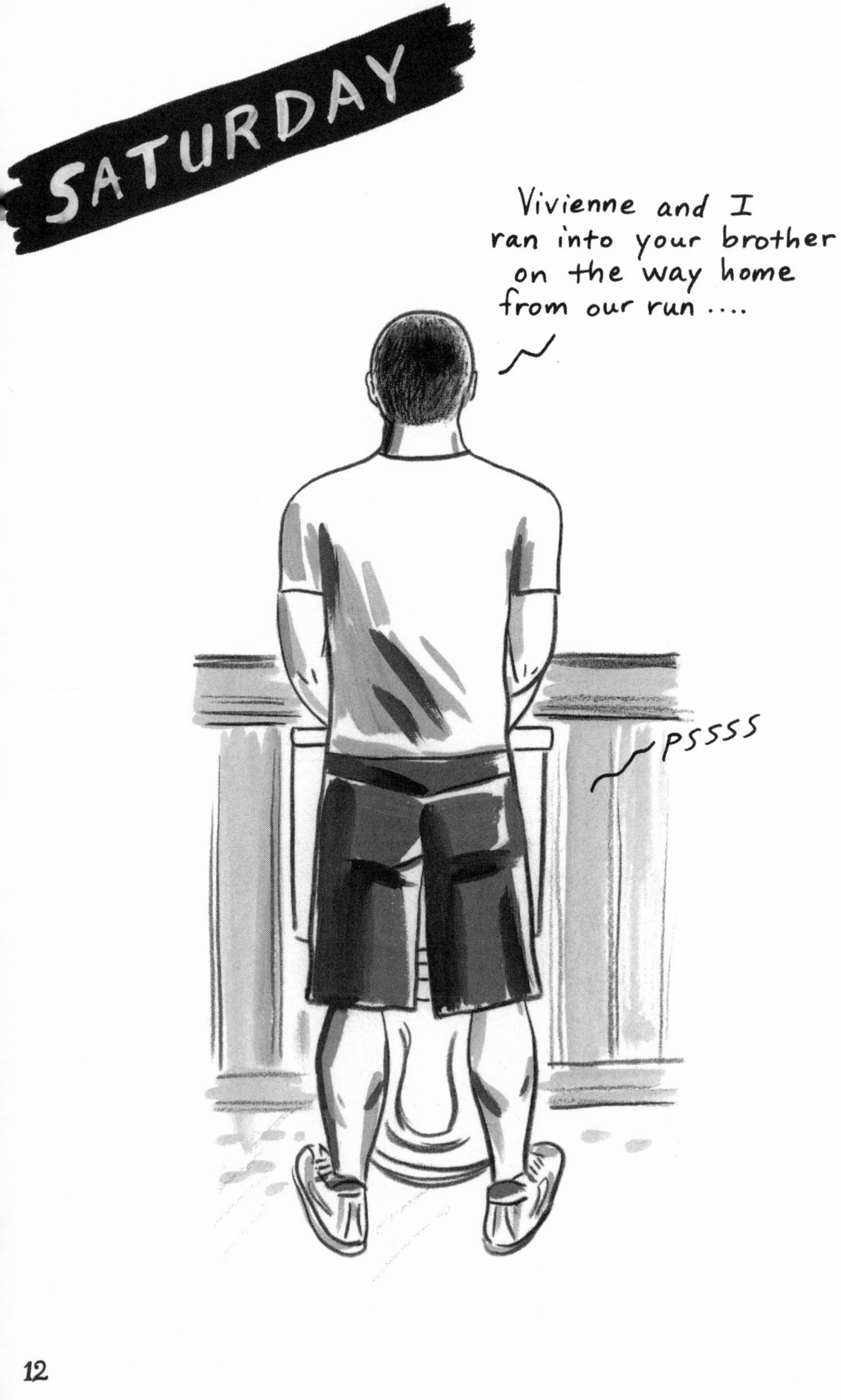
SATURDAY
Vivienne and I ran into your brother on the way home from our run....
PSSSS

A MOMENT OF DEUS EX MACHINA IF THERE EVER WAS...

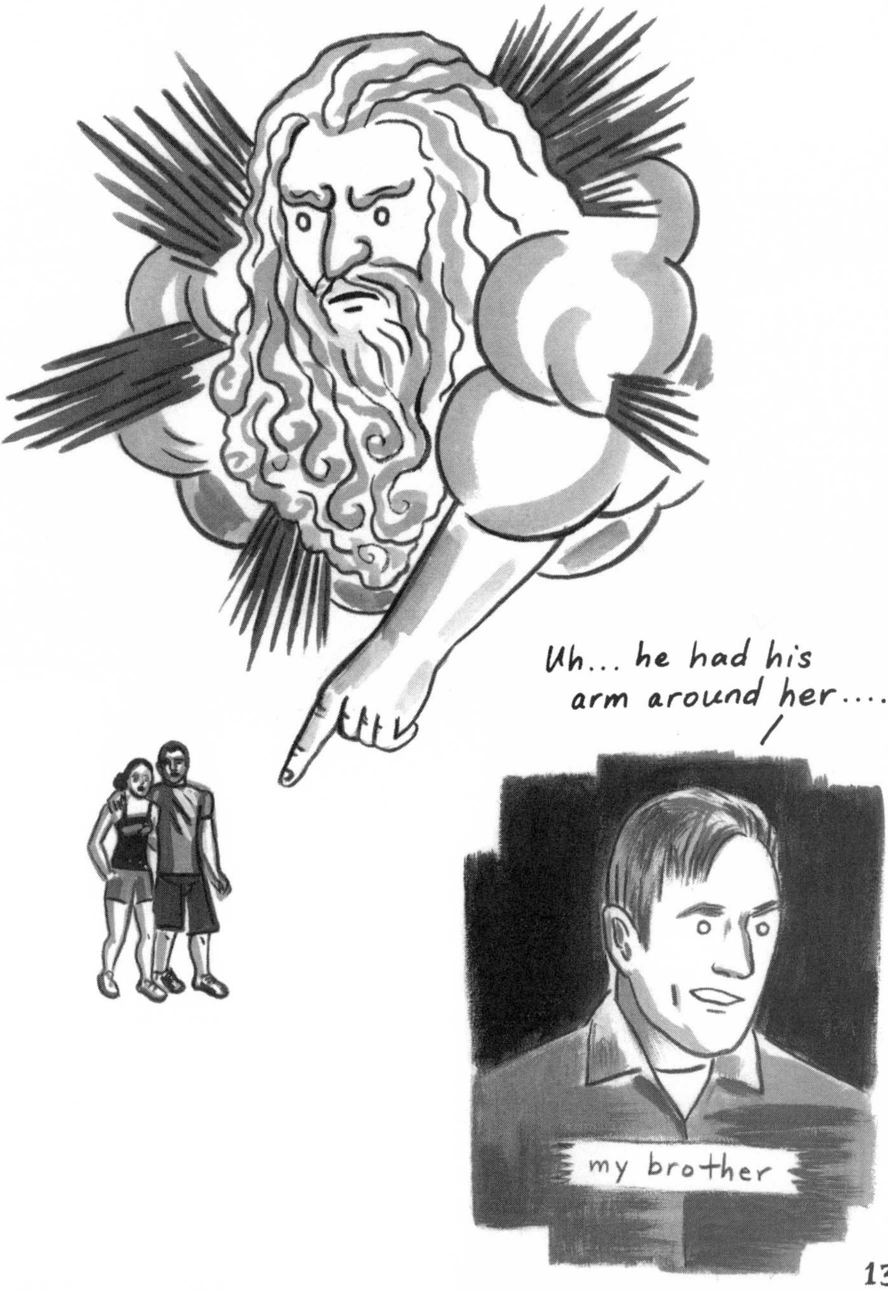
Uh... he had his arm around her....
my brother

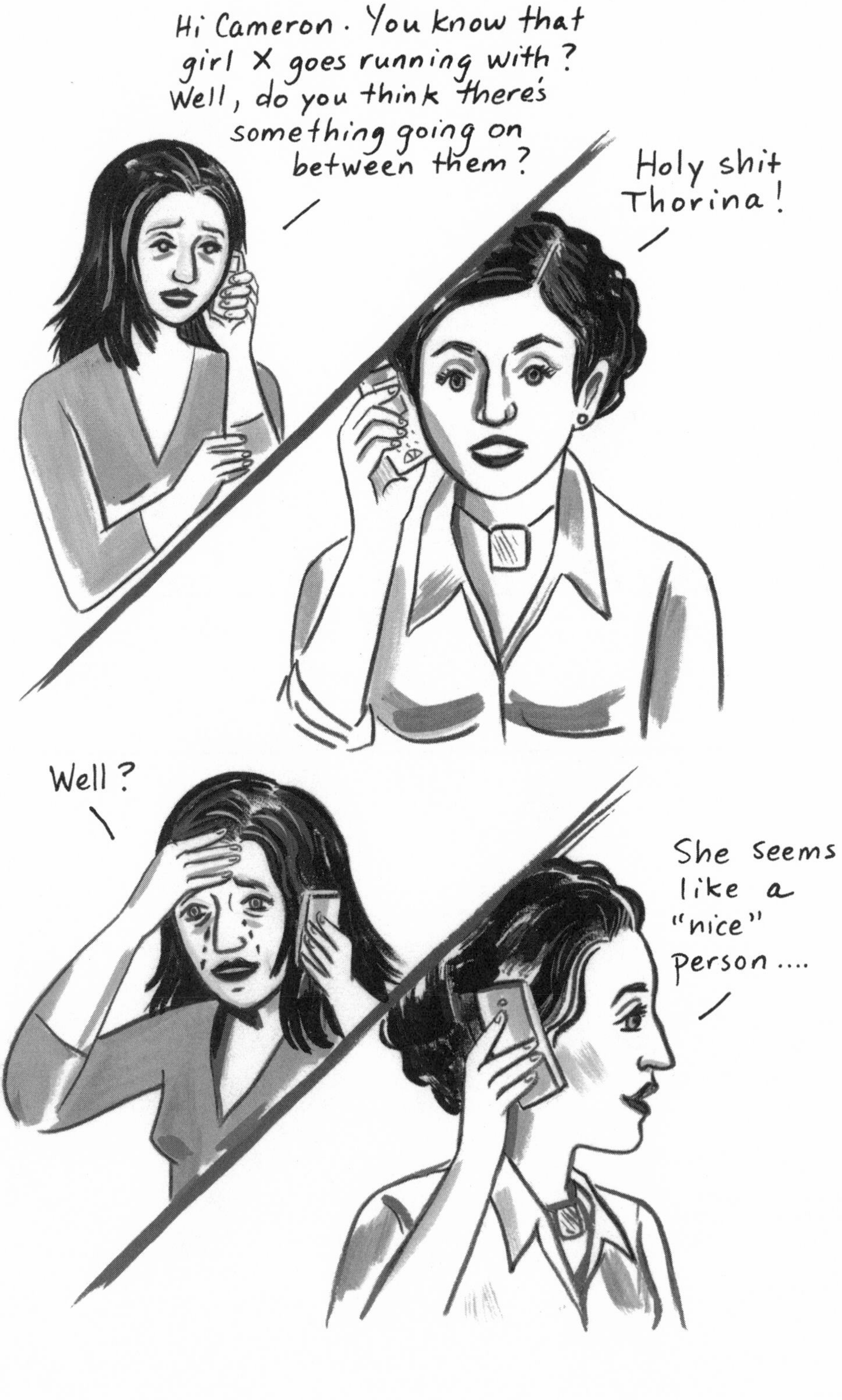

Hi Cameron. You know that girl X goes running with? Well, do you think there's something going on between them?
Holy shit Thorina!
Well?
She seems like a "nice" person....

I CONSIDER THE SPECTER of

Infidelity

A DARK and SCARY NIGHT

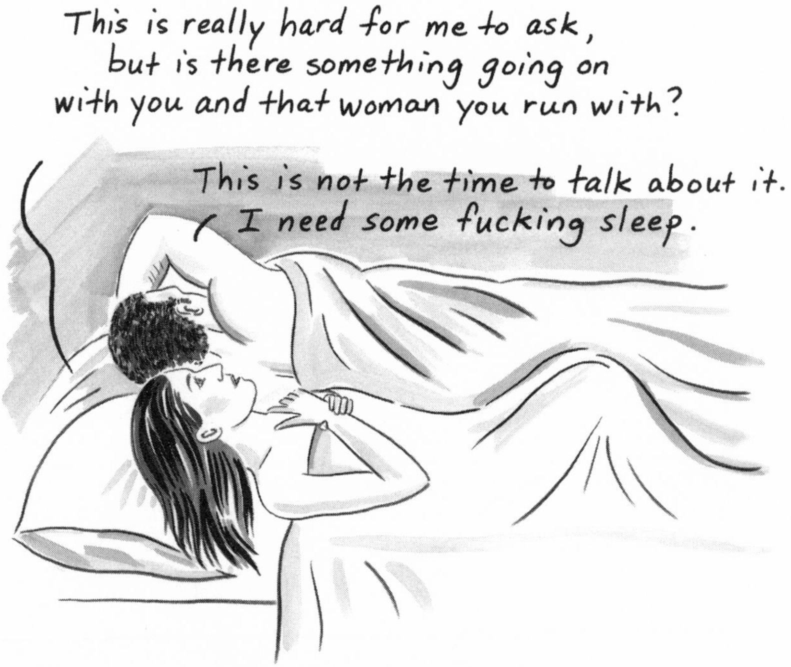

This is really hard for me to ask, but is there something going on with you and that woman you run with?
This is not the time to talk about it. I need some fucking sleep.

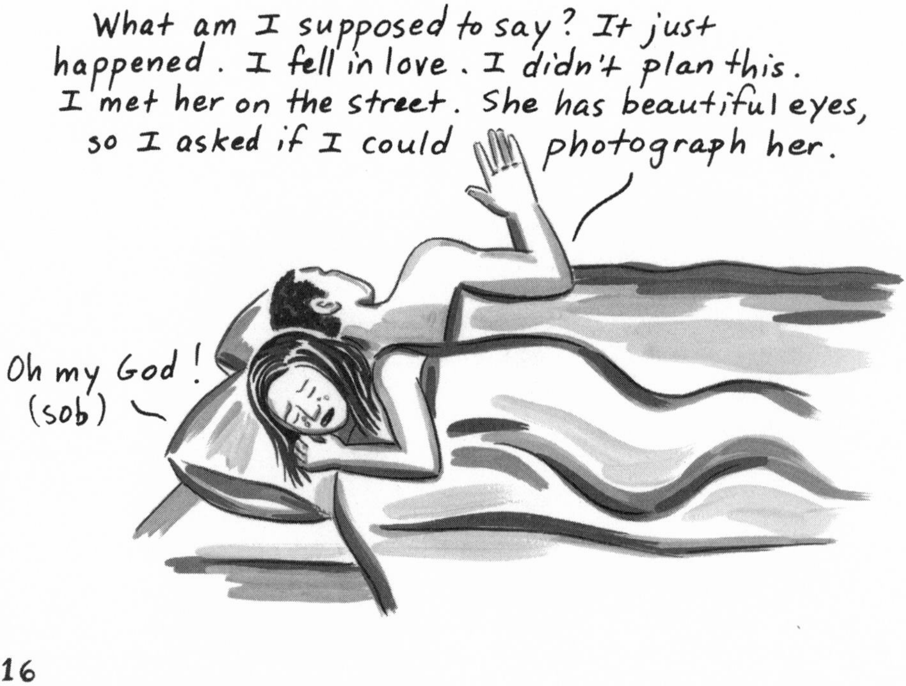

What am I supposed to say? It just happened. I fell in love. I didn't plan this. I met her on the street. She has beautiful eyes, so I asked if I could photograph her.
Oh my God! (sob)

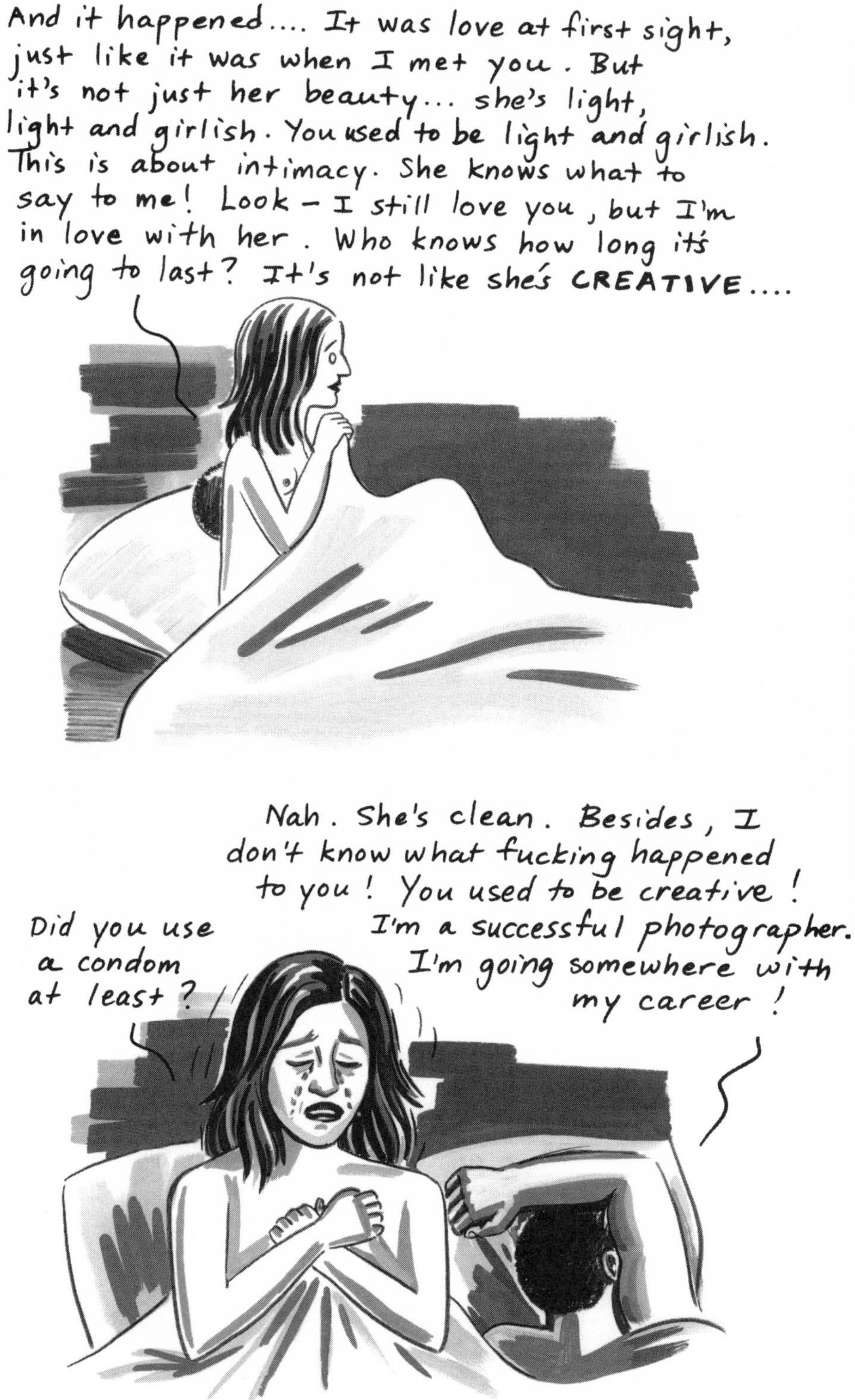
And it happened.... It was love at first sight, just like it was when I met you. But it's not just her beauty... she's light, light and girlish. You used to be light and girlish. This is about intimacy. She knows what to say to me! Look – I still love you, but I'm in love with her. Who knows how long it's going to last? It's not like she's CREATIVE....
Did you use a condom at least?
Nah. She's clean. Besides, I don't know what fucking happened to you! You used to be creative! I'm a successful photographer. I'm going somewhere with my career!

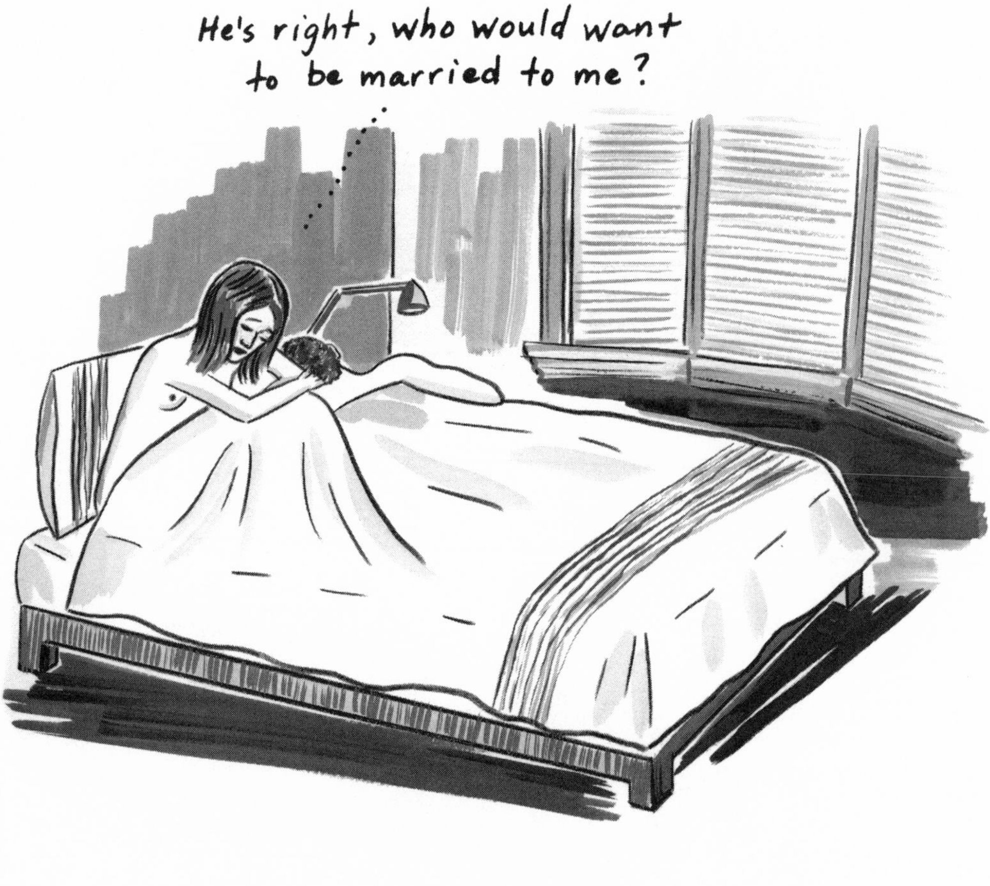
He's right, who would want to be married to me?

WORDS OF WISE WOMEN

"I have yet to hear a man ask
for advice on how to combine
marriage and a career."

GLORIA STEINEM

WHAT ARE MY CHOICES?

1. I can put up with him having a mistress.
2. I can ask him to leave.
3. I can fight to win him back.

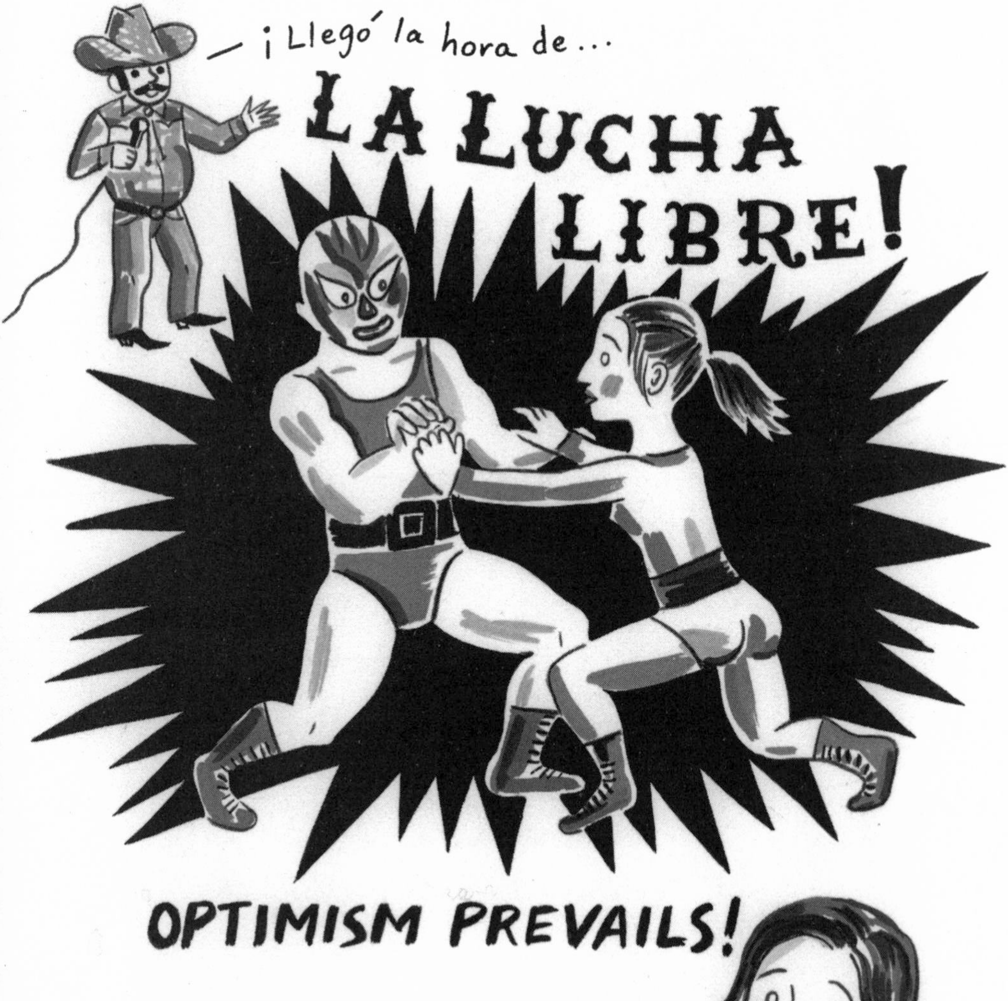
¡Llegó la hora de...
LA LUCHA LIBRE!

OPTIMISM PREVAILS!

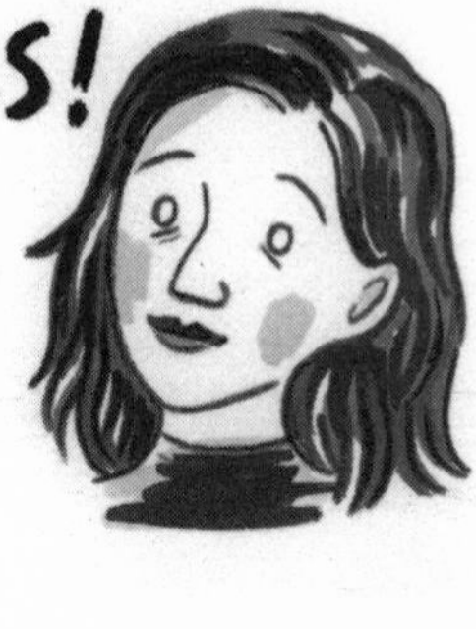

Conquering this obstacle .....

will strengthen our relationship.

I'LL SHOW HIM JUST HOW MUCH I LOVE HIM.

HE'LL REALIZE WHAT HE IS GIVING UP.

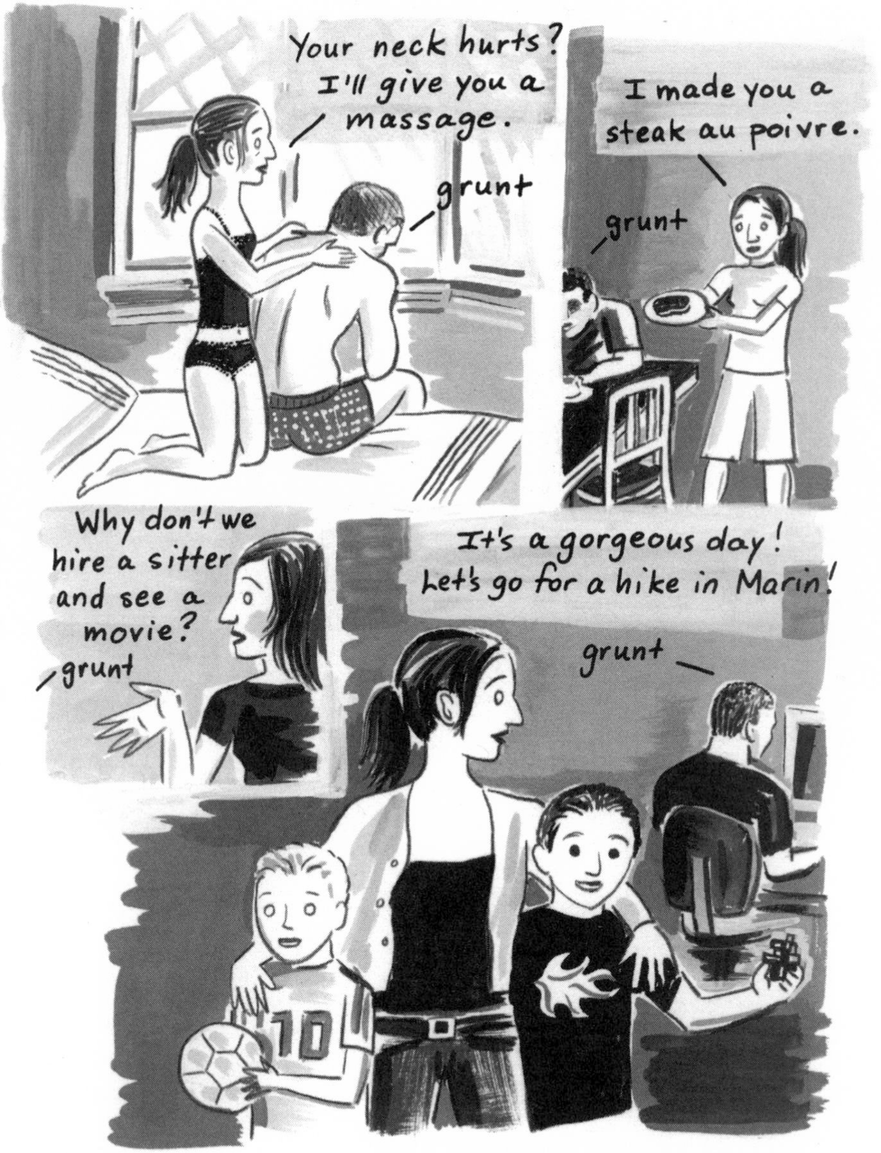
Your neck hurts? I'll give you a massage.
grunt
I made you a steak au poivre.
grunt
Why don't we hire a sitter and see a movie?
grunt
It's a gorgeous day! Let's go for a hike in Marin!
grunt
10

BUT SEEING HIM IN RUNNING GEAR SENDS ME INTO A PAROXYSM of ANXIETY.

Where are you going?
RUNNING?
With **her**?
Oh, she's out of town?
You swear you're going alone?
When are you coming back?
... I hate being a nag.
I want to trust him.
Is that his cell phone on the counter?
Hand has life of its own.

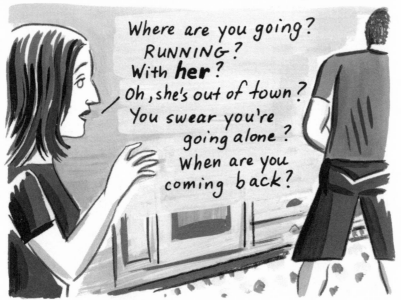

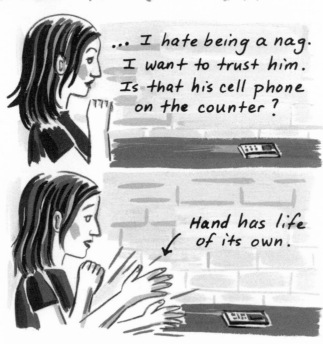

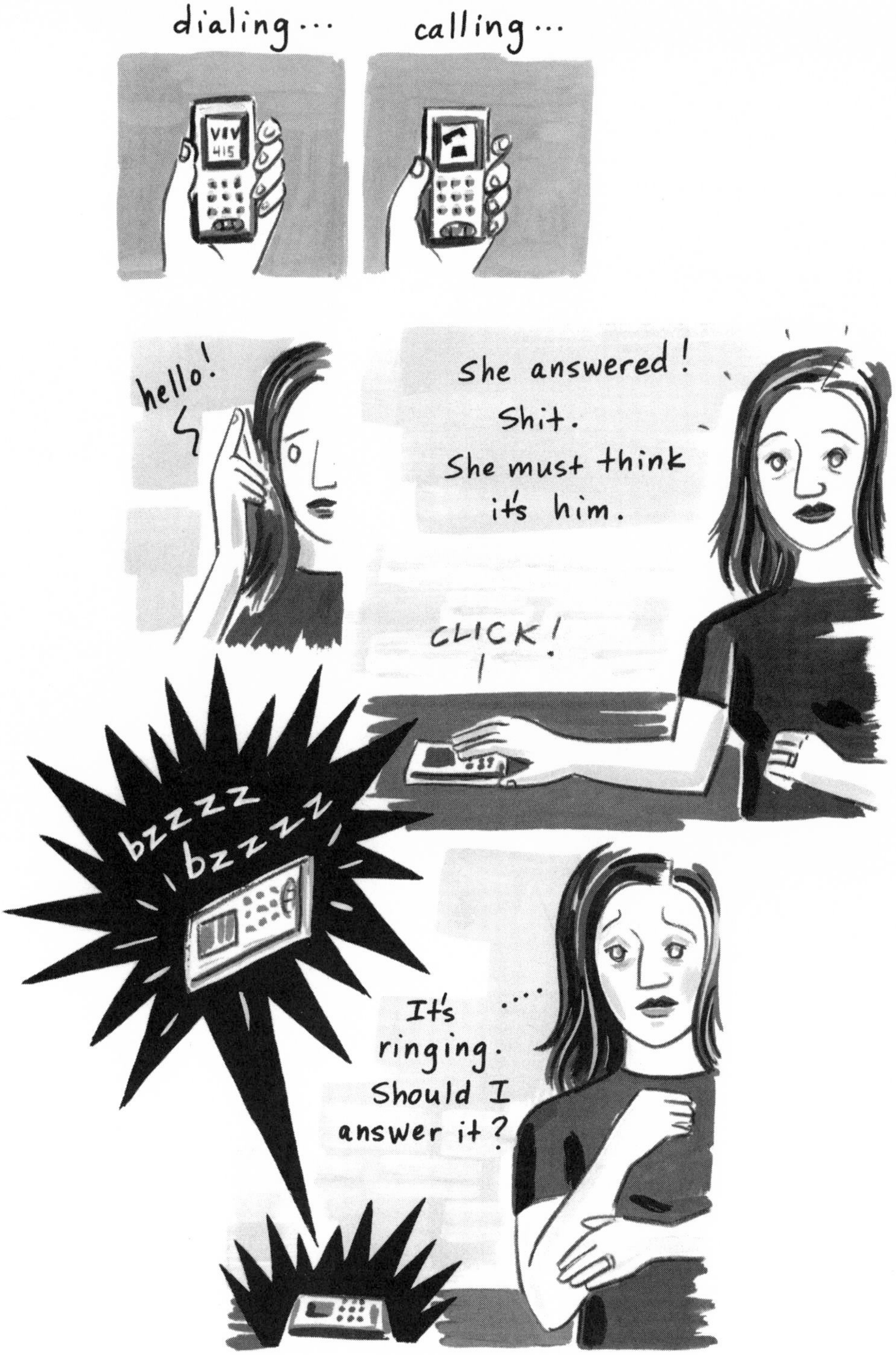
dialing...
calling...
hello!
She answered!
Shit.
She must think it's him.
CLICK!
bzzzz
bzzzz
It's ringing.
Should I answer it?
....

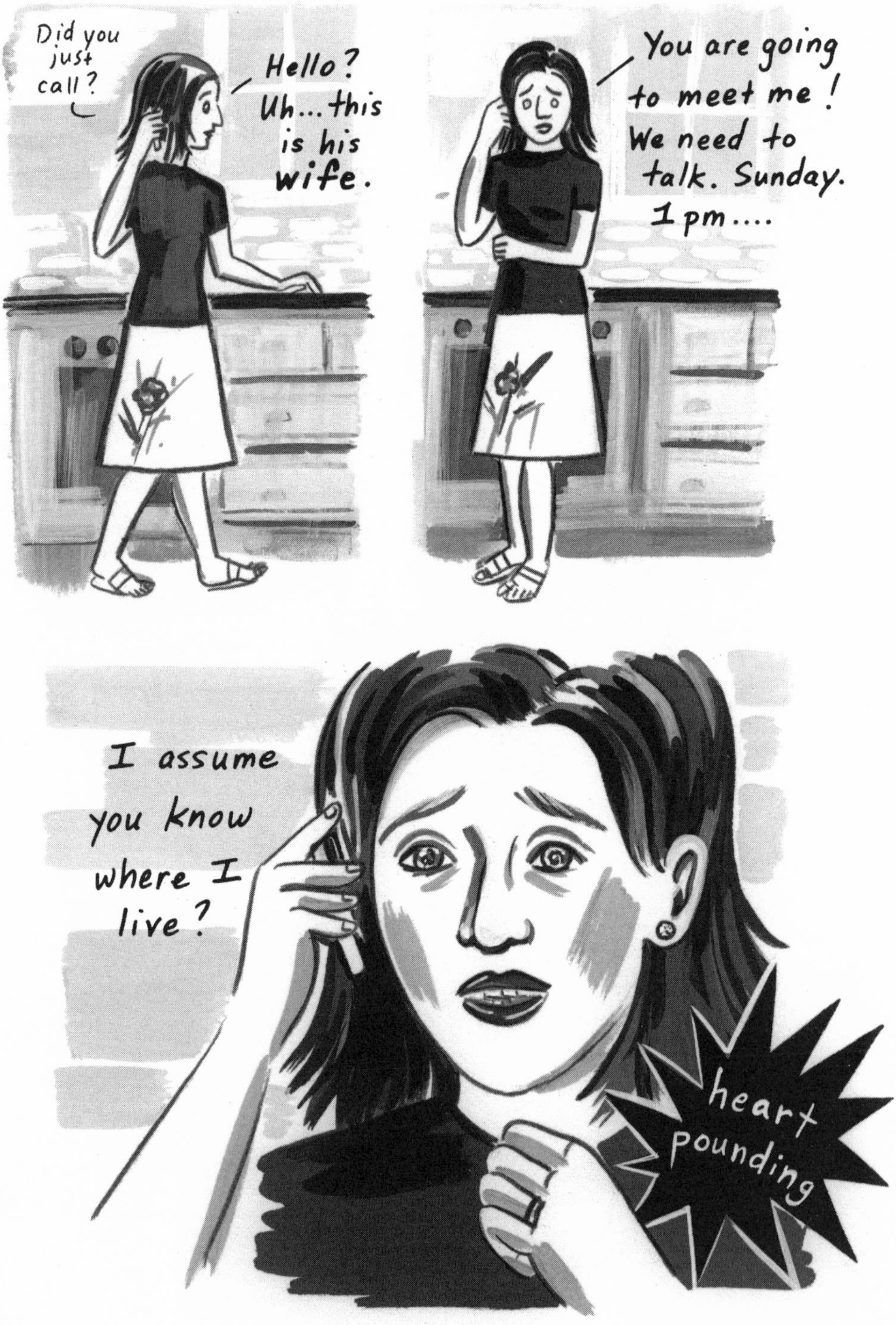
Did you just call?
Hello? Uh... this is his wife.
You are going to meet me! We need to talk. Sunday. 1 pm....
I assume you know where I live?
heart pounding

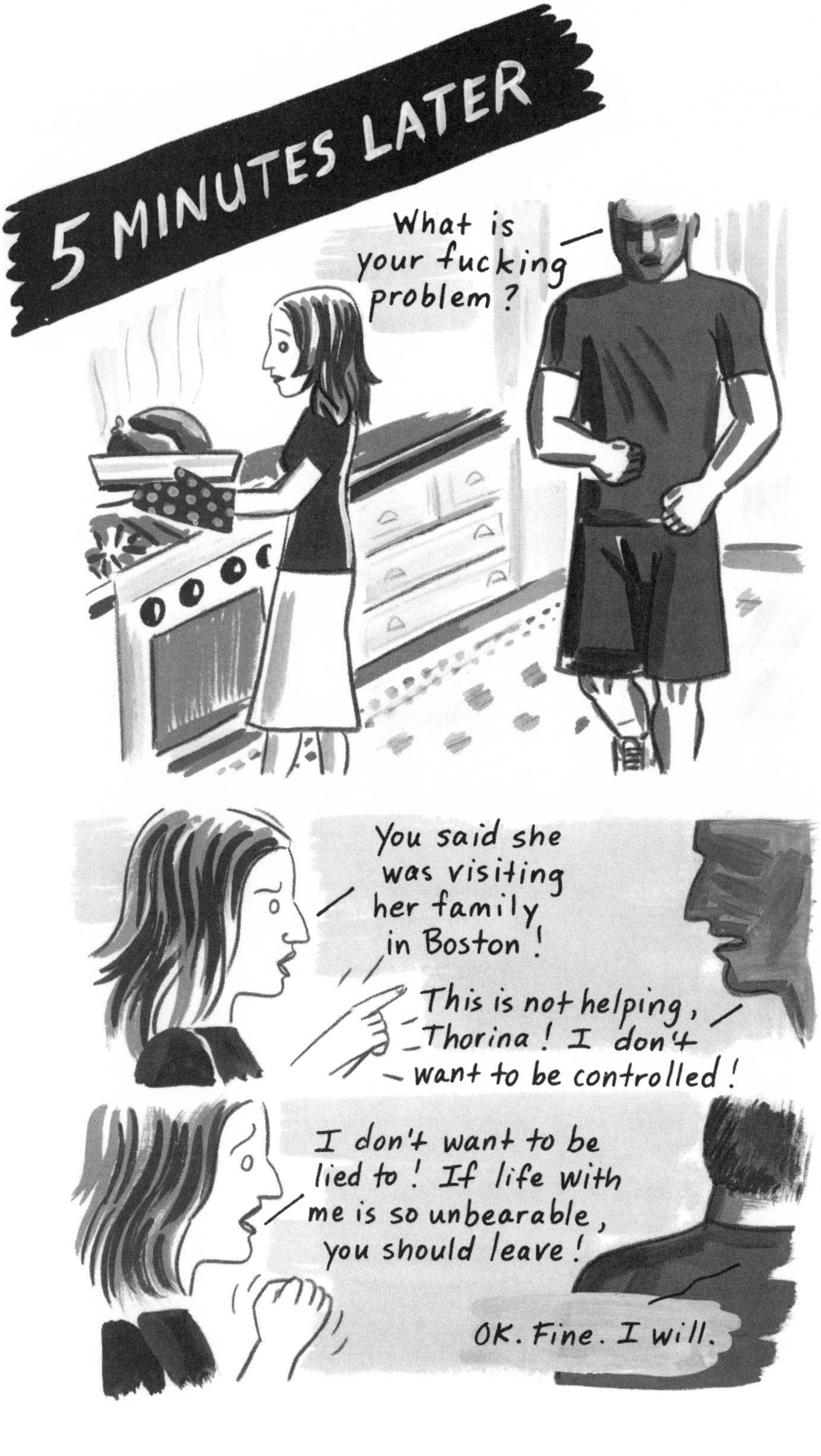
5 MINUTES LATER
What is your fucking problem?
You said she was visiting her family in Boston!
This is not helping, Thorina! I don't want to be controlled!
I don't want to be lied to! If life with me is so unbearable, you should leave!
OK. Fine. I will.

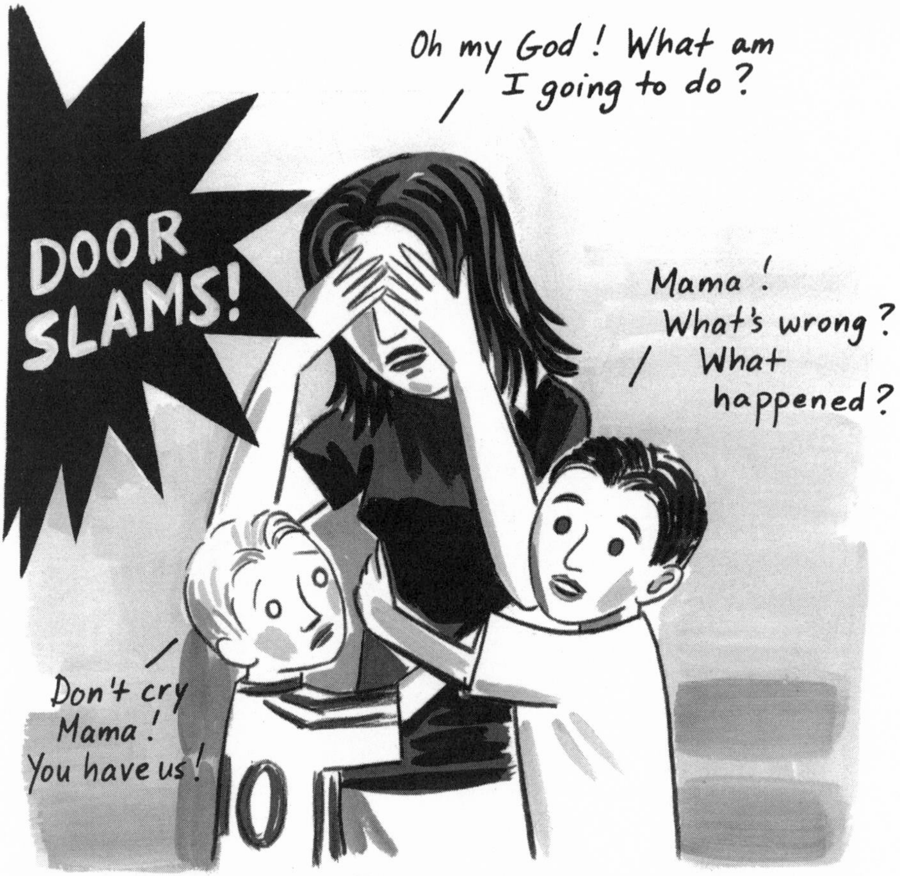
DOOR SLAMS!
Oh my God! What am I going to do?
Mama! What's wrong? What happened?
Don't cry Mama! You have us!

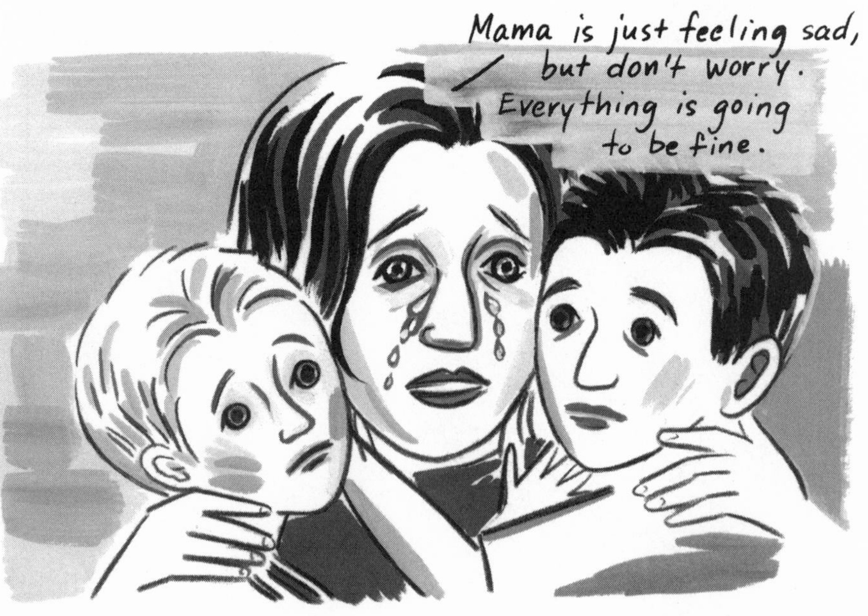
Mama is just feeling sad, but don't worry. Everything is going to be fine.

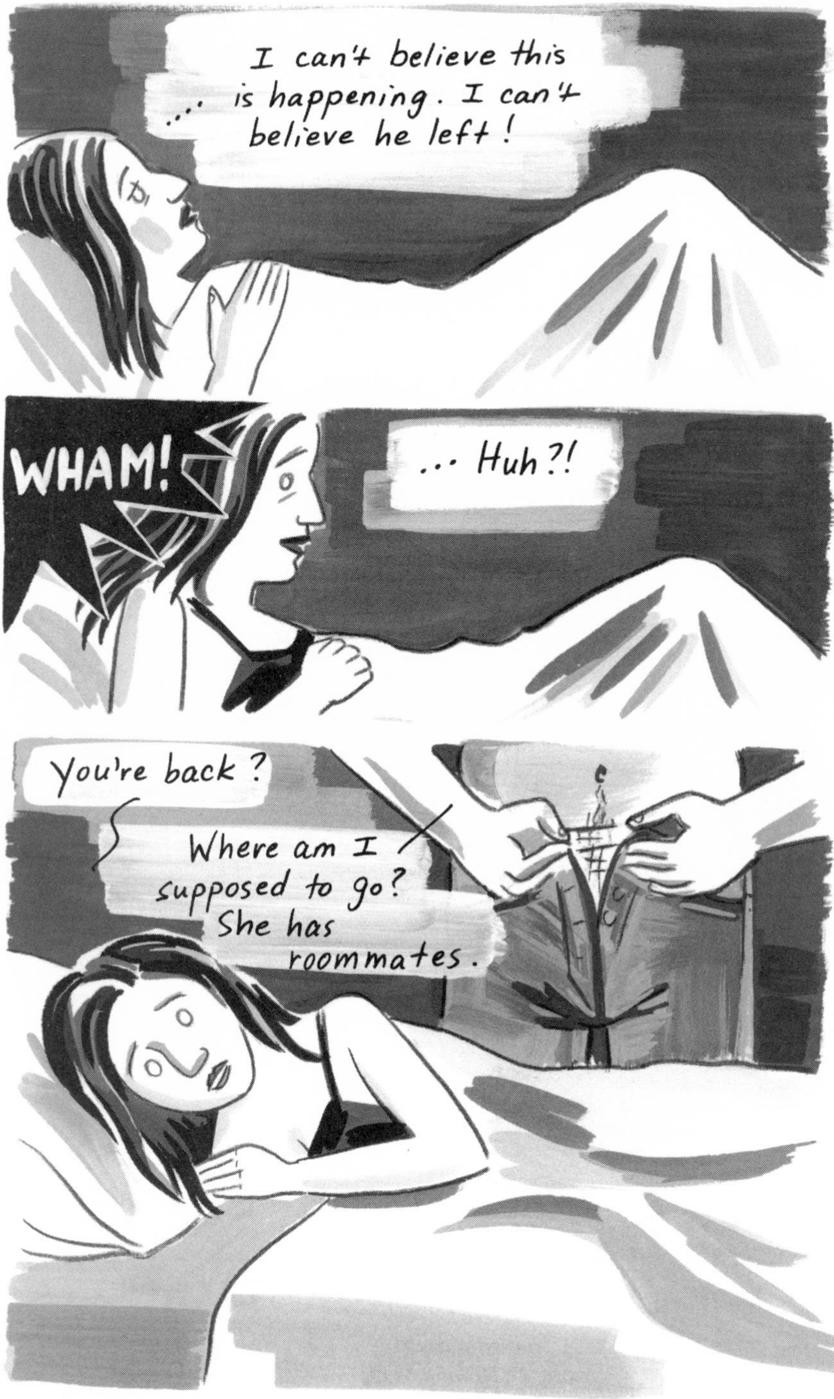
I can't believe this ... is happening. I can't believe he left!
WHAM!
... Huh?!
You're back?
Where am I supposed to go? She has roommates.

SUNDAY

SHE ARRIVES DUTIFULLY ON TIME.

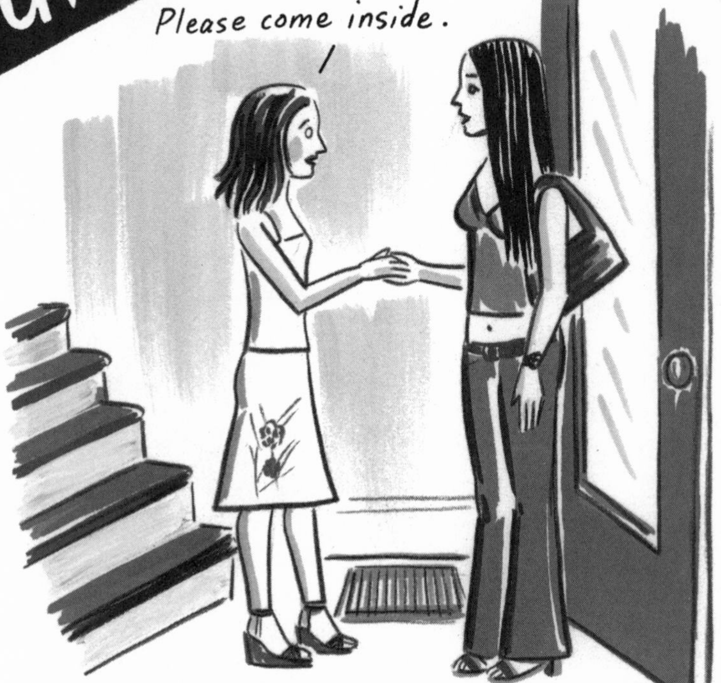
Please come inside.

I DECIDE TO BE IMPECCABLY POLITE AND PUT HER AT EASE...

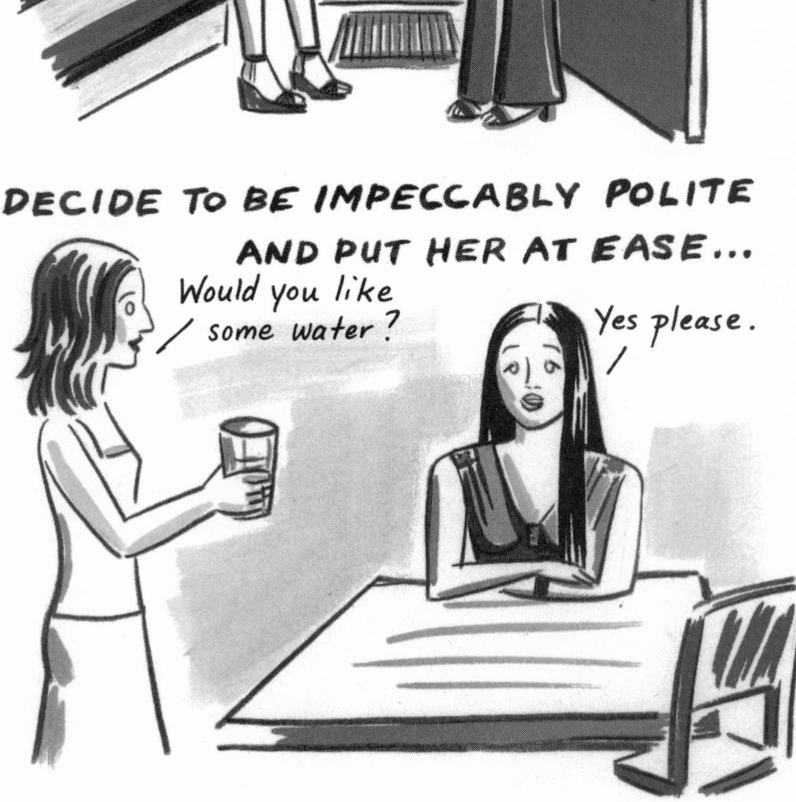
Would you like some water?
Yes please.

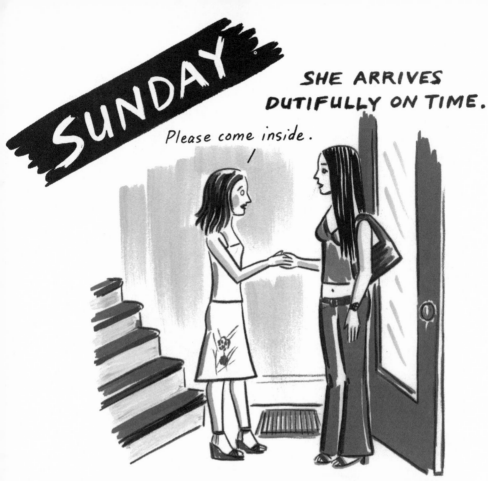

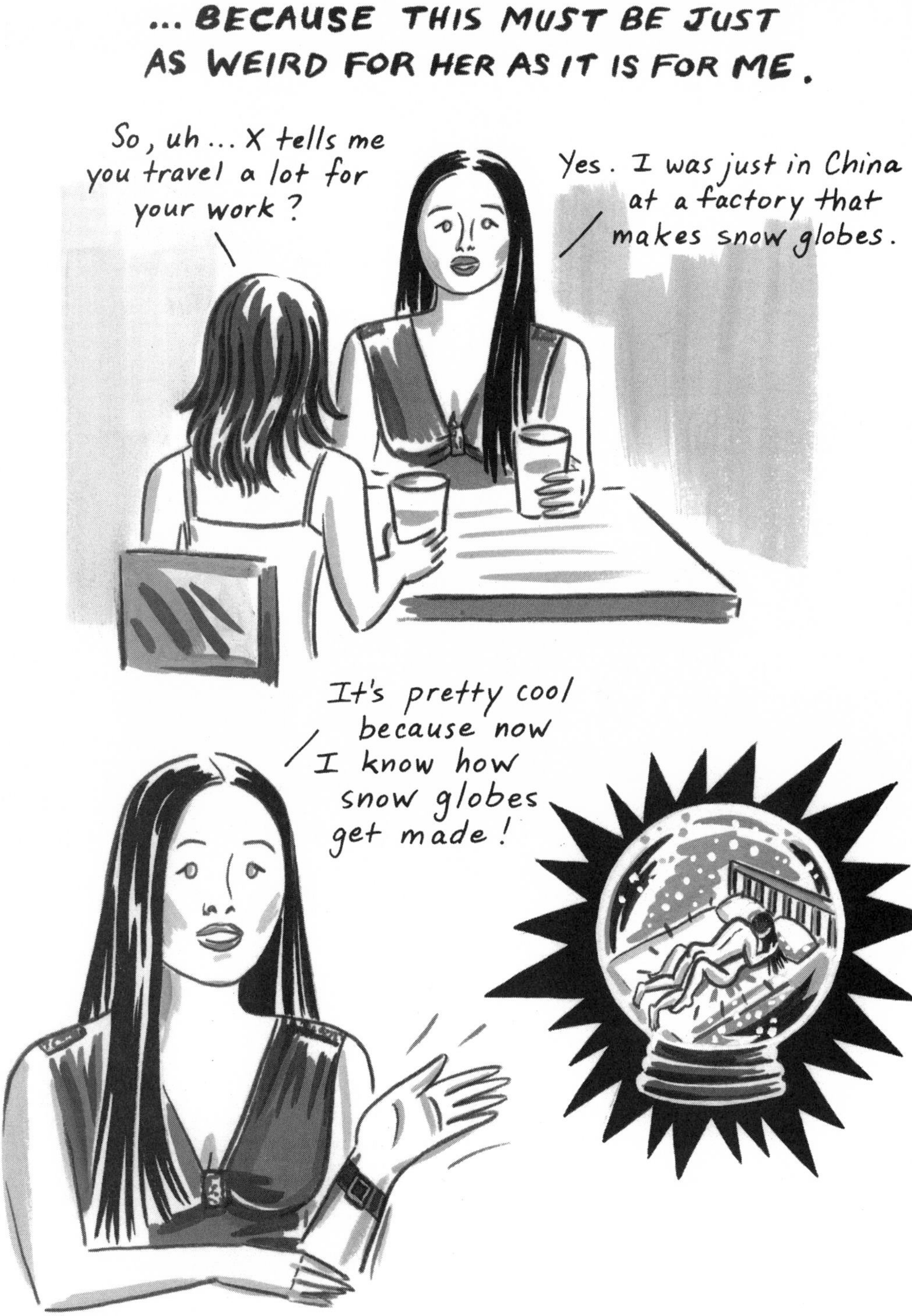
... BECAUSE THIS MUST BE JUST AS WEIRD FOR HER AS IT IS FOR ME.
So, uh ... X tells me you travel a lot for your work?
Yes. I was just in China at a factory that makes snow globes.
It's pretty cool because now I know how snow globes get made!

WHILE SHE TALKS, I ABSORB EVERY DETAIL....

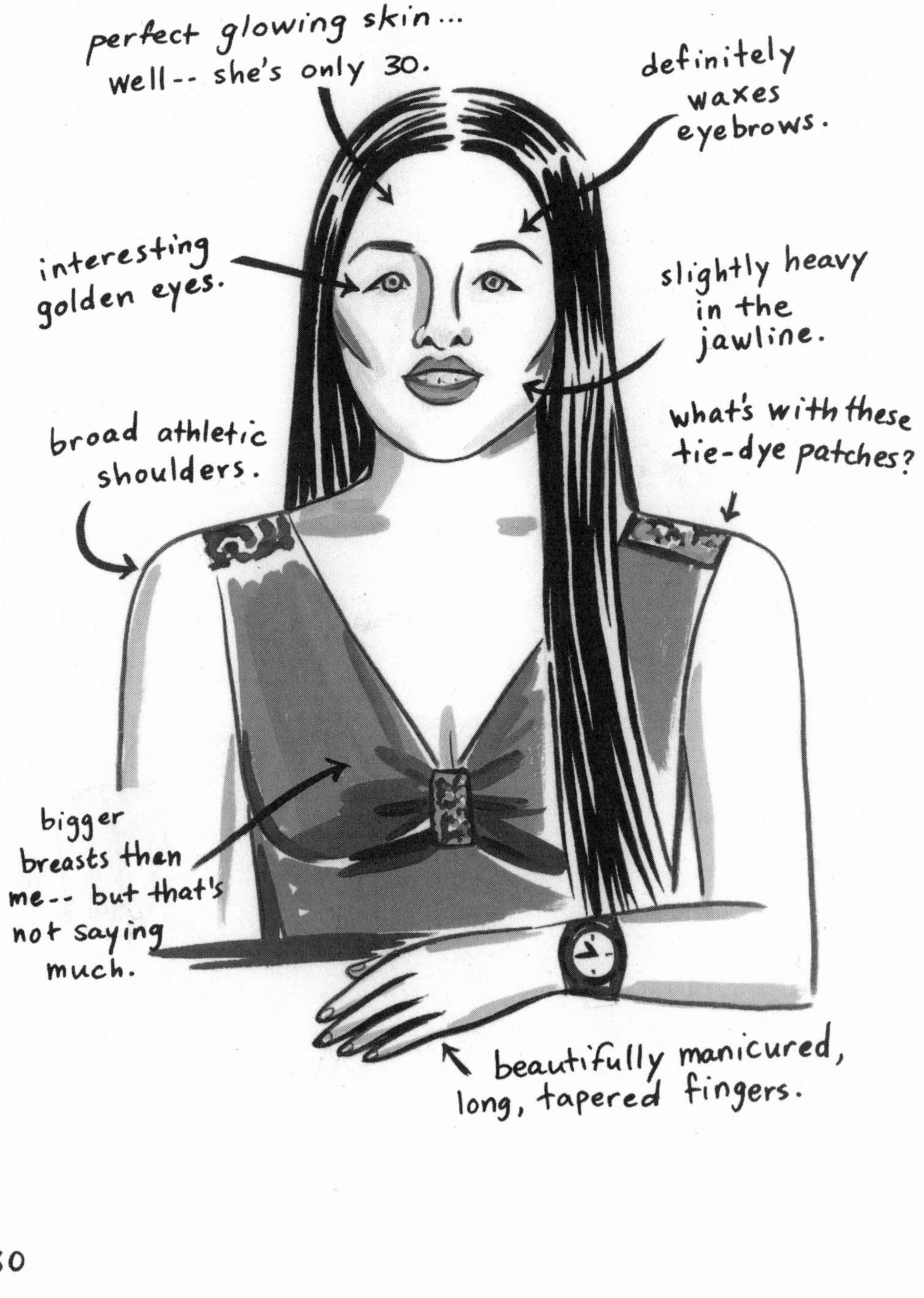
perfect glowing skin... well-- she's only 30.
definitely waxes eyebrows.
interesting golden eyes.
slightly heavy in the jawline.
broad athletic shoulders.
what's with these tie-dye patches?
bigger breasts than me-- but that's not saying much.
beautifully manicured, long, tapered fingers.

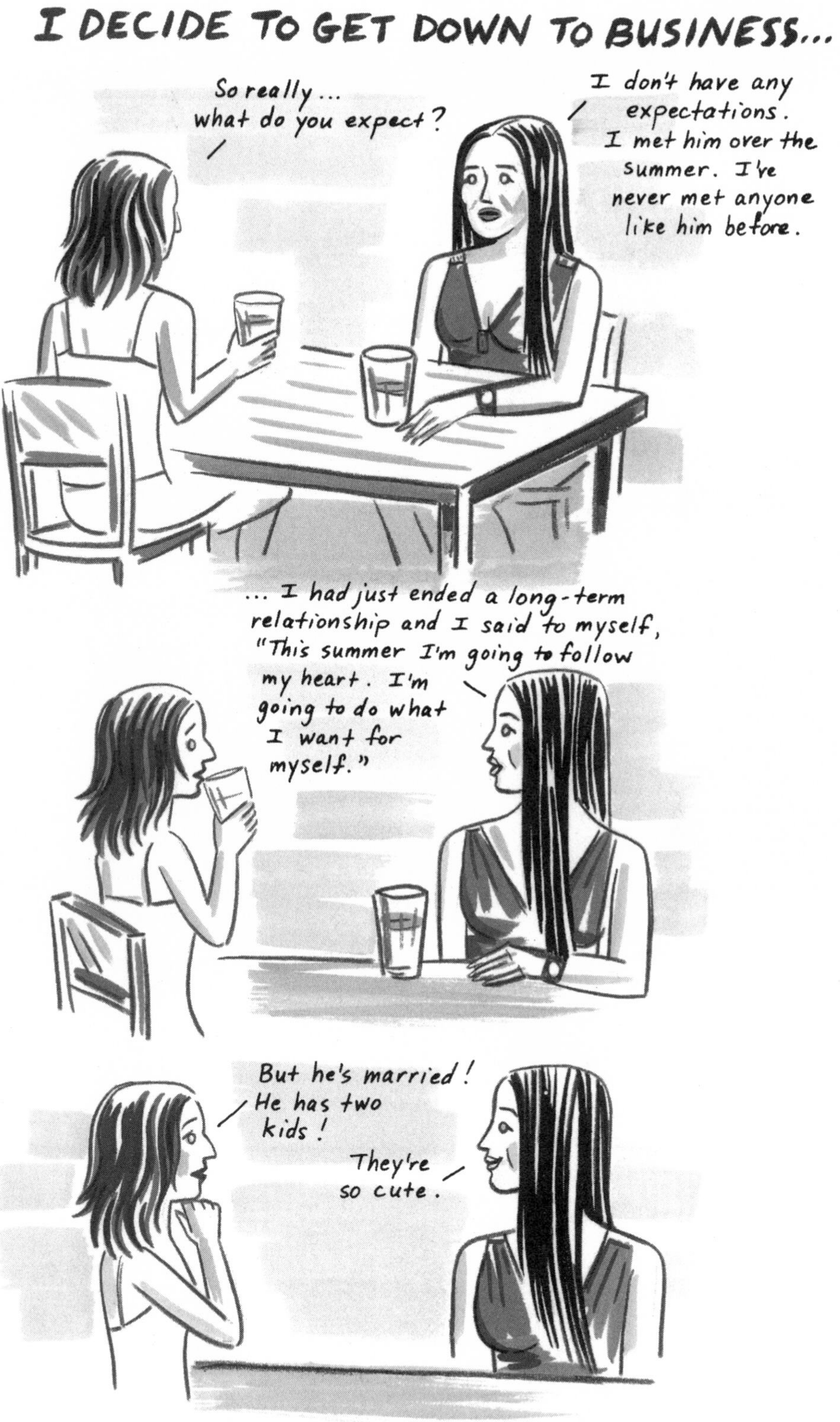
I DECIDE TO GET DOWN TO BUSINESS...
So really... what do you expect?
I don't have any expectations. I met him over the summer. I've never met anyone like him before.
... I had just ended a long-term relationship and I said to myself, "This summer I'm going to follow my heart. I'm going to do what I want for myself."
But he's married! He has two kids!
They're so cute.

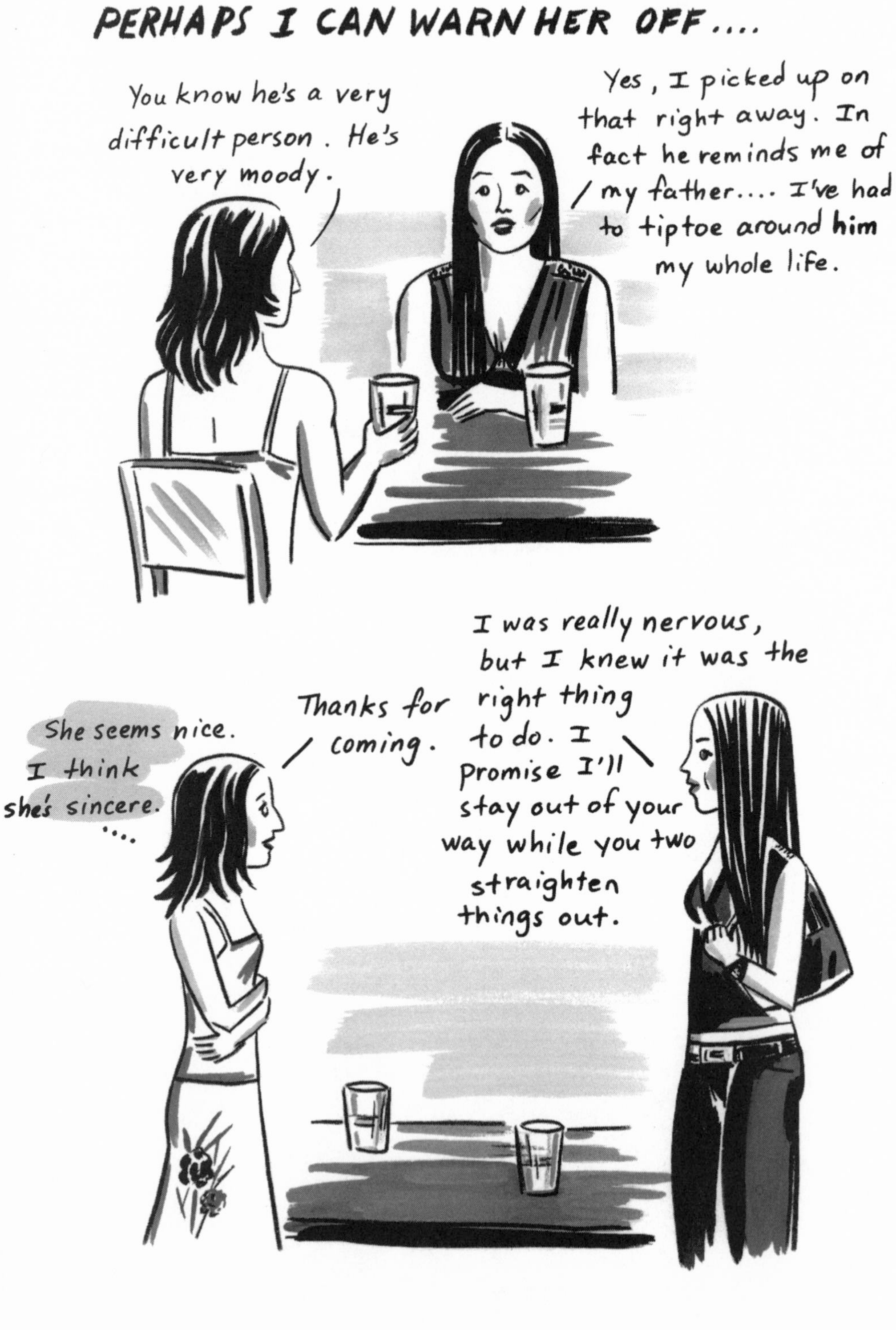
PERHAPS I CAN WARN HER OFF....
You know he's a very difficult person. He's very moody.
Yes, I picked up on that right away. In fact he reminds me of my father.... I've had to tiptoe around **him** my whole life.
She seems nice. I think she's sincere. ....
Thanks for coming.
I was really nervous, but I knew it was the right thing to do. I promise I'll stay out of your way while you two straighten things out.

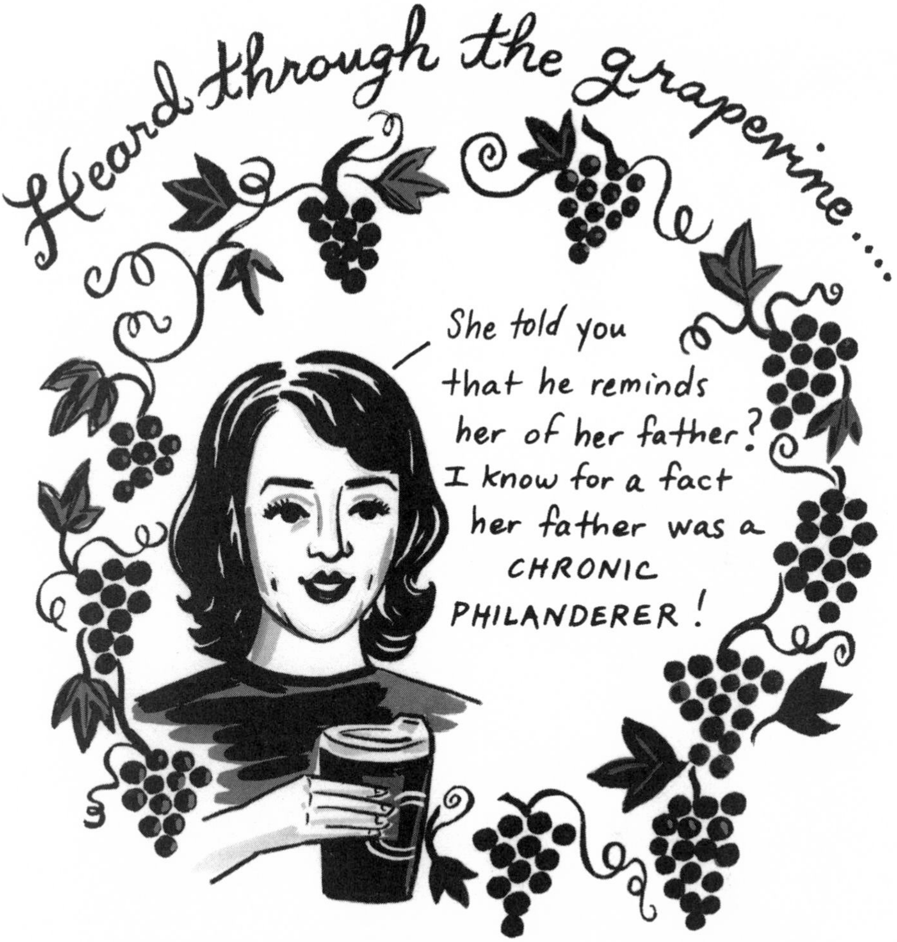
Heard through the grapevine....
She told you that he reminds her of her father? I know for a fact her father was a CHRONIC PHILANDERER!

WHAT WOULD DR. FREUD SAY?

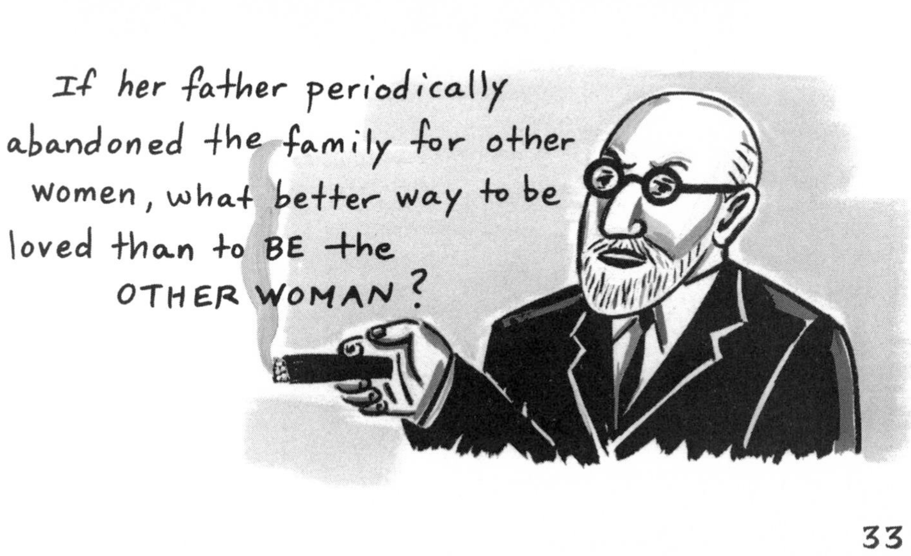
If her father periodically abandoned the family for other women, what better way to be loved than to BE the OTHER WOMAN?

I DECIDE TO APPEAL TO THE SOLIDARITY OF THE SISTERHOOD. IF I WIN HER AFFECTION, HER LOYALTIES WILL BE TORN!

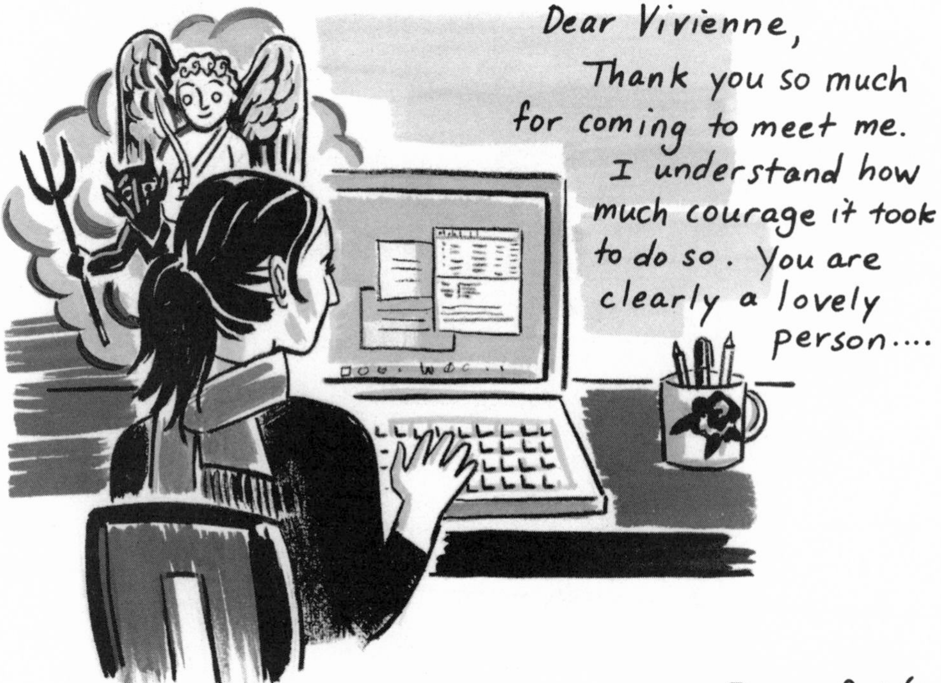

Dear Vivienne,
Thank you so much for coming to meet me. I understand how much courage it took to do so. You are clearly a lovely person....

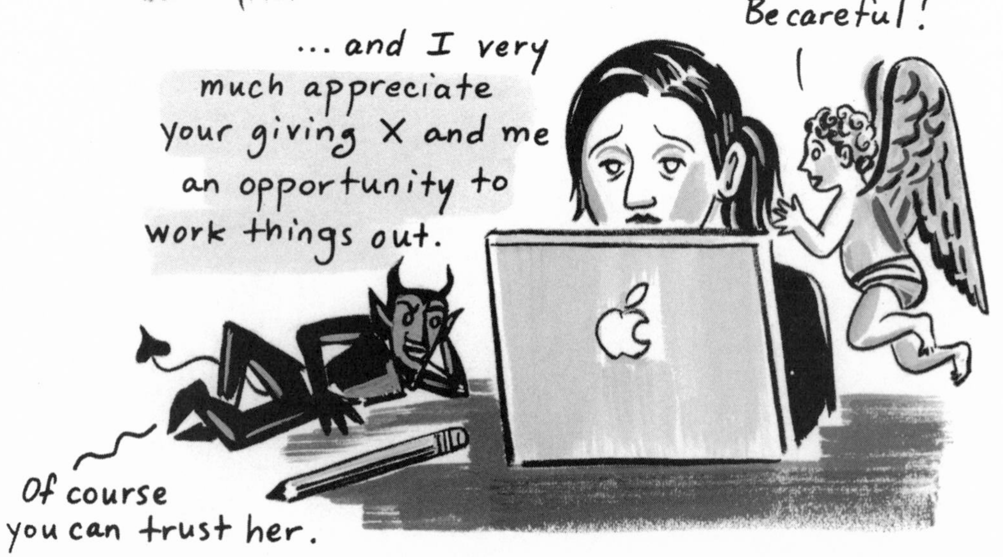

...and I very much appreciate your giving X and me an opportunity to work things out.
Be careful!
Of course you can trust her.

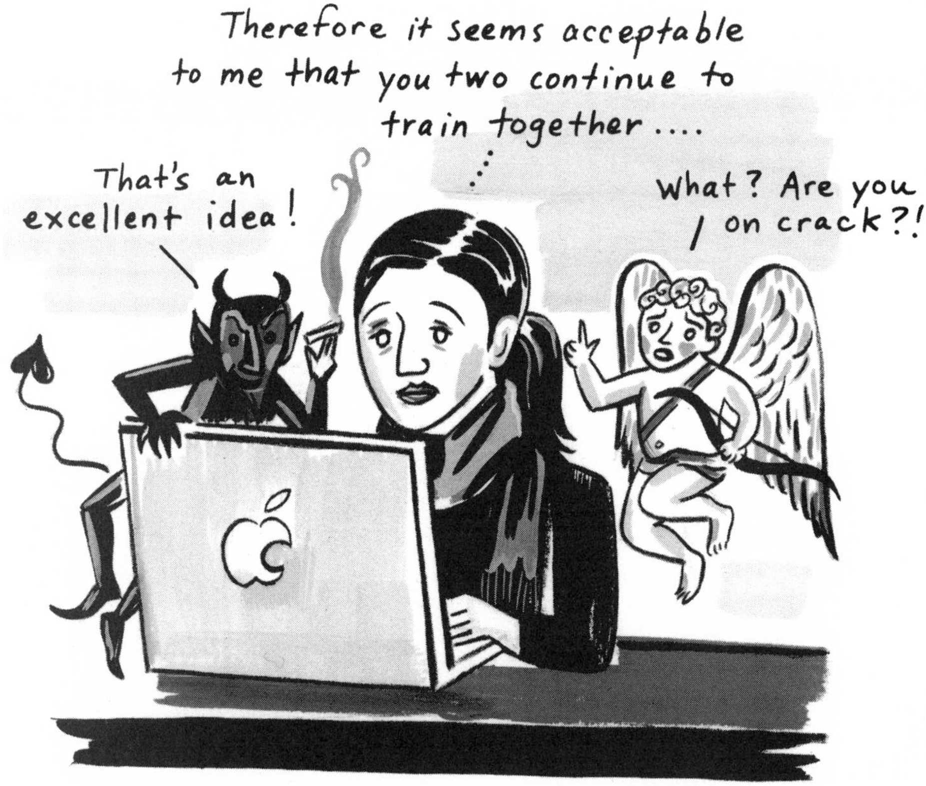
Therefore it seems acceptable to me that you two continue to train together....
That's an excellent idea!
What? Are you on crack?!

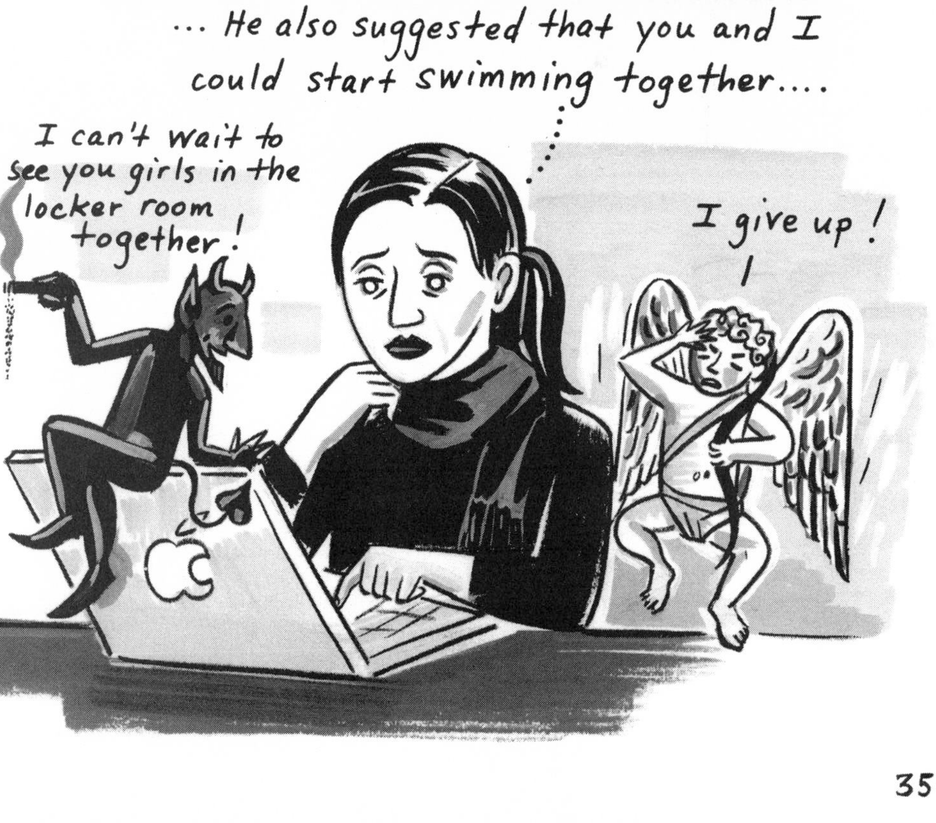
... He also suggested that you and I could start swimming together....
I can't wait to see you girls in the locker room together!
I give up!

THE ADVENT OF HALLOWEEN SHAKES ME FROM MY STUPOR.

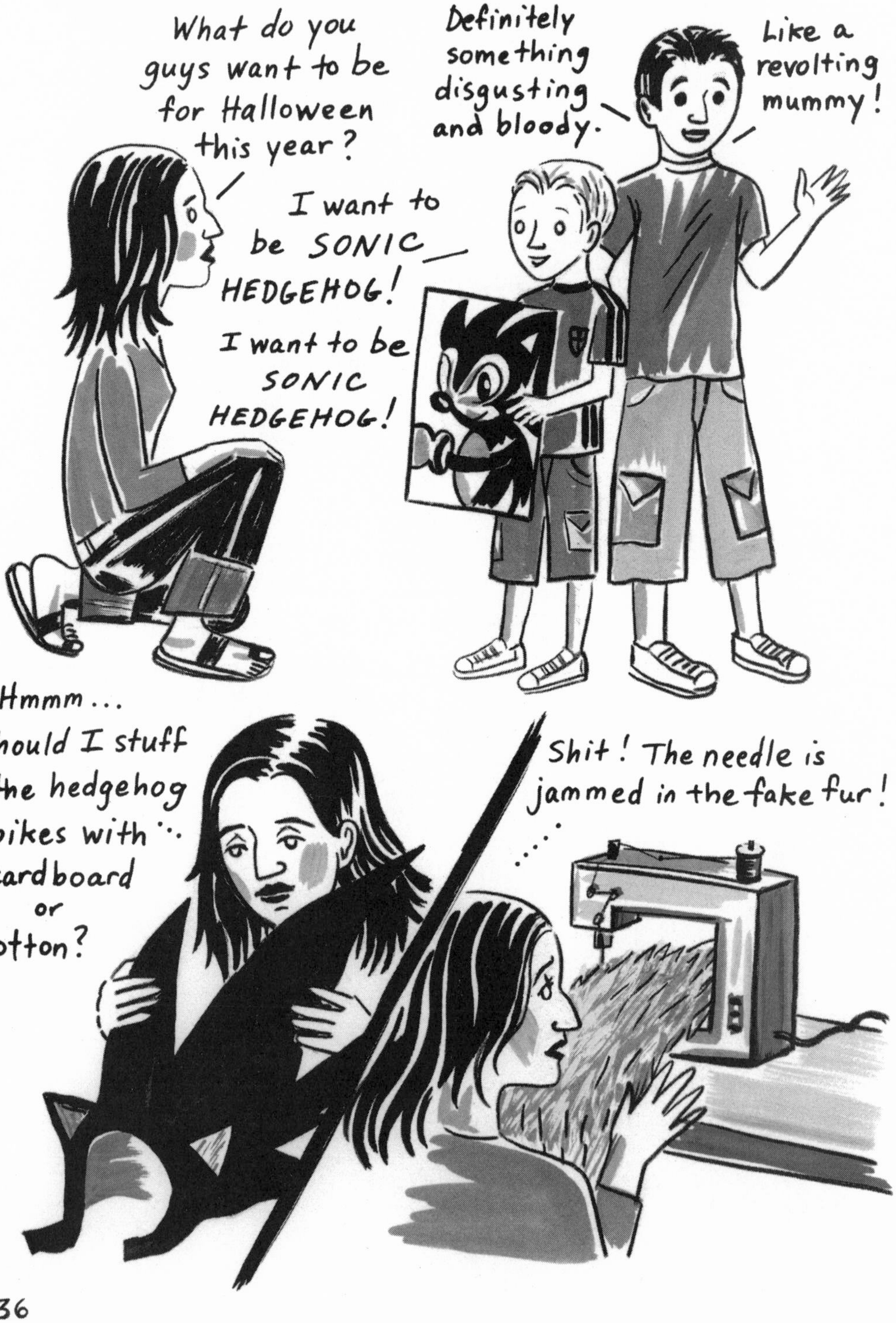
What do you guys want to be for Halloween this year?
Definitely something disgusting and bloody.
Like a revolting mummy!
I want to be SONIC HEDGEHOG!
I want to be SONIC HEDGEHOG!
Hmmm... Should I stuff the hedgehog spikes with cardboard or cotton?
Shit! The needle is jammed in the fake fur!

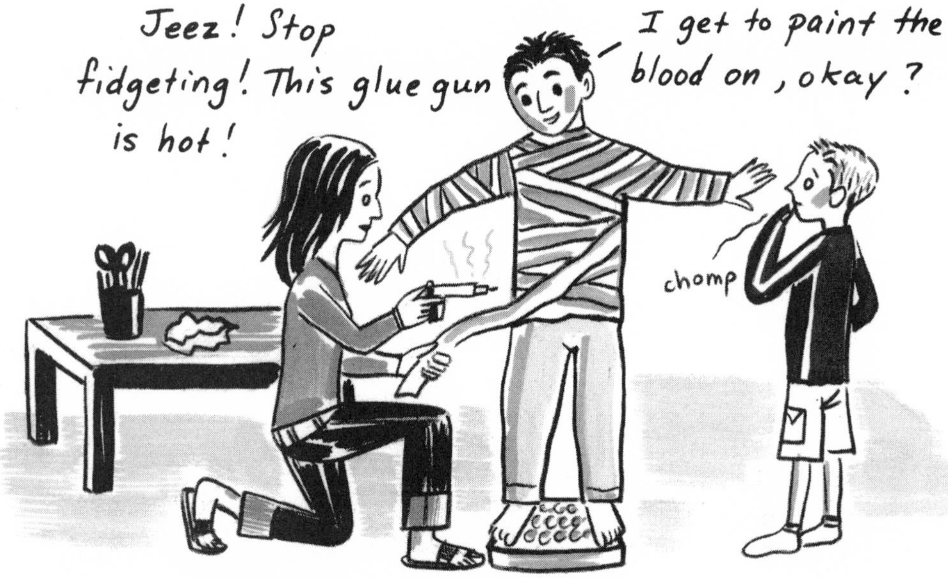
Jeez! Stop fidgeting! This glue gun is hot!
I get to paint the blood on, okay?
chomp

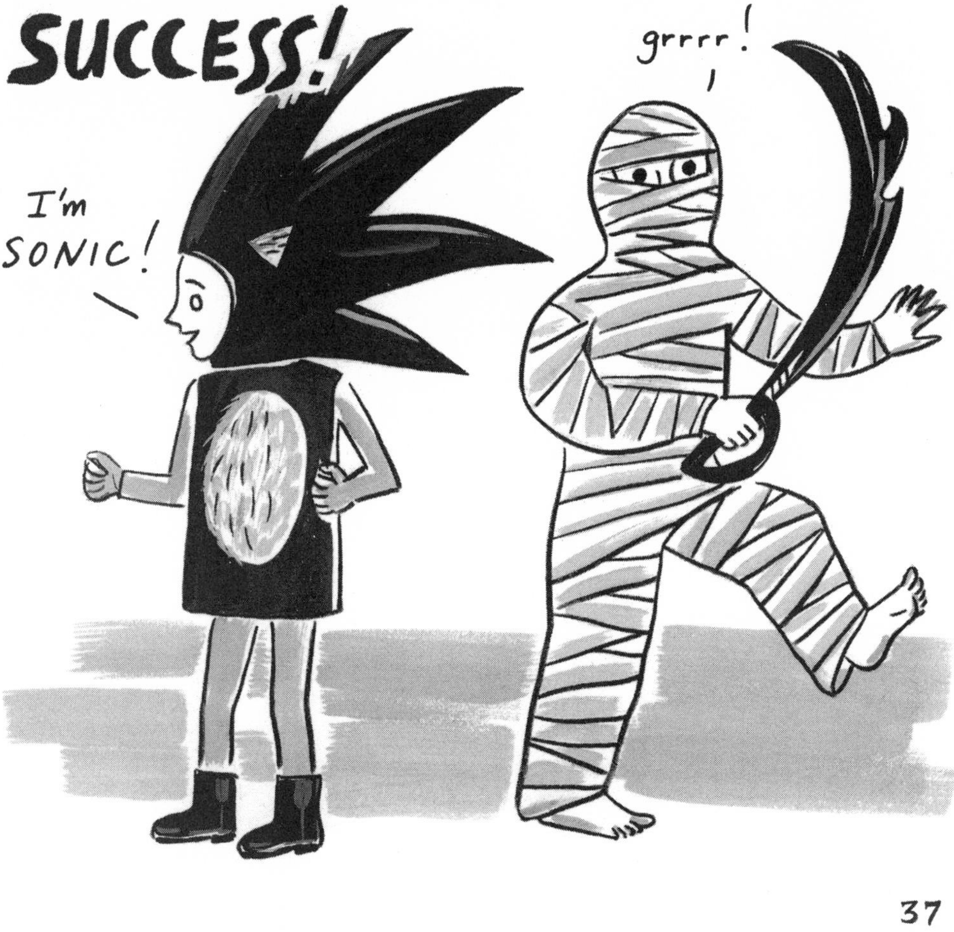
SUCCESS!
grrrr!
I'm SONIC!

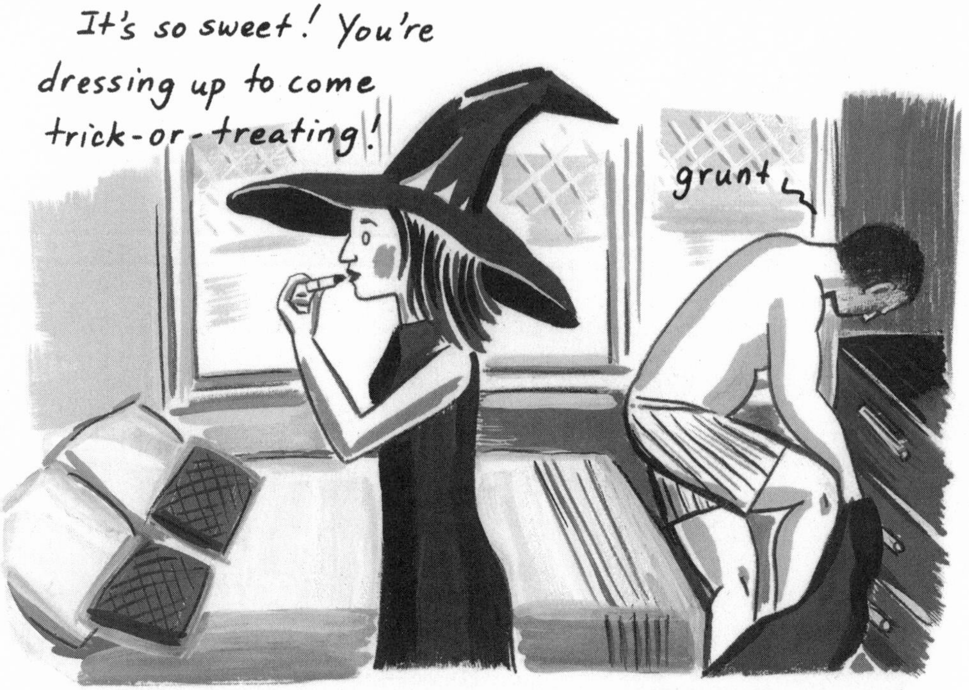

It's so sweet! You're dressing up to come trick-or-treating!
grunt

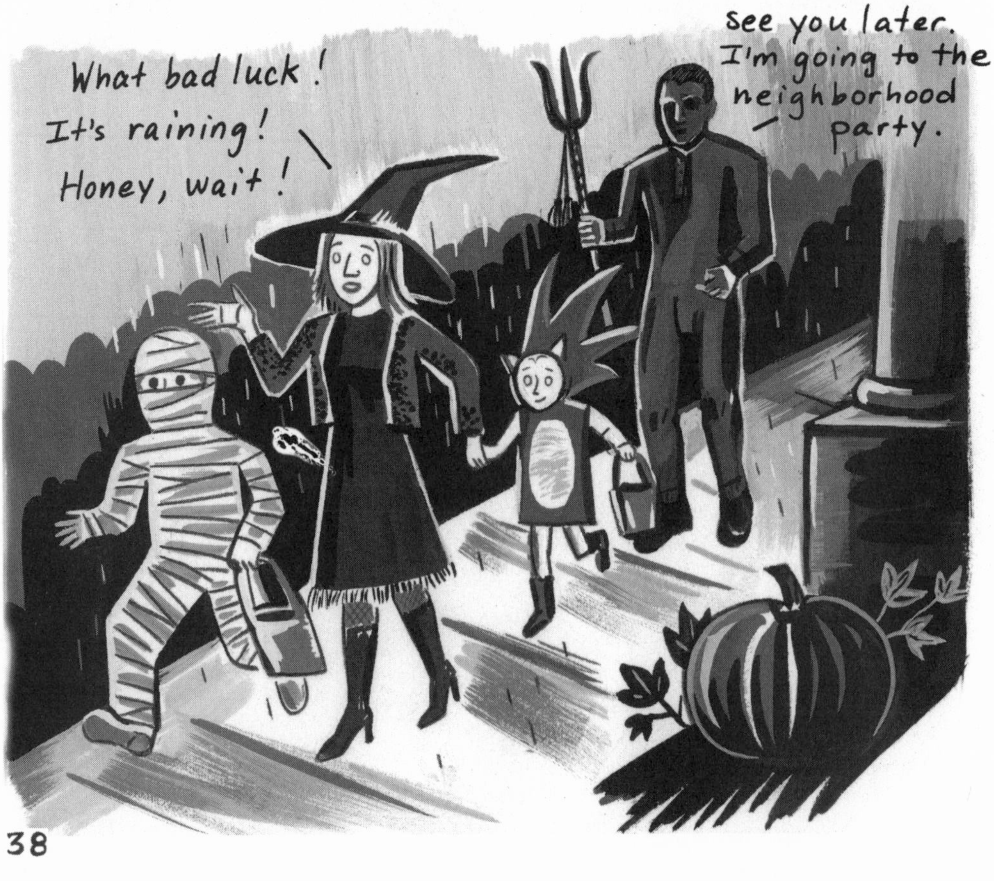

What bad luck! It's raining! Honey, wait!
see you later. I'm going to the neighborhood party.

AS THE EVENING PROGRESSES, HE NEVER APPEARS!

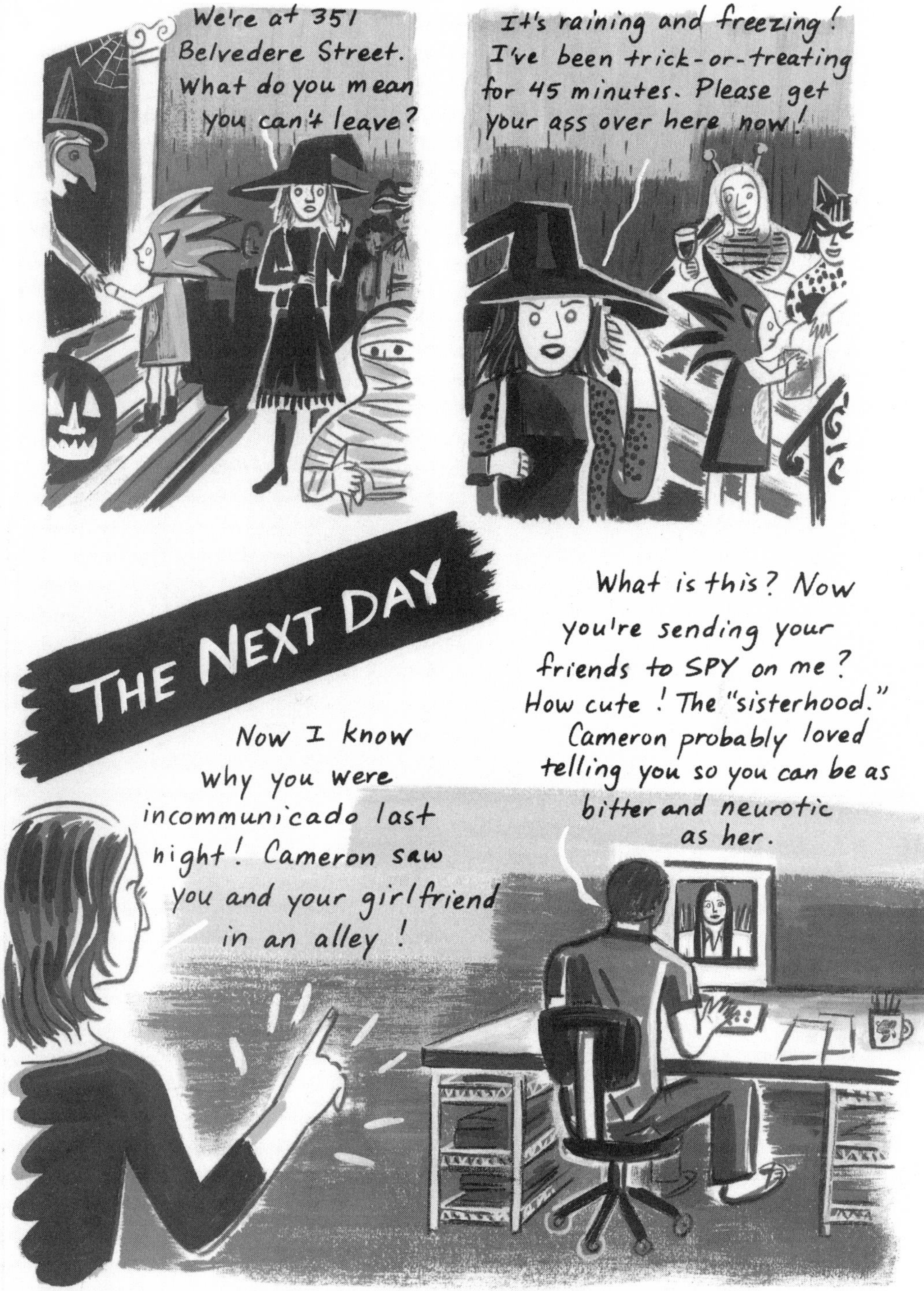
We're at 351 Belvedere Street. What do you mean you can't leave?
It's raining and freezing! I've been trick-or-treating for 45 minutes. Please get your ass over here now!
THE NEXT DAY
Now I know why you were incommunicado last night! Cameron saw you and your girlfriend in an alley!
What is this? Now you're sending your friends to SPY on me? How cute! The "sisterhood." Cameron probably loved telling you so you can be as bitter and neurotic as her.

IN ALL HONESTY, I MUST BE UNBEARABLE TO LIVE WITH. I'M TRACKING HIS EVERY TWITCH LIKE A HYENA STALKING A WILDEBEEST.

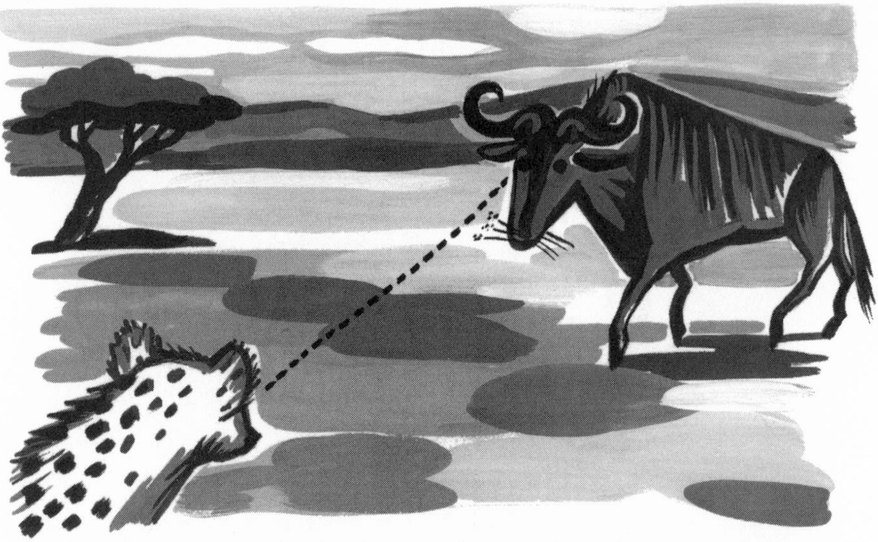

BUT THE MORE I TRY TO HOLD ON, THE MORE ELUSIVE HE BECOMES.

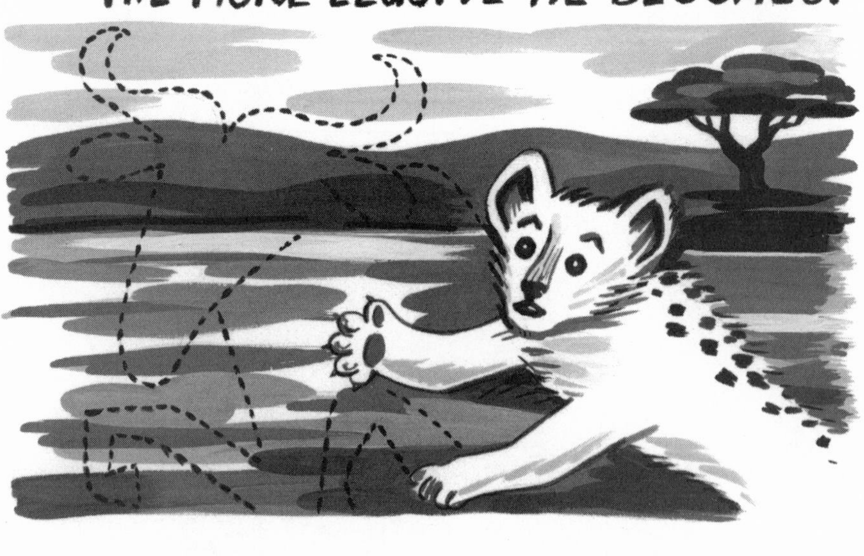

WORDS of WISE WOMEN

*"Love is suffering.
One side always loves more."*

Catherine Deneuve

I COMMENCE THE OBSESSIVE-COMPULSIVE PASTIMES OF THE SCORNED WIFE:

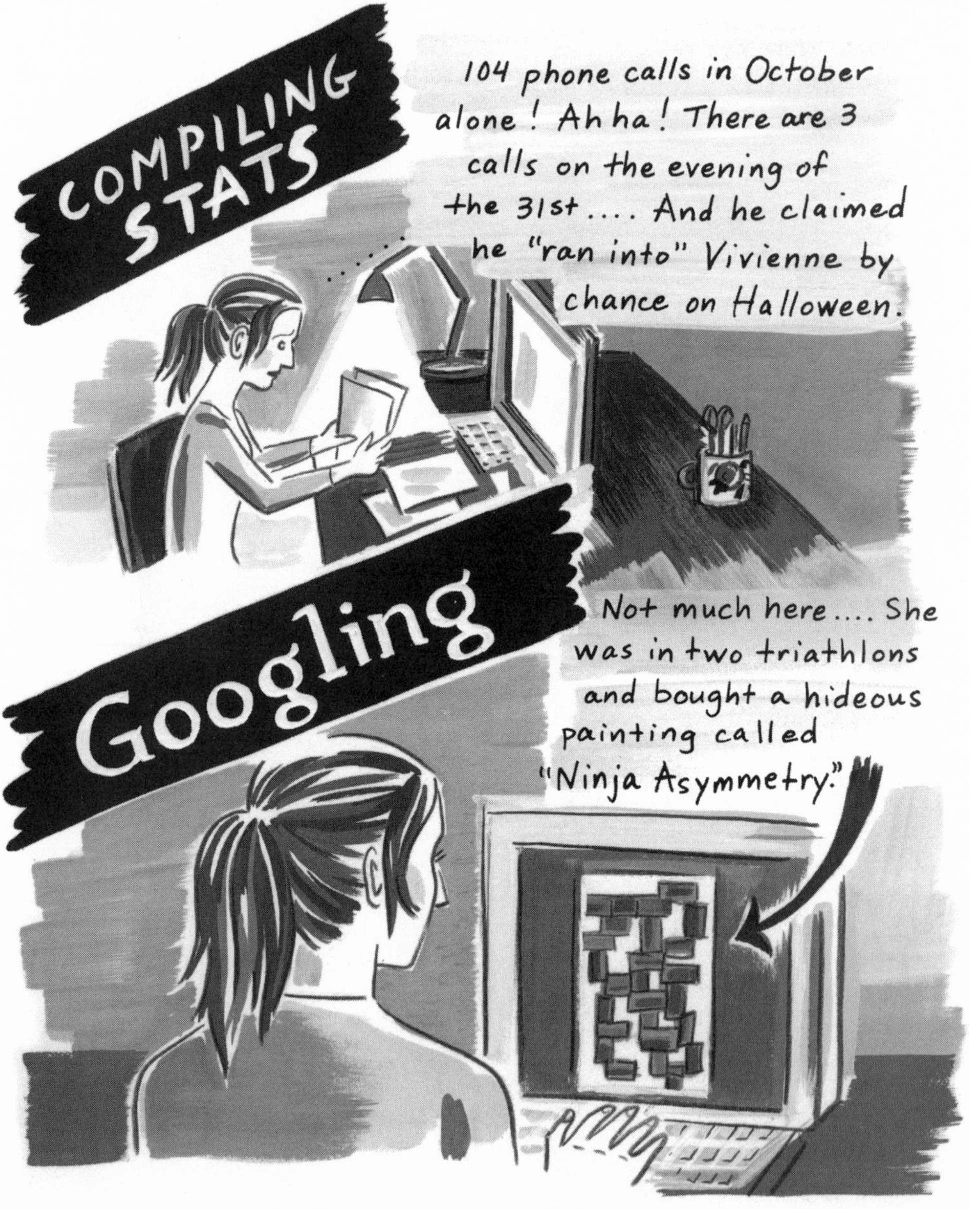
COMPILING STATS
104 phone calls in October alone! Ah ha! There are 3 calls on the evening of the 31st.... And he claimed he "ran into" Vivienne by chance on Halloween.
Googling
Not much here.... She was in two triathlons and bought a hideous painting called "Ninja Asymmetry."

WHY THE HECK WOULD MY HUSBAND LEAVE ME FOR A JOCK WITH BAD TASTE IN ART?

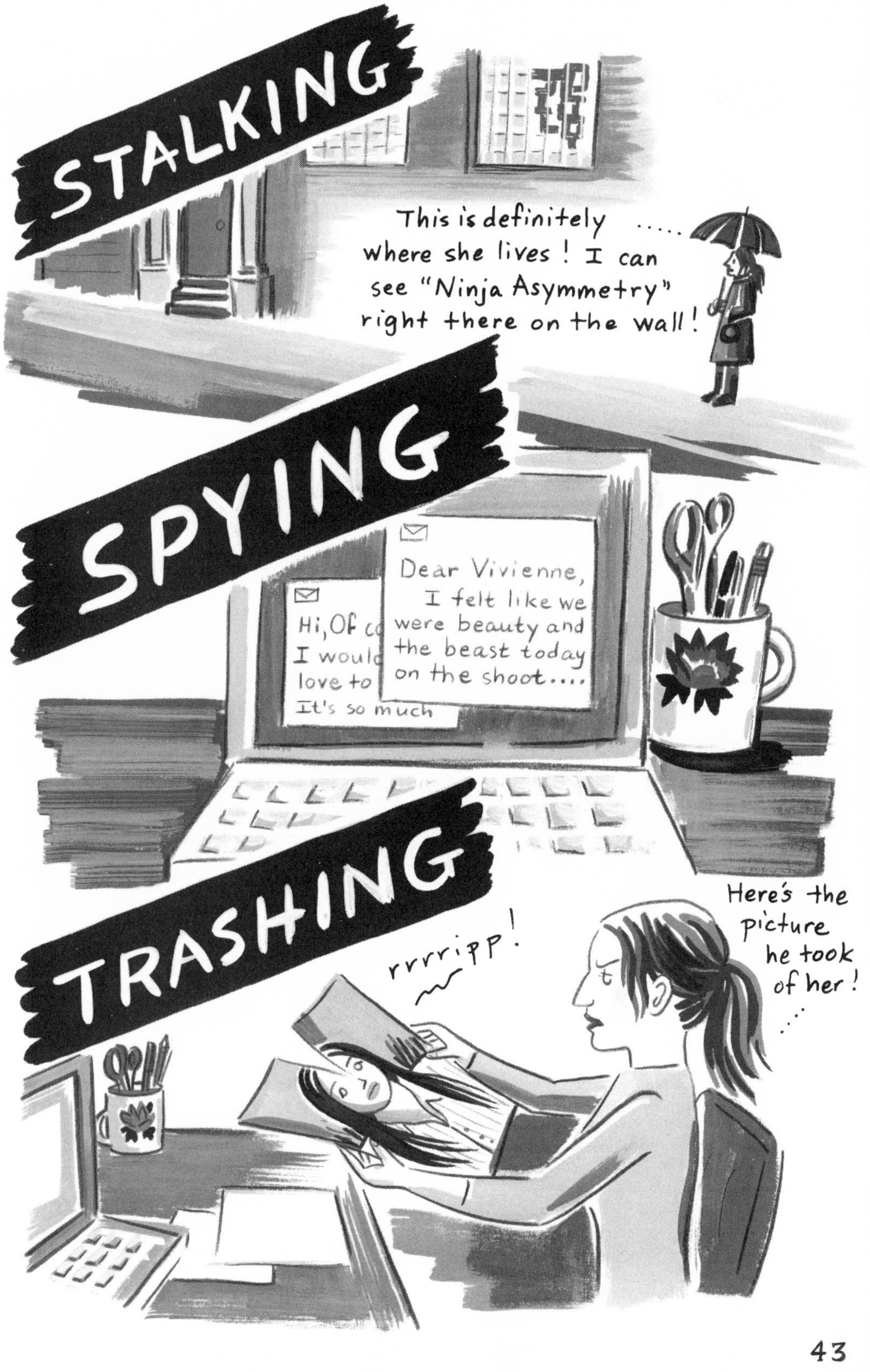
STALKING
This is definitely where she lives! I can see "Ninja Asymmetry" right there on the wall!
SPYING
Hi, Of co I would love to It's so much
Dear Vivienne, I felt like we were beauty and the beast today on the shoot....
TRASHING
rrrripp!
Here's the picture he took of her!

ARMED WITH IRREFUTABLE DATA I CONFRONT HIM WITH MY RESEARCH.

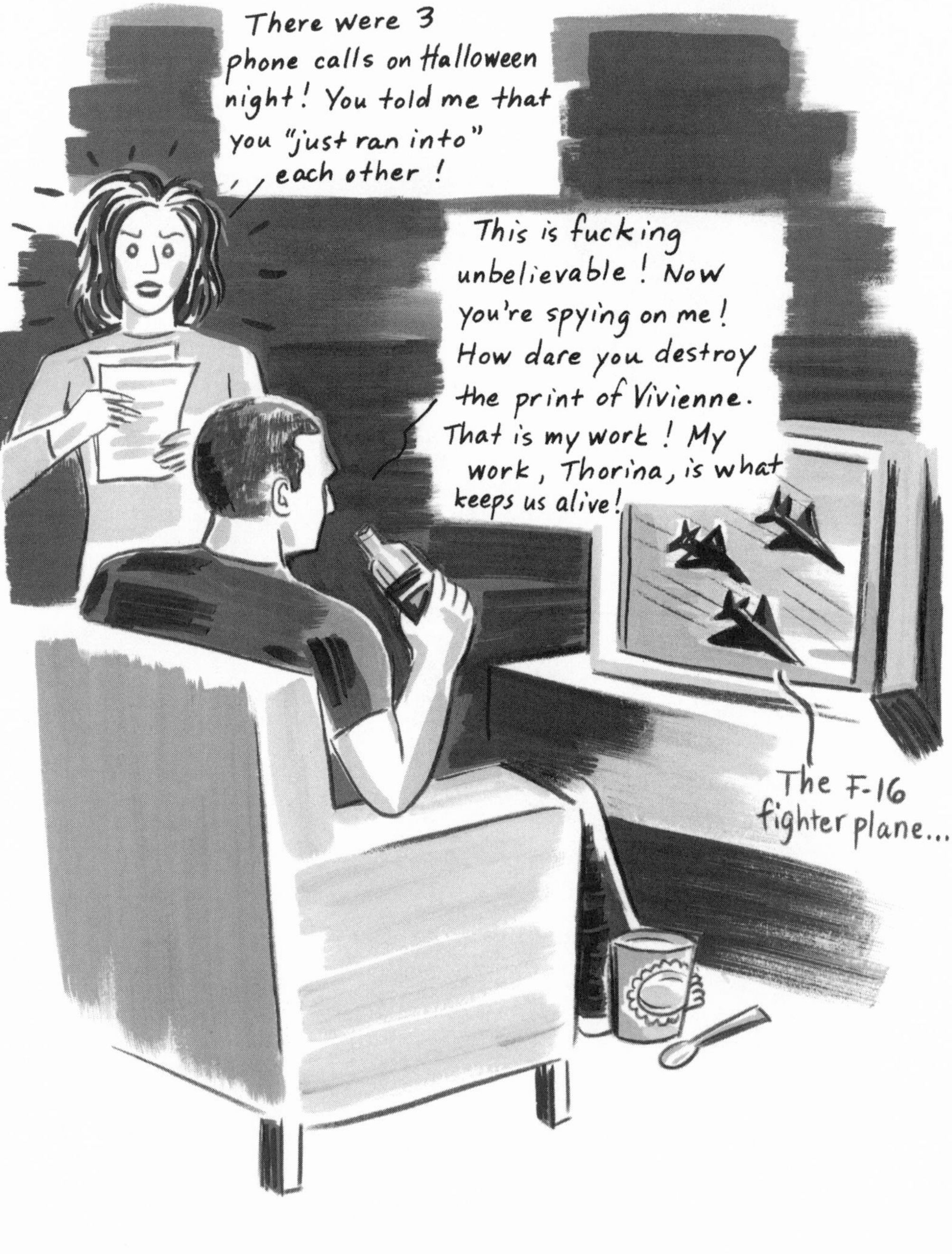
There were 3 phone calls on Halloween night! You told me that you "just ran into" each other!
This is fucking unbelievable! Now you're spying on me! How dare you destroy the print of Vivienne. That is my work! My work, Thorina, is what keeps us alive!
The F-16 fighter plane...

Words of Wise Women

"The way I see it, if you want the rainbow, you gotta put up with the rain."

Dolly Parton

NOW IS NO TIME FOR DIGNITY, I KEEL PITIABLY TOWARD A COMFORTING EMBRACE.

COPING MECHANISM #1
FRIENDS

MY BEST FRIEND CAMERON WAS A GOOD PLACE TO START.

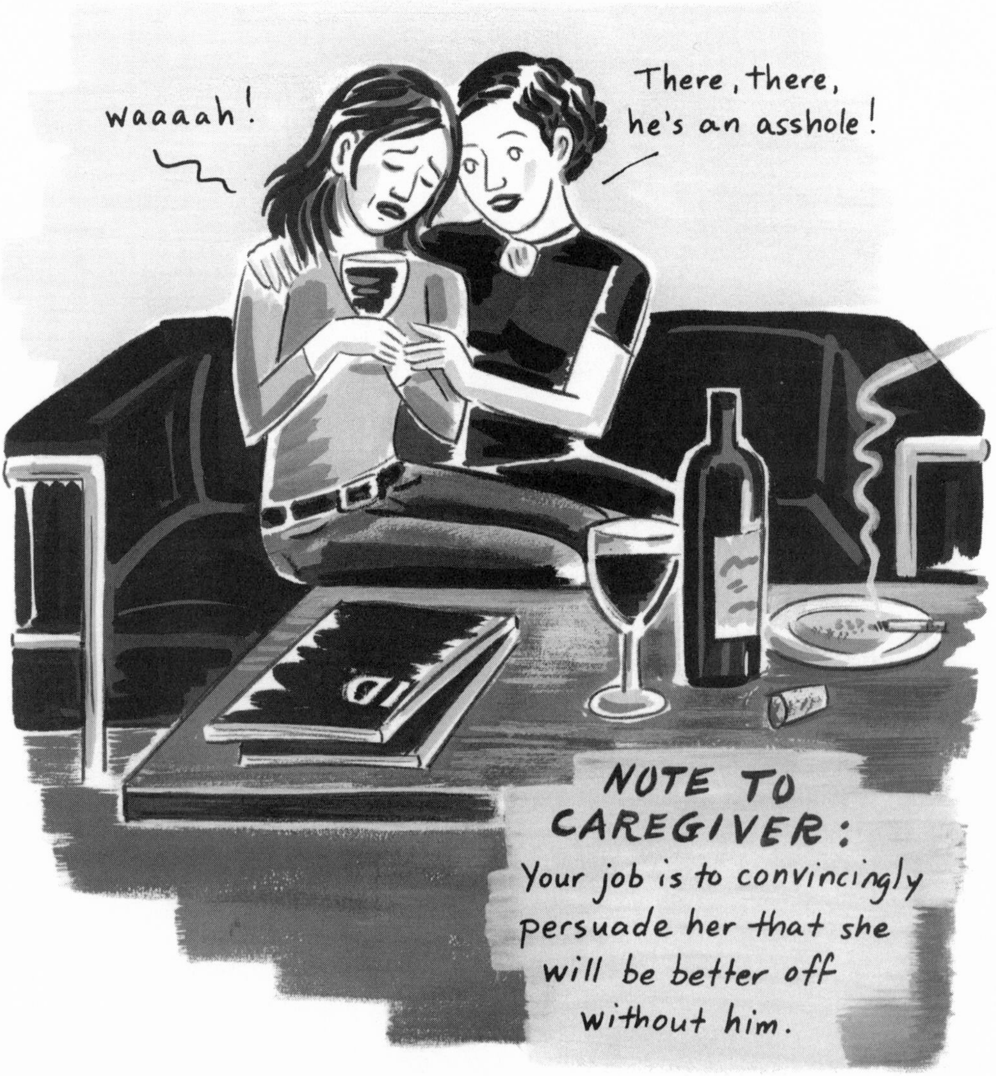
waaaah!
There, there, he's an asshole!
NOTE TO CAREGIVER:
Your job is to convincingly persuade her that she will be better off without him.

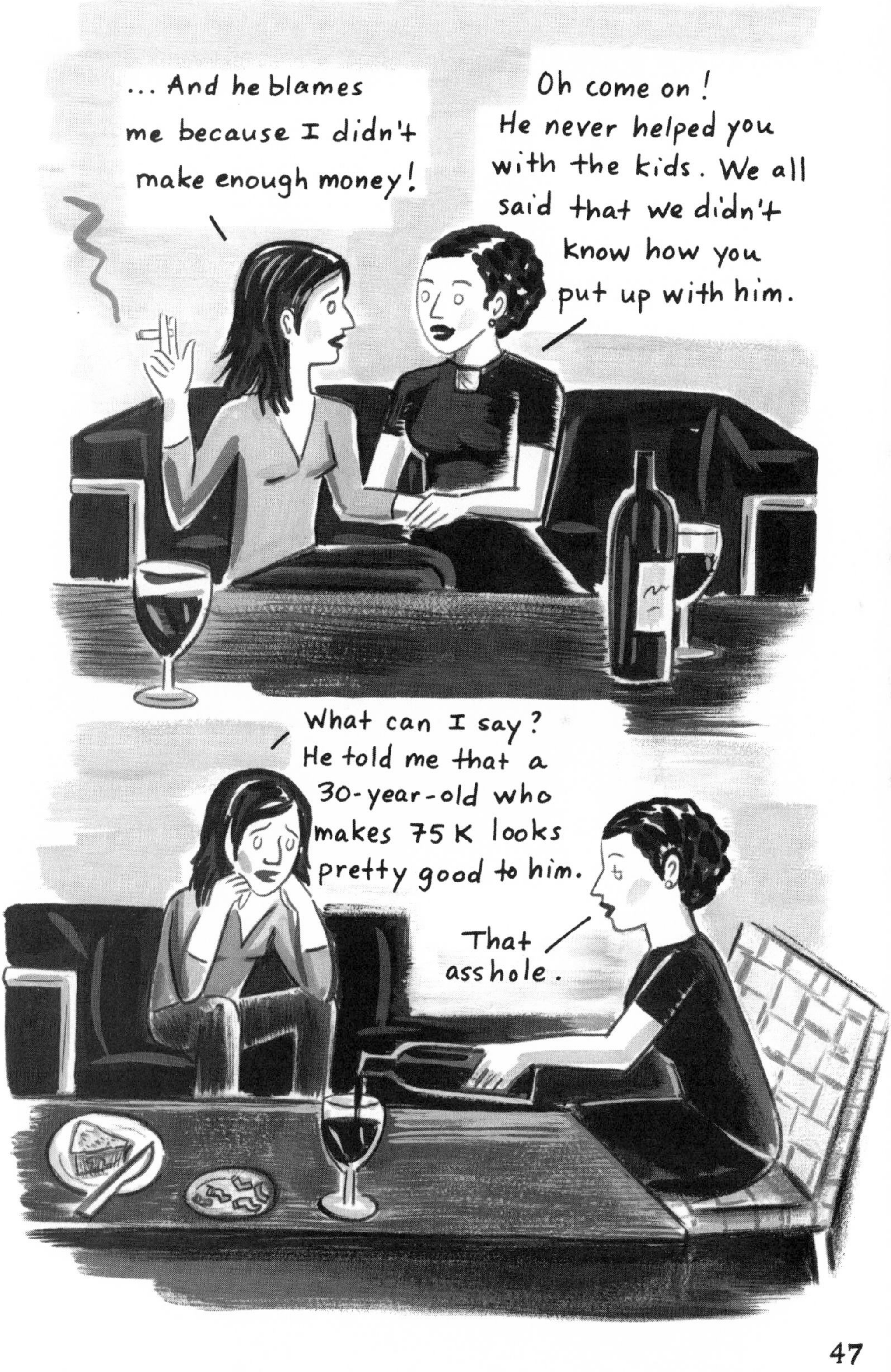
... And he blames me because I didn't make enough money!
Oh come on! He never helped you with the kids. We all said that we didn't know how you put up with him.
What can I say? He told me that a 30-year-old who makes 75 K looks pretty good to him.
That asshole.

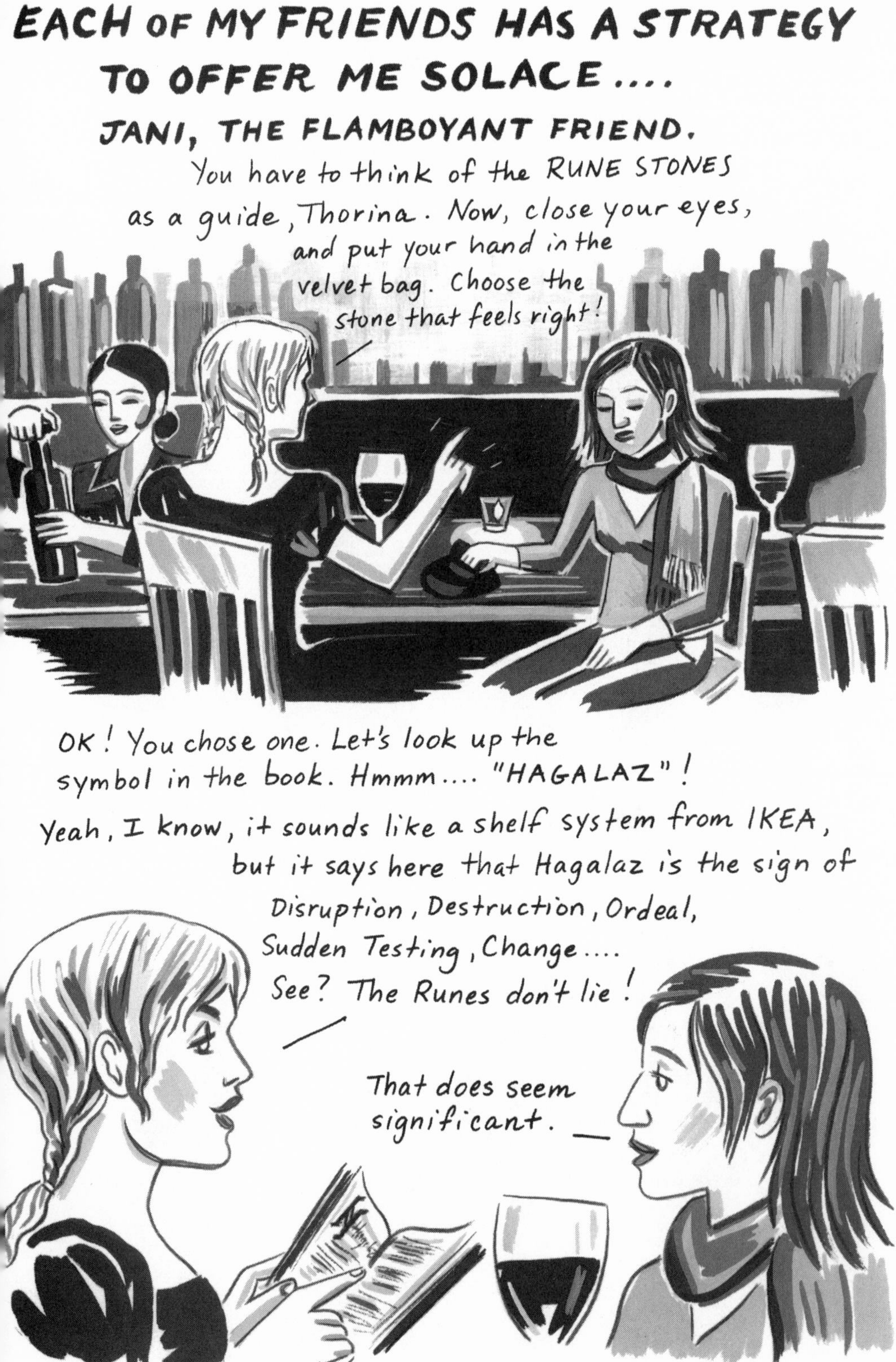
EACH OF MY FRIENDS HAS A STRATEGY TO OFFER ME SOLACE....
JANI, THE FLAMBOYANT FRIEND.
You have to think of the RUNE STONES as a guide, Thorina. Now, close your eyes, and put your hand in the velvet bag. Choose the stone that feels right!
OK! You chose one. Let's look up the symbol in the book. Hmmm.... "HAGALAZ"!
Yeah, I know, it sounds like a shelf system from IKEA, but it says here that Hagalaz is the sign of Disruption, Destruction, Ordeal, Sudden Testing, Change.... See? The Runes don't lie!
That does seem significant.

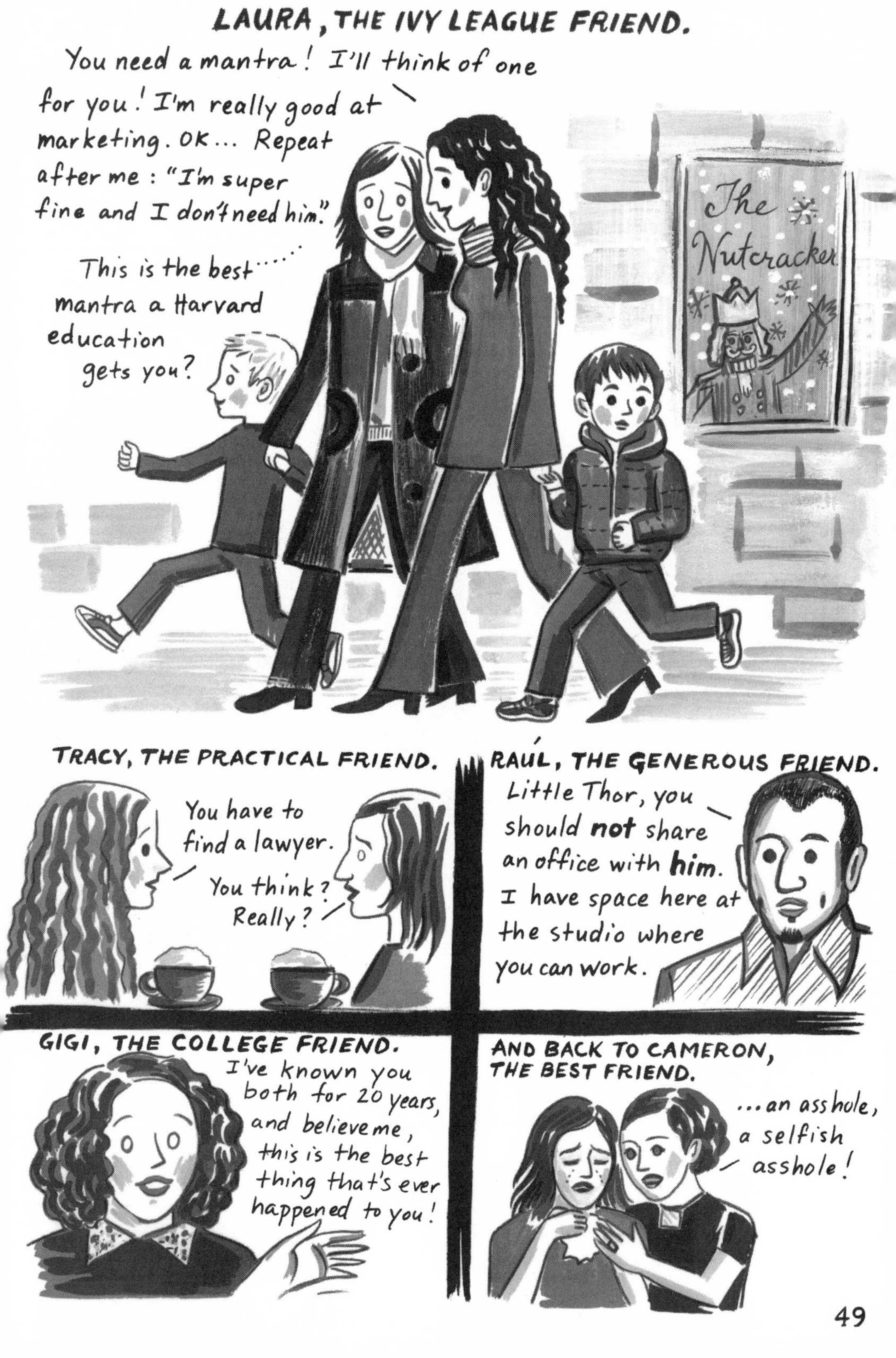
LAURA, THE IVY LEAGUE FRIEND.
You need a mantra! I'll think of one for you! I'm really good at marketing. OK... Repeat after me: "I'm super fine and I don't need him."
This is the best...... mantra a Harvard education gets you?
The Nutcracker
TRACY, THE PRACTICAL FRIEND.
You have to find a lawyer.
You think? Really?
RAÚL, THE GENEROUS FRIEND.
Little Thor, you should **not** share an office with **him**. I have space here at the studio where you can work.
GIGI, THE COLLEGE FRIEND.
I've known you both for 20 years, and believe me, this is the best thing that's ever happened to you!
AND BACK TO CAMERON, THE BEST FRIEND.
...an asshole, a selfish asshole!

MY FRIENDS' UNDERSTANDING AND EMPATHY MAKES ME FEEL SO MUCH BETTER, I DEVOTE MYSELF ENTHUSIASTICALLY TO SPREADING THE WORD!

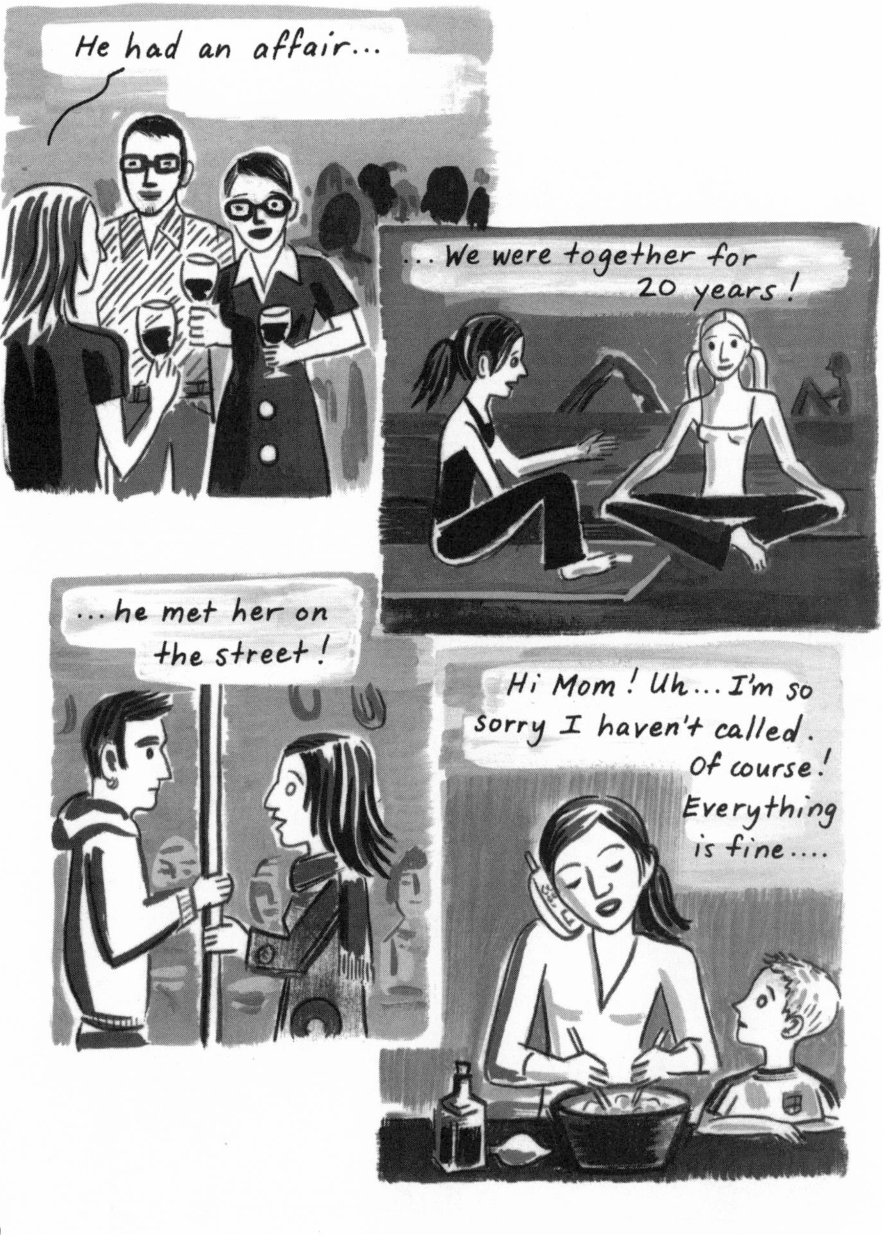

He had an affair...
...We were together for 20 years!
...he met her on the street!
Hi Mom! Uh... I'm so sorry I haven't called. Of course! Everything is fine....

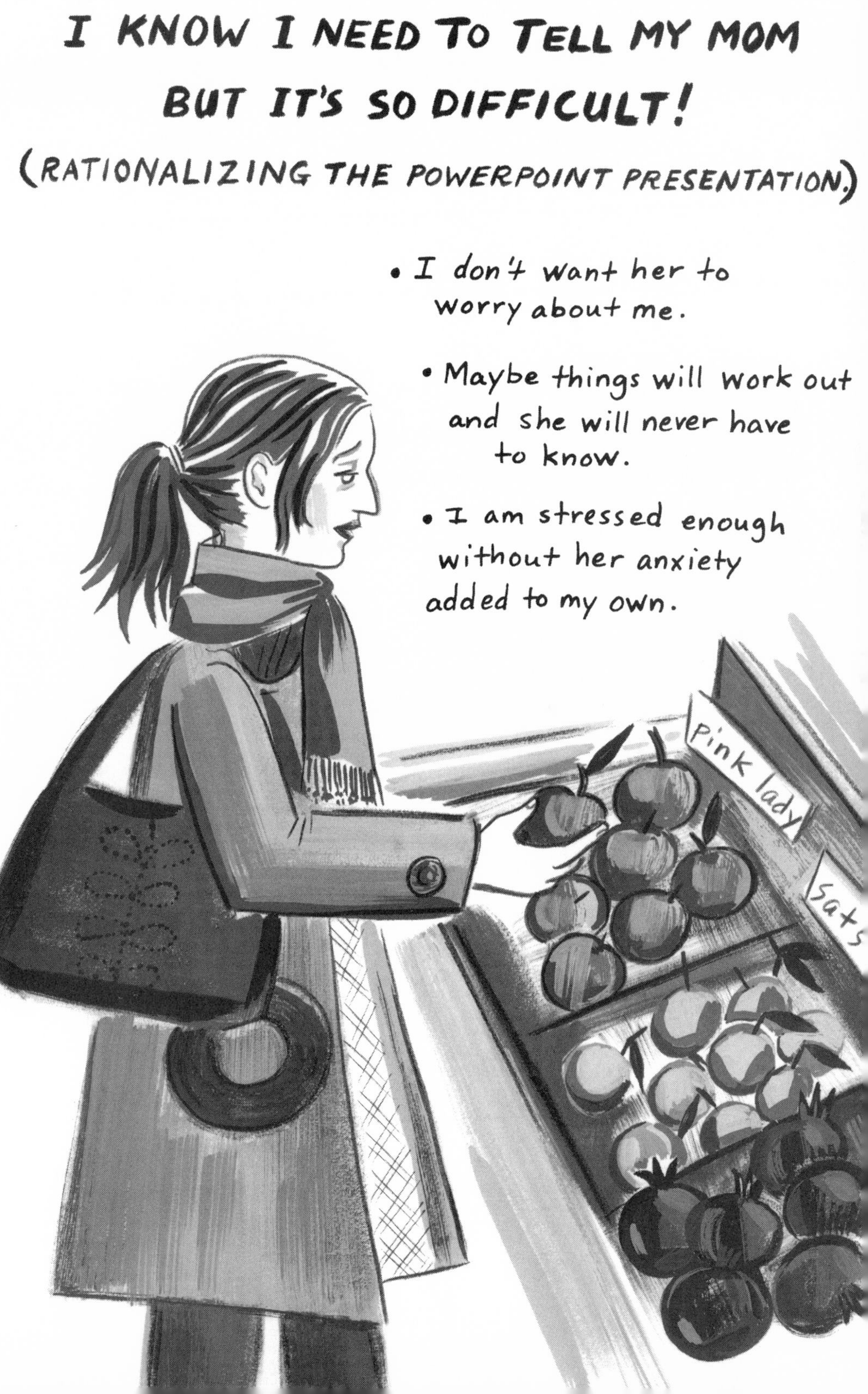
I KNOW I NEED TO TELL MY MOM BUT IT'S SO DIFFICULT!
(RATIONALIZING THE POWERPOINT PRESENTATION.)
• I don't want her to worry about me.
• Maybe things will work out and she will never have to know.
• I am stressed enough without her anxiety added to my own.
Pink lady
Sats

MEANWHILE EVERYONE AROUND ME IS EAGER TO OPINE ABOUT MY PREDICAMENT AND ABOUT THE DRAMATIC PERSONAE.

THE CHORUS

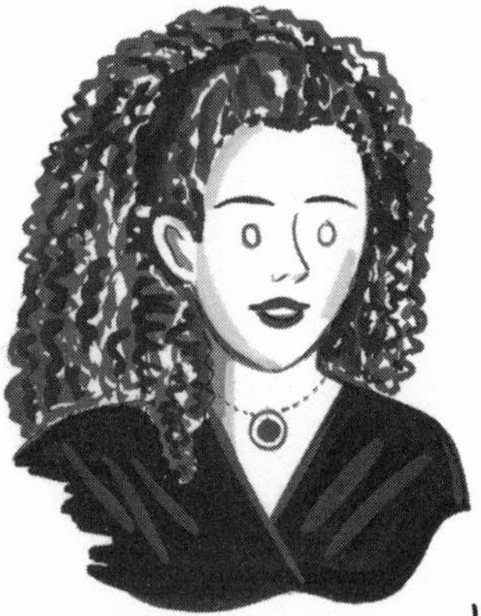

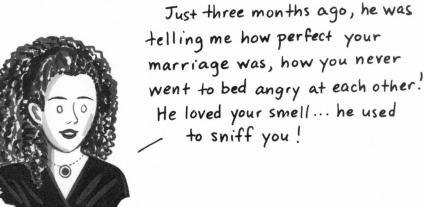

Just three months ago, he was telling me how perfect your marriage was, how you never went to bed angry at each other! He loved your smell... he used to sniff you!

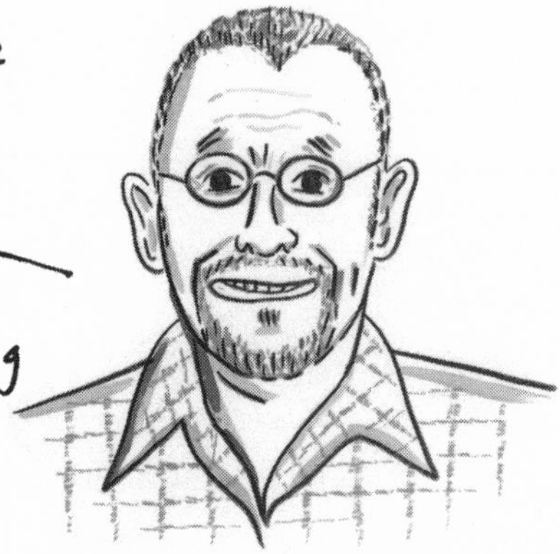

Have you met the girlfriend? I'm just so curious! It's like watching a train wreck waiting to happen....

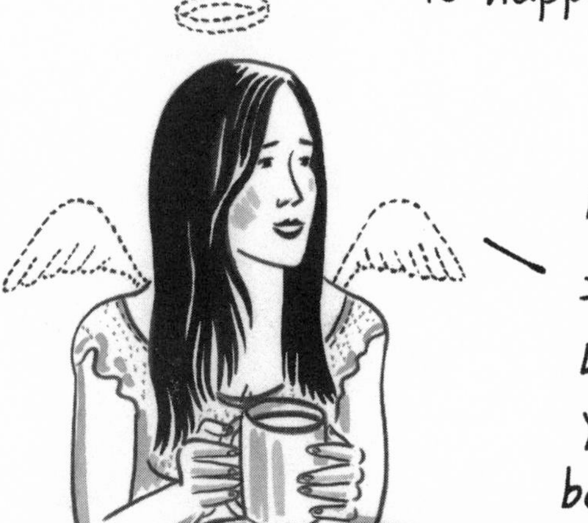

He will NEVER leave you! I want you to know that he LOVES you! The proof of your love is those two beautiful children of yours!

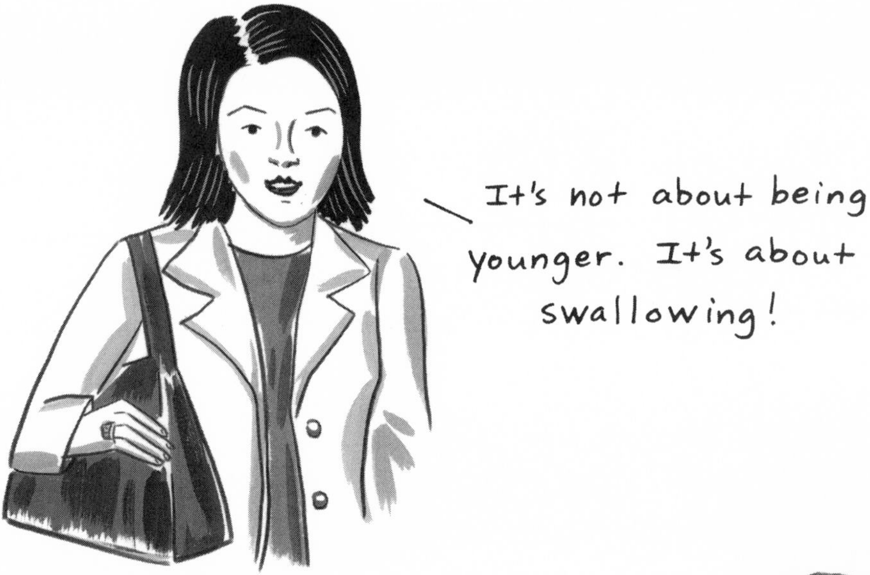
It's not about being younger. It's about swallowing!

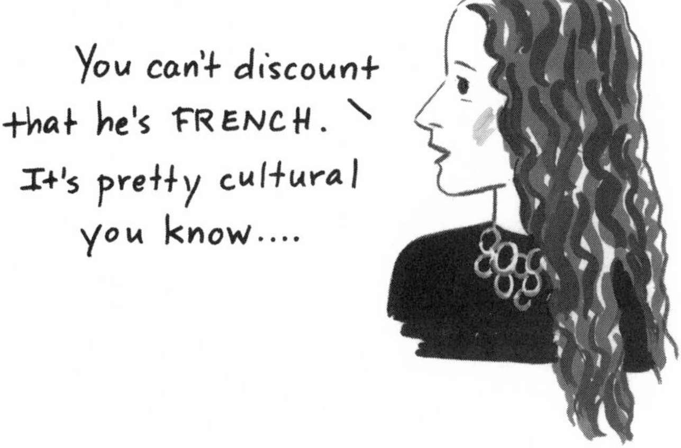
You can't discount that he's FRENCH. It's pretty cultural you know....

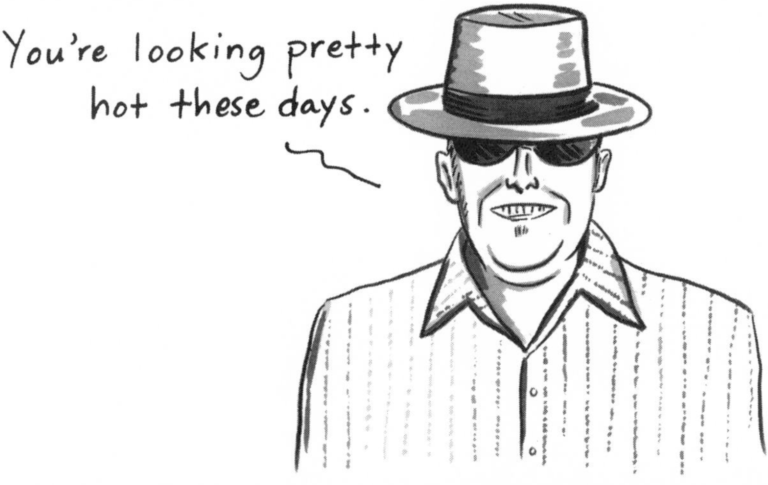
You're looking pretty hot these days.

HAVING WALLOWED LONG ENOUGH ON MY BEST FRIEND'S COUCH, I DECIDE IT'S TIME TO WALLOW ON A PROFESSIONAL'S COUCH.

SHRINKAGE

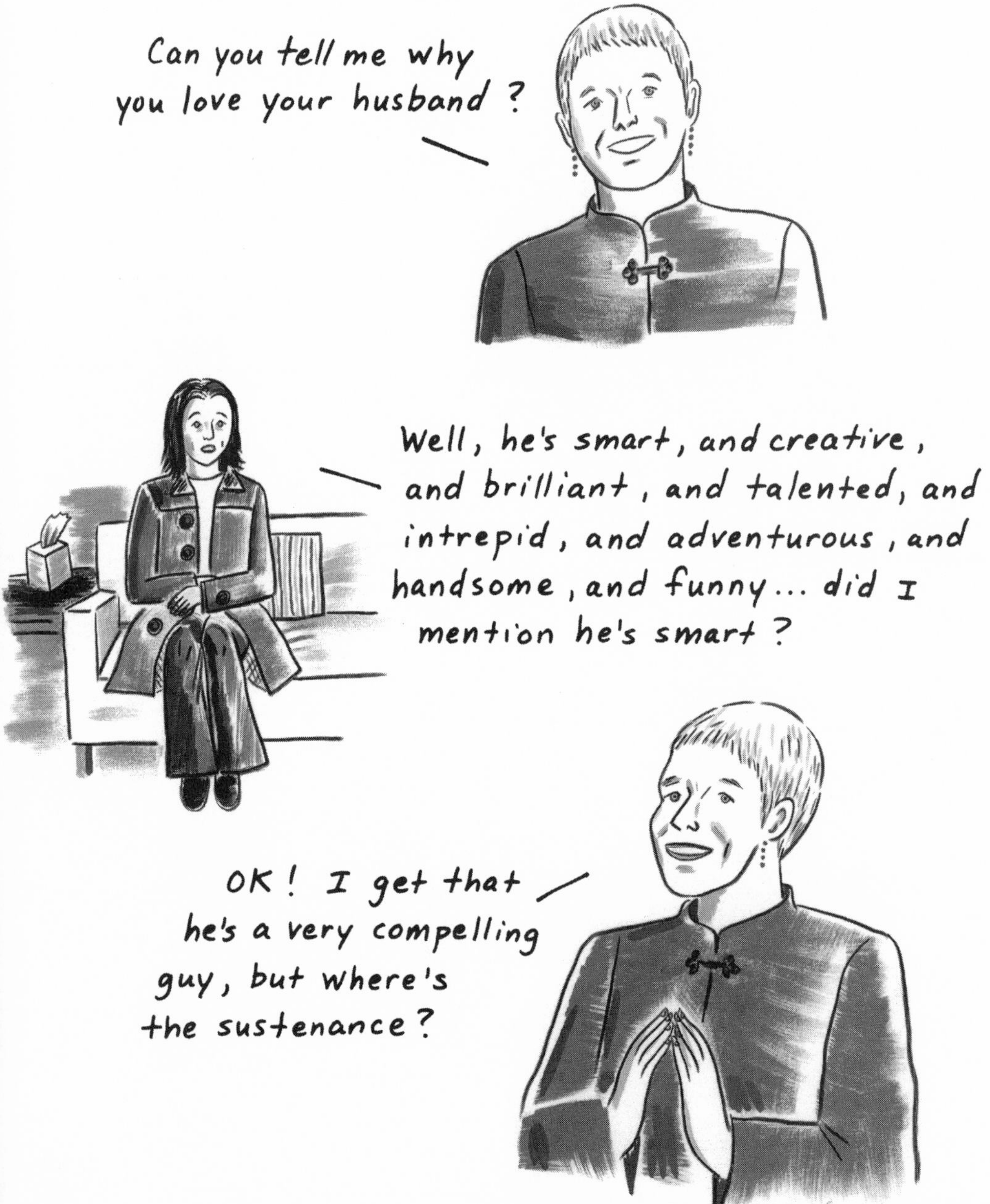

Can you tell me why you love your husband?
Well, he's smart, and creative, and brilliant, and talented, and intrepid, and adventurous, and handsome, and funny... did I mention he's smart?
OK! I get that he's a very compelling guy, but where's the sustenance?

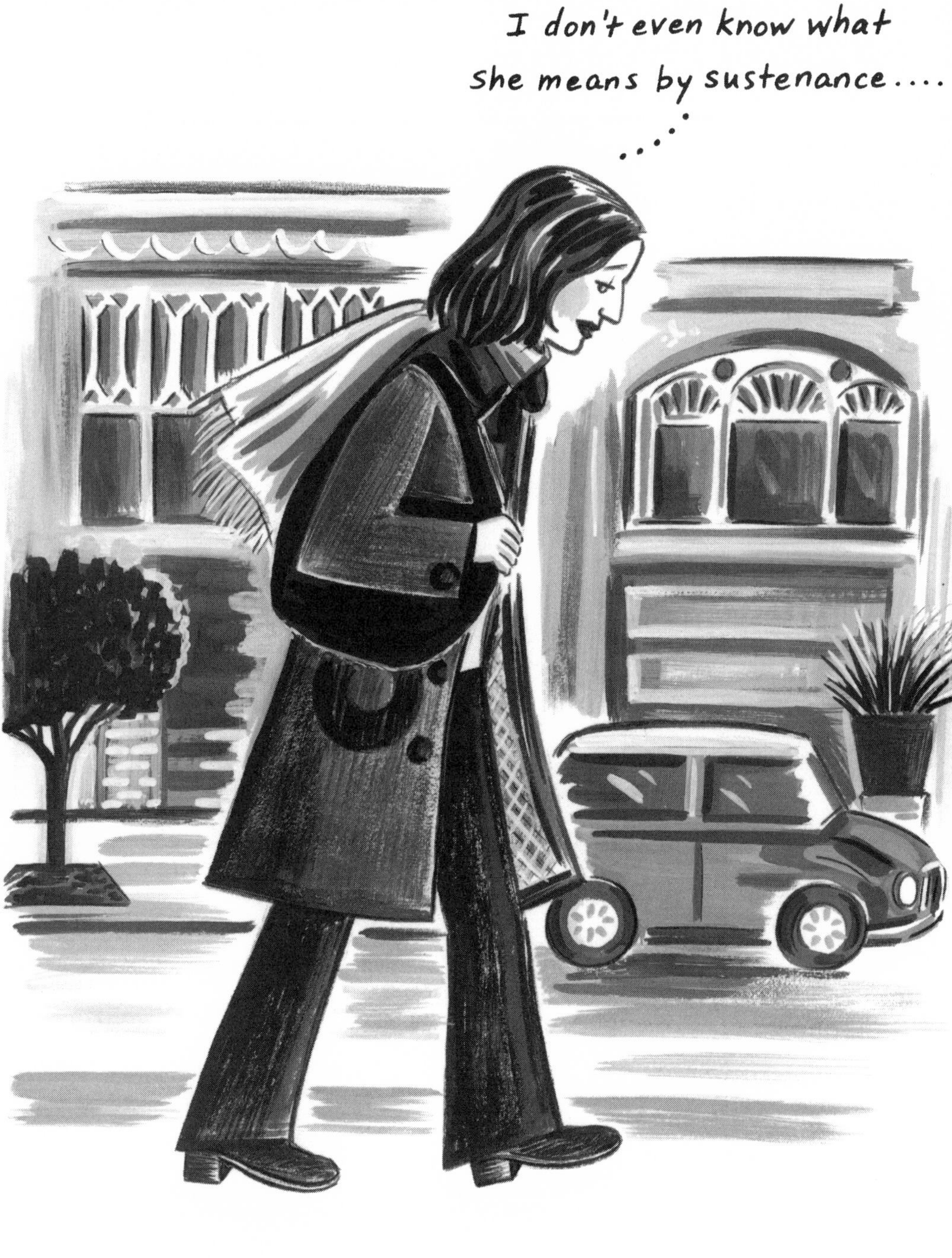
I don't even know what she means by sustenance....

THE UPSIDE OF LIVING WITH CONSTANT ANXIETY IS THAT THE **HEARTBREAK DIET** BURNS CALORIES FASTER THAN TREKKING THE ANNAPURNA CIRCUIT. CLEARLY SIGNIFICANT PHYSIOLOGICAL CHANGES ARE OCCURRING.

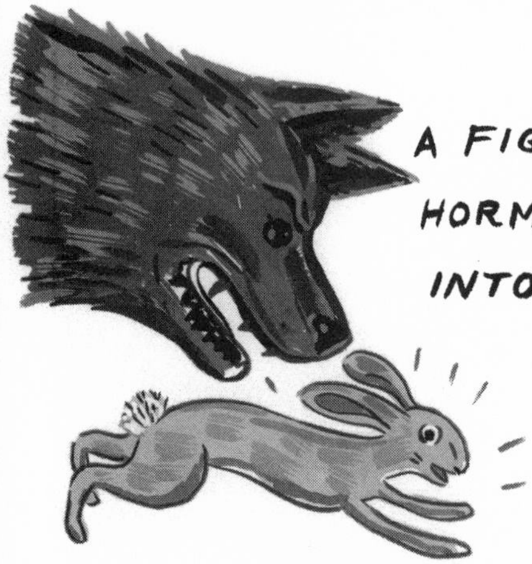

A FIGHT-OR-FLIGHT EFFECT SHOOTS HORMONES SUCH AS ADRENALINE INTO THE SYSTEM....

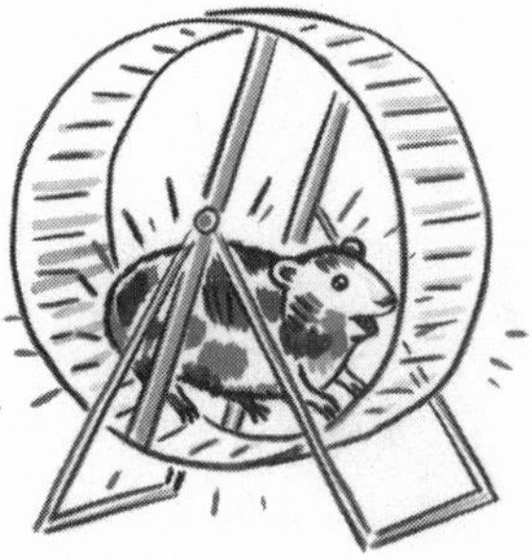

BLOOD SUGAR LEVELS RISE...

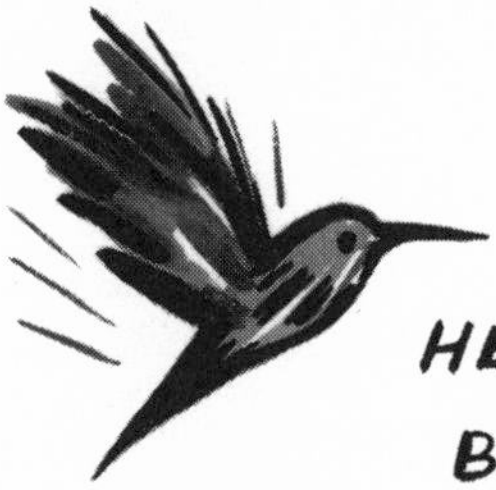

...AND AN INCREASED HEART RATE PUMPS MORE BLOOD TO THE MUSCLES.

AND PERHAPS MOST IMPORTANT, FORMERLY SIGNIFICANT ACTIVITIES SUCH AS LUNCH NOW SEEM UTTERLY IRRELEVANT.

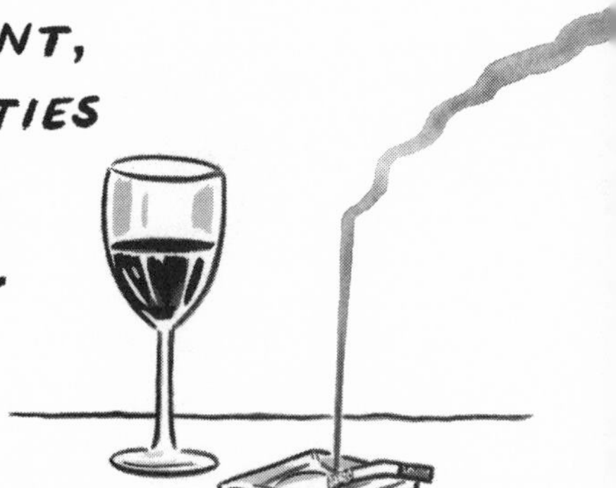

THERE IS ACTUALLY SUCH A THING AS
"*BROKEN HEART SYNDROME.*"
THE MEDICAL TERM IS STRESS CARDIOMYOPATHY.
IT PRIMARILY AFFECTS OLDER WOMEN AND IS
BROUGHT ABOUT BY SHOCK. A DEATH OF A LOVED
ONE OR THE ABANDONMENT OF A SPOUSE CAN
TRIGGER THE ADRENAL SYSTEM TO REACT
SUDDENLY AND **SOMETIMES FATALLY. YES, THE
VICTORIAN** NOVELISTS WERE RIGHT ....
A PERSON CAN DIE FROM A BROKEN HEART.

I FEEL MISERABLE, BUT I LOOK HOT, IS THE INESCAPABLE CONCLUSION THAT LEADS PREDICTABLY TO:

COPING MECHANISM #2

Retail Therapy

My butt hasn't looked like this since I was on the high-school gymnastics scene.

Hence, new jeans.

New shoes to go with the new jeans.

Red is such a cheerful color. I need cheering up. $500 is a lot to spend on a coat, but if I wear it every day that's only $1.36 per day!

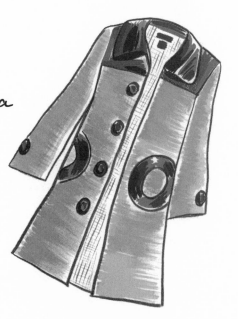

BUT ULTIMATELY RETAIL THERAPY LEAVES ME FEELING EMPTY, GUILT-RIDDEN, AND BROKE....

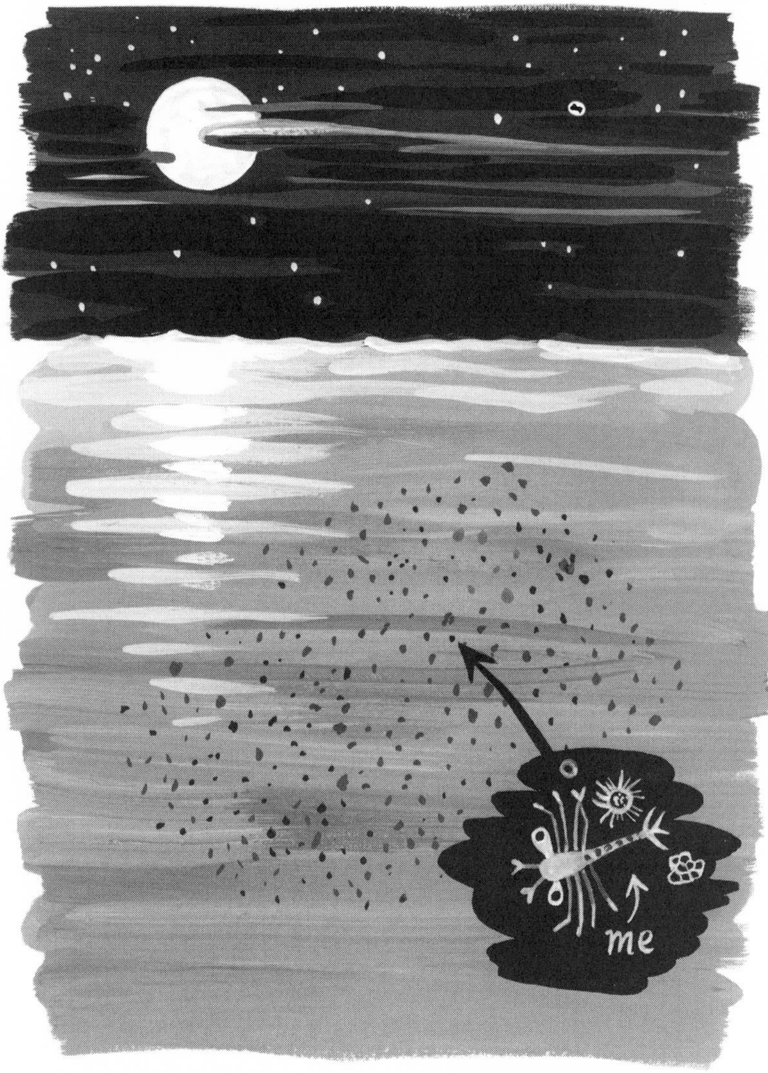
me

WHAT DOES LIFE MEAN ANYWAY? WE'RE NO MORE SIGNFICANT THAN BITS OF PLANKTON FLOATING IN THE VASTNESS OF THE SEA.

I DECIDE THAT THIS IS AS GOOD A TIME AS ANY TO BECOME ENLIGHTENED....

COPING MECHANISM #3
Cultivating Inner Peace

For the first time in my life I find myself drifting down **that** aisle in the bookstore.

Expectations cause suffering.

Even scientists say meditation provides quantifiable benefits....

inhale
exhale
inhale
exhale
what's for lunch?
inhale

MY YOGA TEACHER IS INCREDIBLY PROFOUND. I FIND THAT EVERYTHING HE SAYS RELATES TO MY PERSONAL CRISIS.

~ Focus and find that place of stillness in your turbulent life. Much as the center of a spinning wheel is a place of stillness.

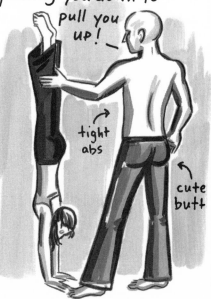

Use GRAVITY! Use the force that is pulling you down to pull you up! ~

tight abs

cute butt

Yes! I AM a peaceful warrior!

I perform a METTA meditation for X.... I accept with compassion his right to choose the path that will bring him happiness.

61

ONE EVENING, I RETURN FROM YOGA, BRIMMING WITH SERENITY AND COMPASSION....

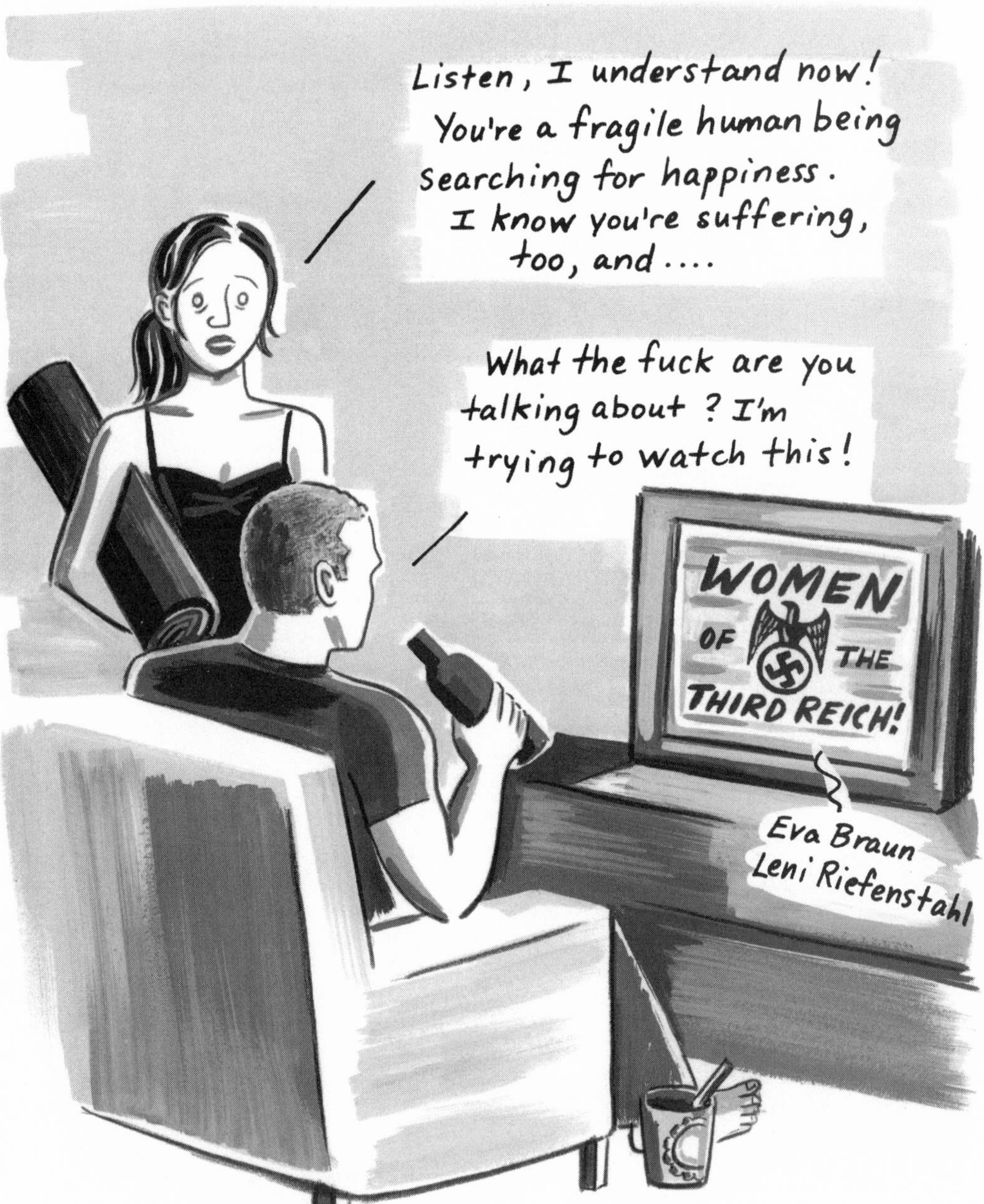

Listen, I understand now! You're a fragile human being searching for happiness. I know you're suffering, too, and....
What the fuck are you talking about? I'm trying to watch this!
WOMEN OF THE THIRD REICH!
Eva Braun
Leni Riefenstahl

Words of Wise Women

"No more tears now! I will
think about revenge!"

Mary, Queen of Scots

SO MUCH FOR COMPASSION....

COPING MECHANISM #4

REVENGE FANTASIES!

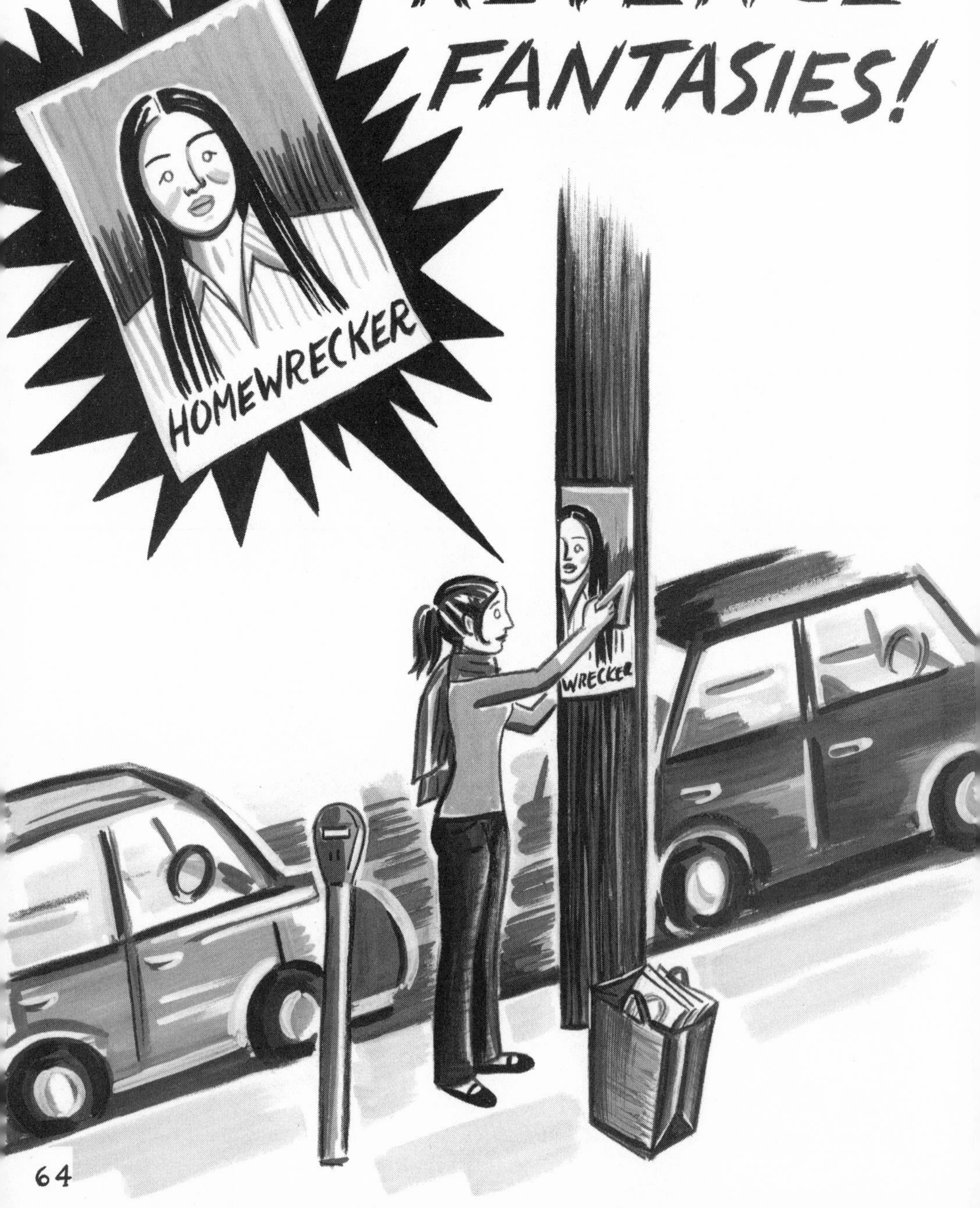
HOMEWRECKER
WRECKER

PUBLIC HUMILIATION!
THE PURITANS WERE ON TO SOMETHING!

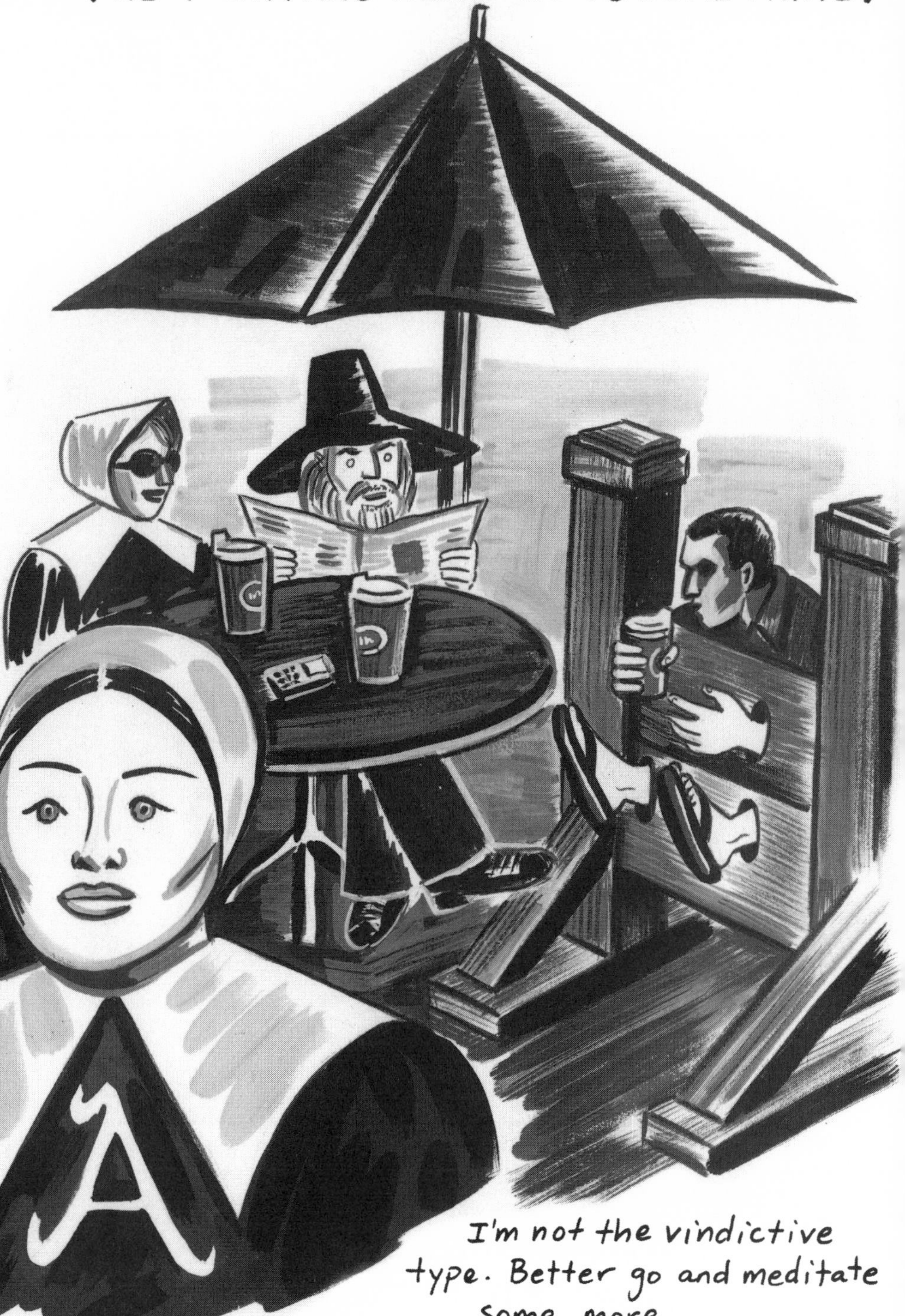
I'm not the vindictive type. Better go and meditate some more ....

IF ONLY I HAD THE **CHUTZPAH** TO EXECUTE MY ELABORATE SCHEMES!

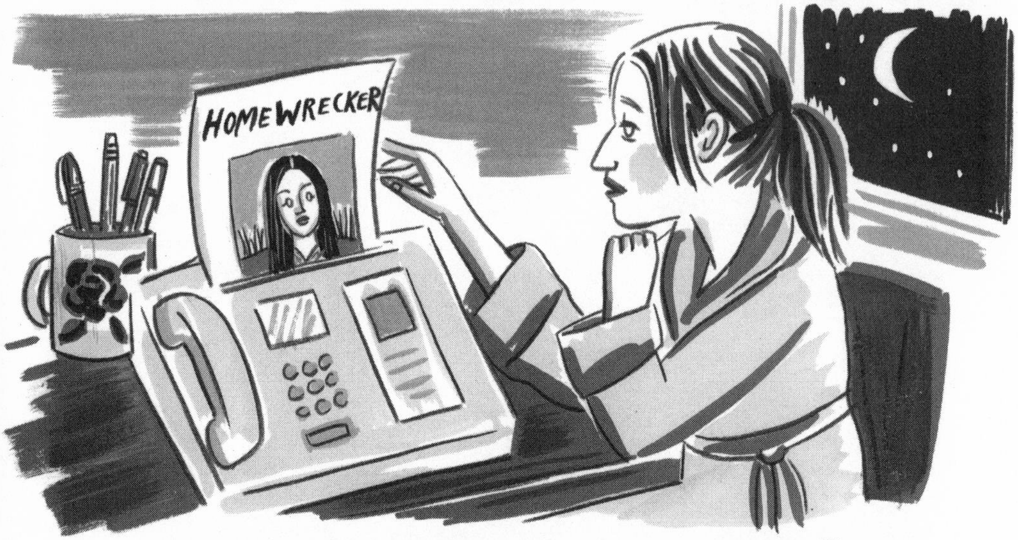
HOMEWRECKER

AT THE GIRLFRIEND'S WORKPLACE THE NEXT MORNING:

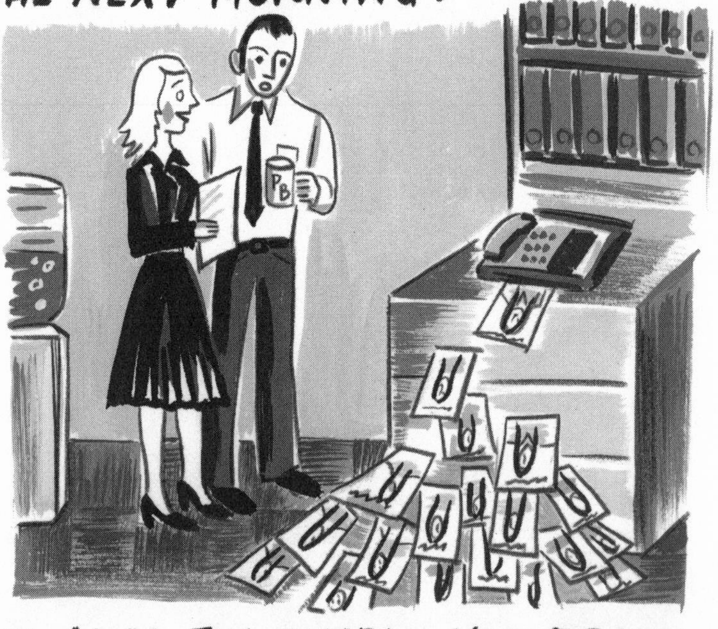
PB

BUT ALAS I'M SIMPLY NOT BRAVE OR ENERGETIC (OR NUTS) ENOUGH TO FEED A FAX MACHINE ALL NIGHT.

WHY DO I FIXATE ON **HER**? SHE DIDN'T BETRAY ME! I'M SURE IT HAS SOMETHING TO DO WITH EVOLUTION.... IN THE QUEST FOR SURVIVAL, THE "OTHER WOMAN" POSES A CLEAR THREAT TO MY GENETIC HERITAGE. IF SHE REPRODUCES WITH MY MATE, THEN HER OFFSPRING COME INTO DIRECT COMPETITION FOR PRECIOUS RESOURCES WITH MY OFFSPRING.

CONCLUSION: SHE MUST BE DESTROYED!

PRIMARILY I CONCENTRATE ON

COPING MECHANISM #5 DENIAL

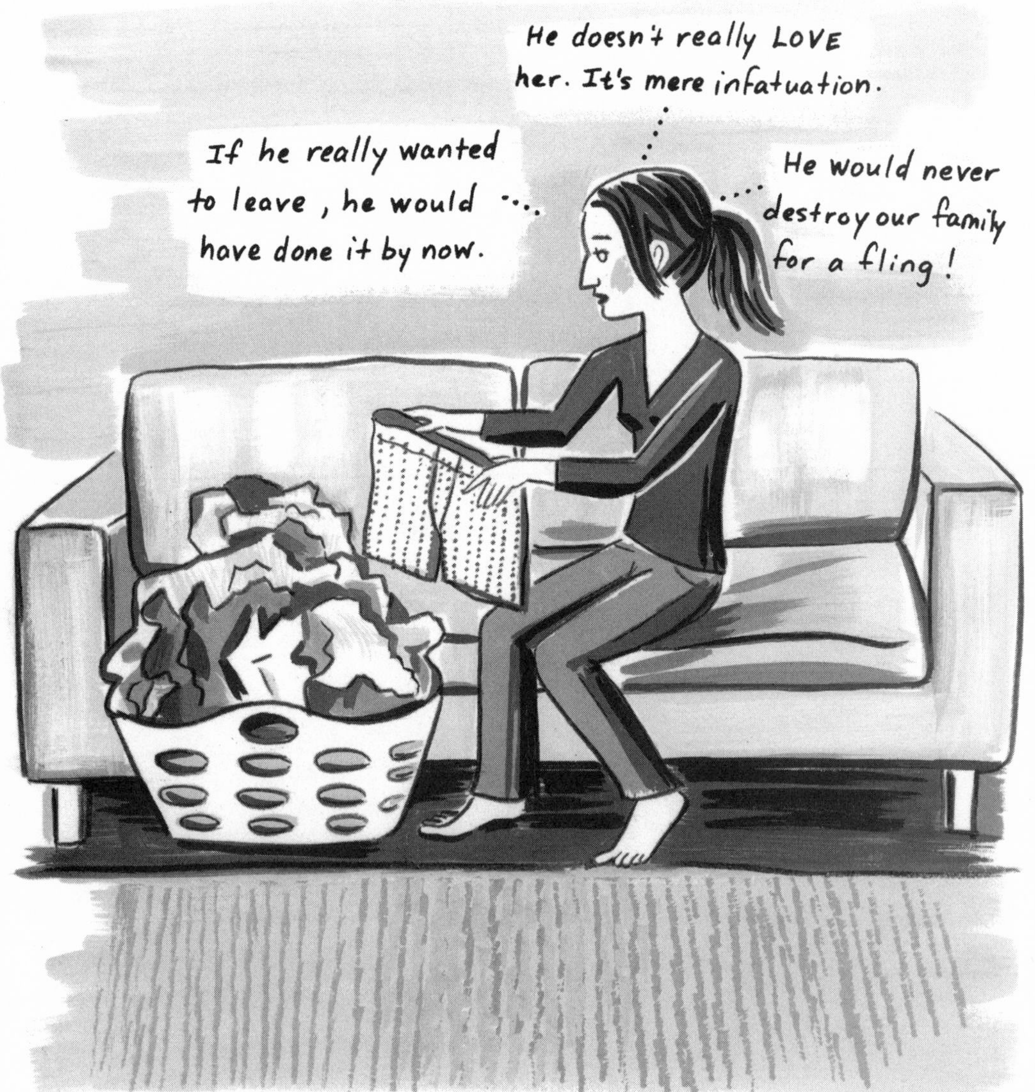
If he really wanted to leave, he would have done it by now.
He doesn't really LOVE her. It's mere infatuation.
He would never destroy our family for a fling!

Words of Wise Women

"I believe in denial. Denial is
a marvelous thing."

Kitty Carlisle Hart

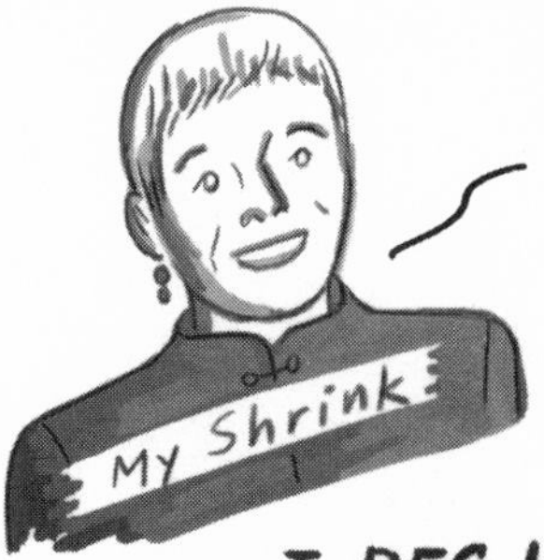
My Shrink

Now that the apple cart is tipped over, you may as well look at the apples!

I BEG HIM TO TRY COUPLES' COUNSELING. X RELUCTANTLY AGREES....

SHRINKAGE

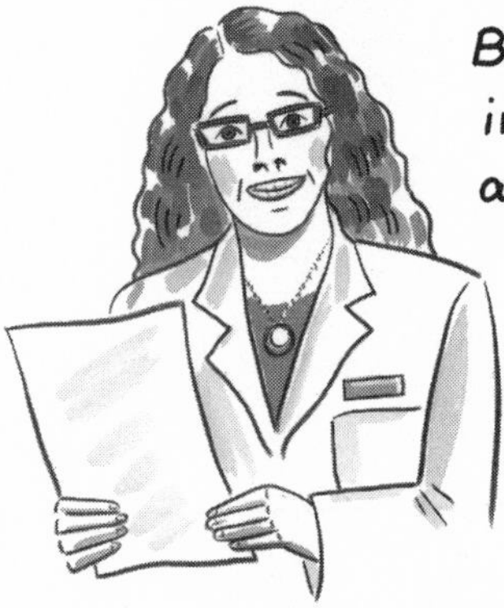

Before we start, please sign these forms in triplicate to acknowledge that you are aware that I am an intern....

FORGET THE H.M.O., IT'S TIME FOR THE BIG GUNS

I've been doing this for twenty years, and triangles are tricky. If X wants to salvage the marriage, he needs to say goodbye to the third party TODAY and devote 100 percent of his energy to working on the relationship with Thorina. However, in my experience, most people, maybe 98 percent, choose to move on to the new relationship. Well, our time is up. Next week X will tell us what he decides....

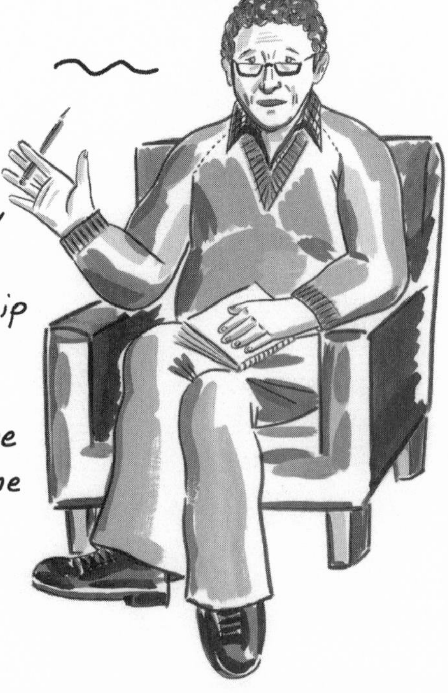

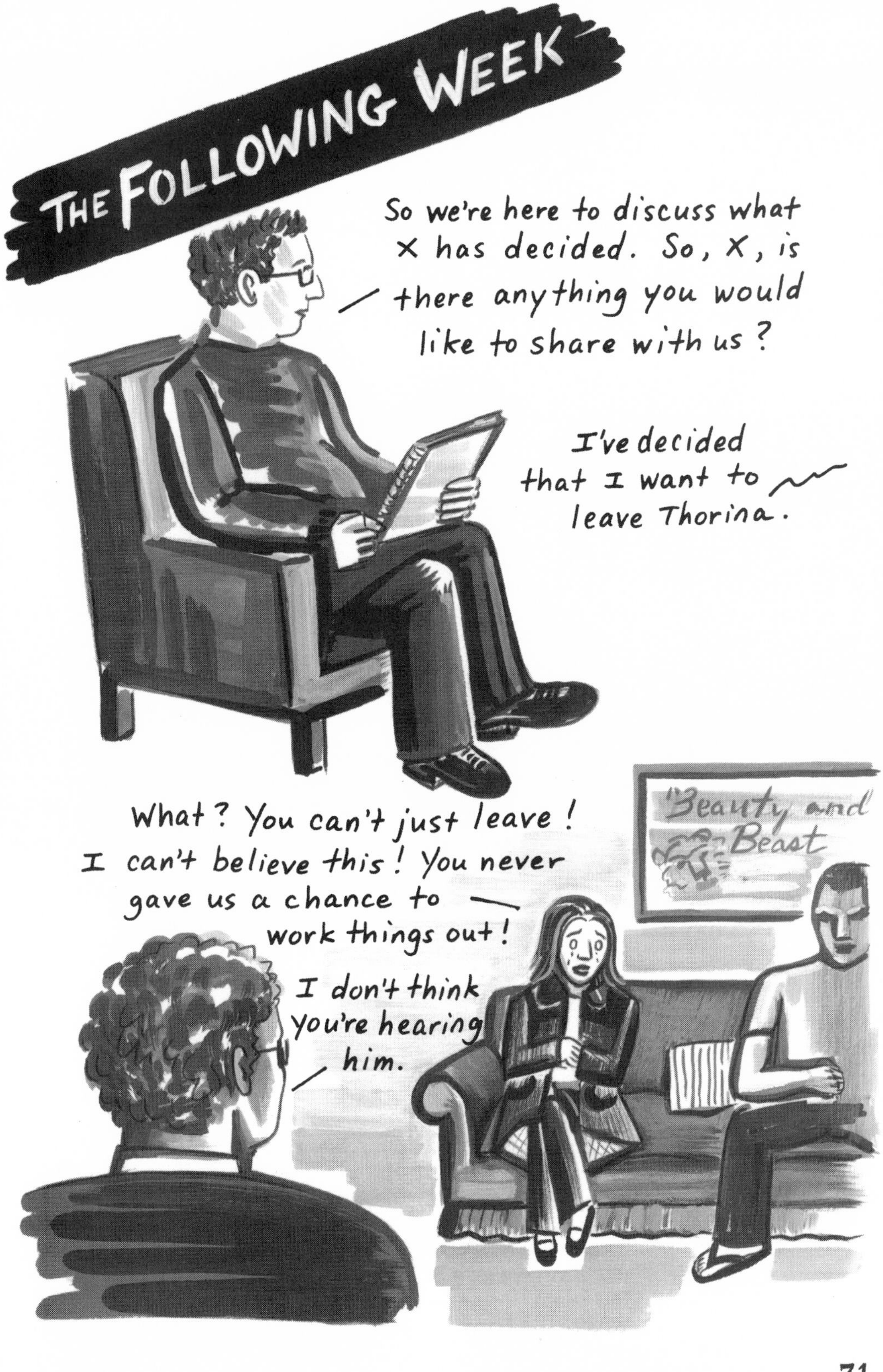
THE FOLLOWING WEEK
So we're here to discuss what X has decided. So, X, is there anything you would like to share with us?
I've decided that I want to leave Thorina.
"Beauty and Beast
What? You can't just leave! I can't believe this! You never gave us a chance to work things out!
I don't think you're hearing him.

MY DEEPLY ENTRENCHED DENIAL IS PUNCTURED BY THE NEED FOR CLARITY.

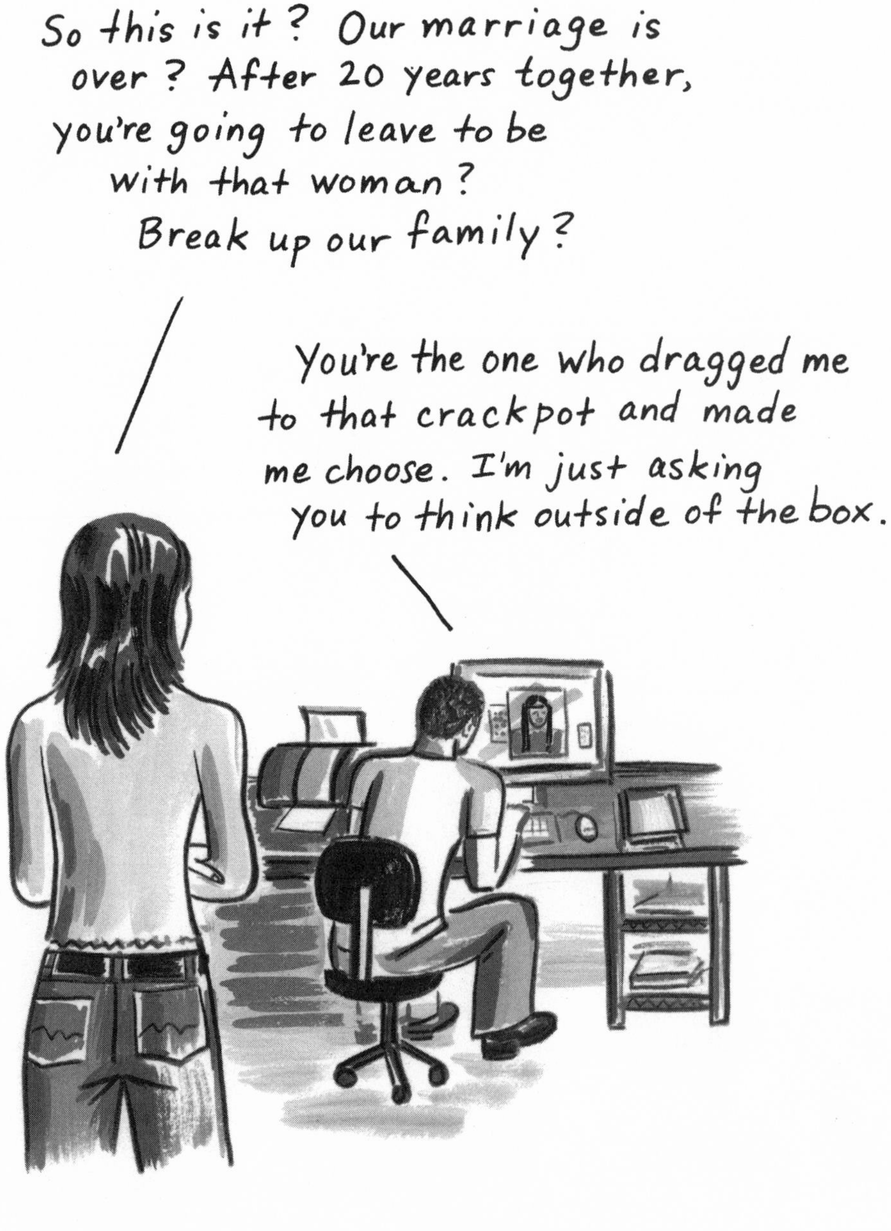
So this is it? Our marriage is over? After 20 years together, you're going to leave to be with that woman? Break up our family?
You're the one who dragged me to that crackpot and made me choose. I'm just asking you to think outside of the box.

OUTSIDE OF THE BOX?

But, what if I like the box?
I'm in the box....
My family is in the box.
Everything I love is in the BOX!

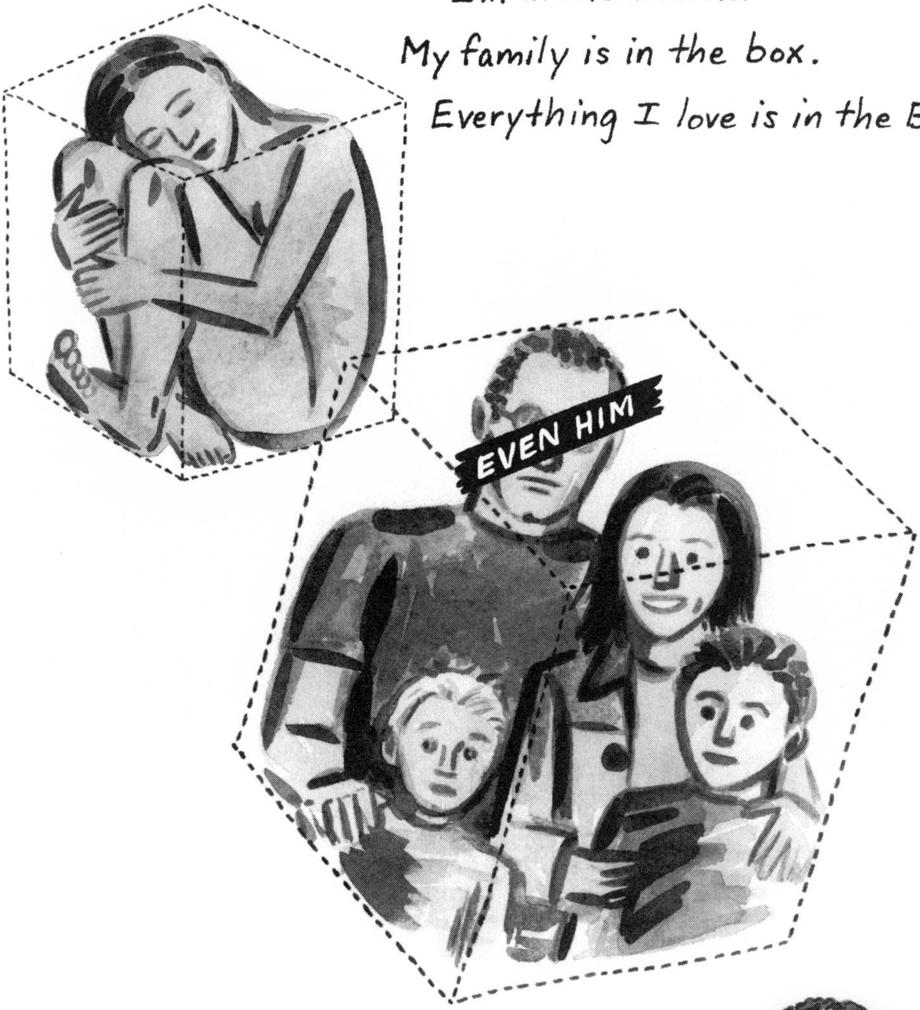
EVEN HIM

Outside of the box?! He said that?
Thorina, it's a marriage, not a start-up.

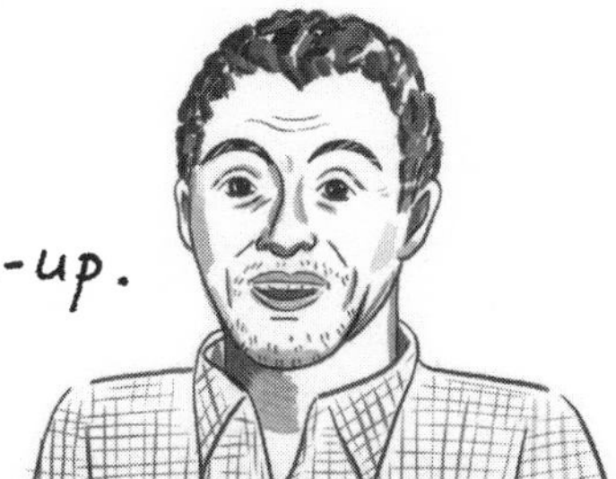
friend

IT'S DEPRESSING, BUT PERHAPS HE'S RIGHT ABOUT MONOGAMY. HOW MANY ANIMAL SPECIES ARE MONOGAMOUS? I'LL Google "ANIMALS THAT MATE FOR LIFE."

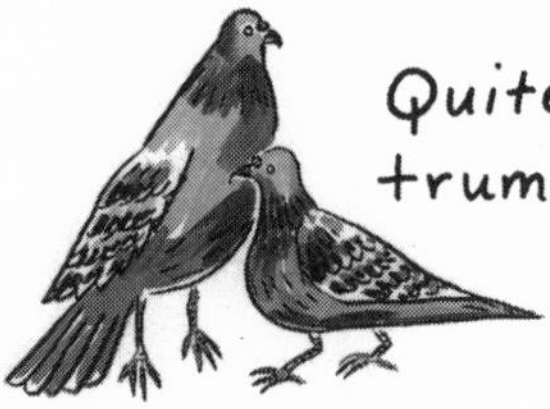

Quite a few birds.... Pigeons, ducks, geese, trumpeter swans, mate for life.

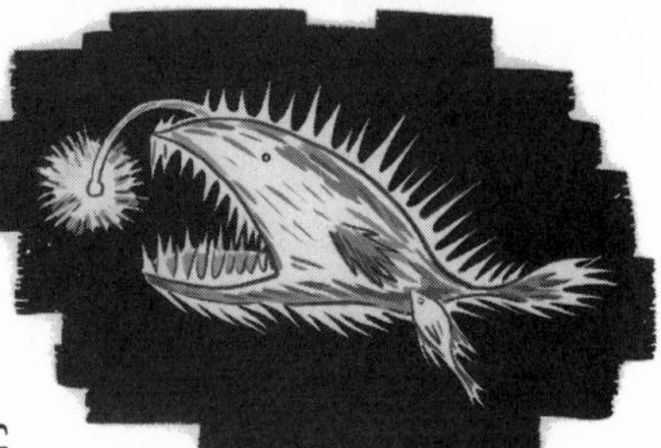

The deep-sea anglerfish is an interesting example of a monogamous creature.... The male locates the female in the blackness of the seafloor by sniffing (do fish sniff?) her pheromones. He then fuses himself to her body. His blood vessels merge with hers. His organs atrophy. He literally becomes an external sperm-producing organ.

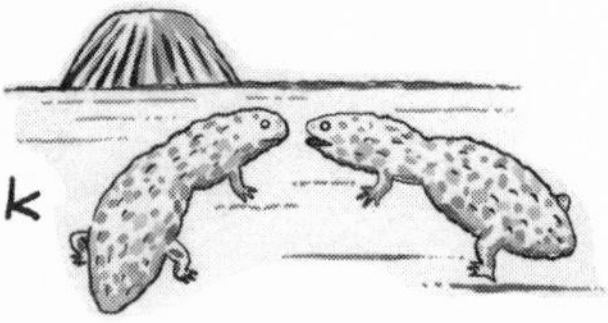

The Australian shingleback skink mates for life. So do the Djungarian hamster and the gray wolf. At least they're mammals.

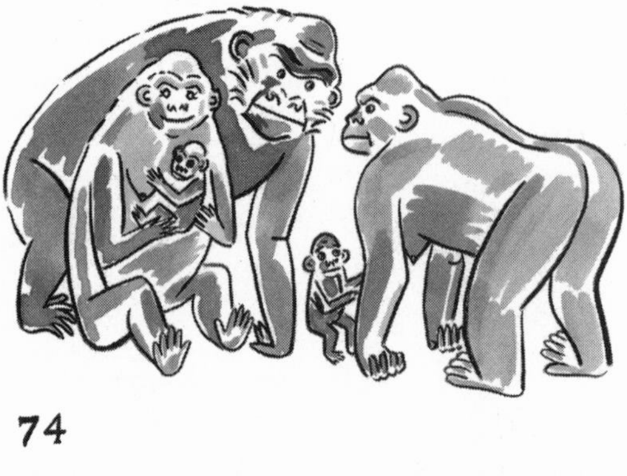

The "Pet Doctor" at the Arizona Zoo proclaims that gorillas are monogamous — except for the males. (huh?)

CLEARLY, IF WE'RE GOING TO APPROACH THIS IN A DARWINISTIC FASHION, MONOGAMY ISN'T MUCH OF A SURVIVAL TACTIC....

Take, for instance, the endangered Andean condor. When its mate dies, the surviving condor never reproduces again. Maybe there should be a "MATCH" site for Andean condors.

"Are you looking for commitment? Meet me for a bite of carrion and let my 12-foot wingspan sweep you away!"

BUT AREN'T WE HUMANS DIFFERENT? ISN'T MONOGAMY KEY TO A STABLE FAMILY? THE FAMILY BEING KEY TO A STABLE SOCIETY?

I CONTEMPLATE WHAT **OUTSIDE** OF THE **BOX** WOULD LOOK LIKE....

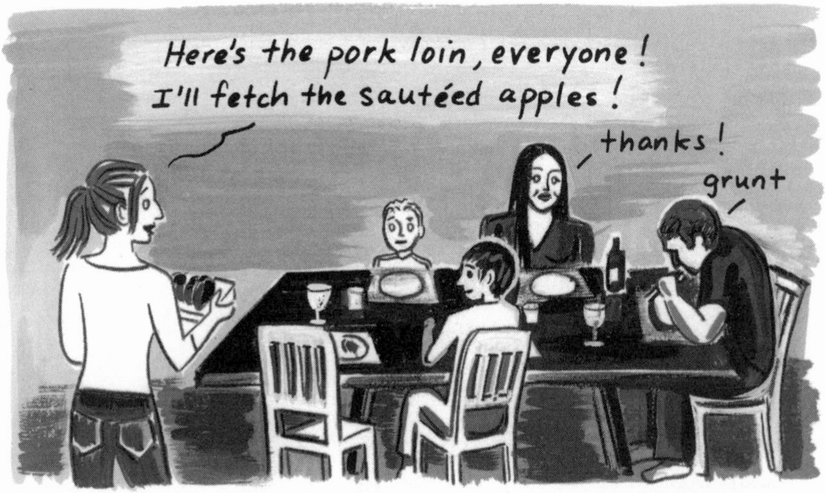

Here's the pork loin, everyone! I'll fetch the sautéed apples!
thanks!
grunt

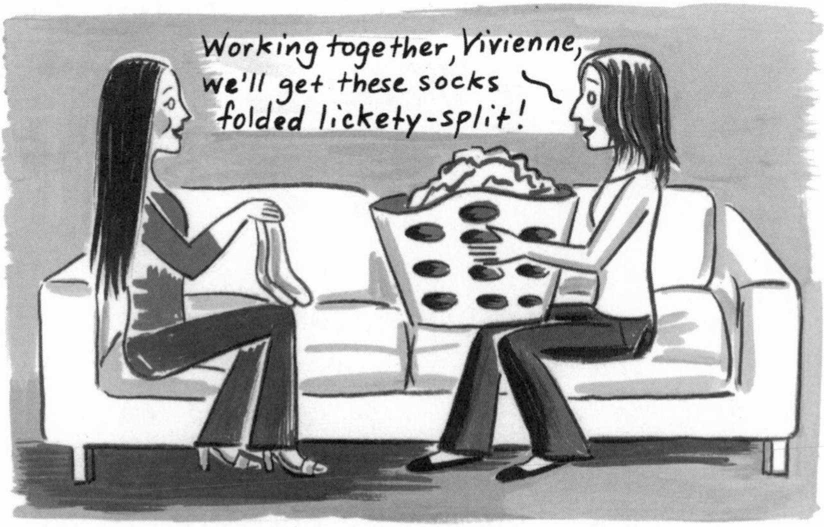

Working together, Vivienne, we'll get these socks folded lickety-split!

IT WOULD TAKE SOME ORGANIZATION....

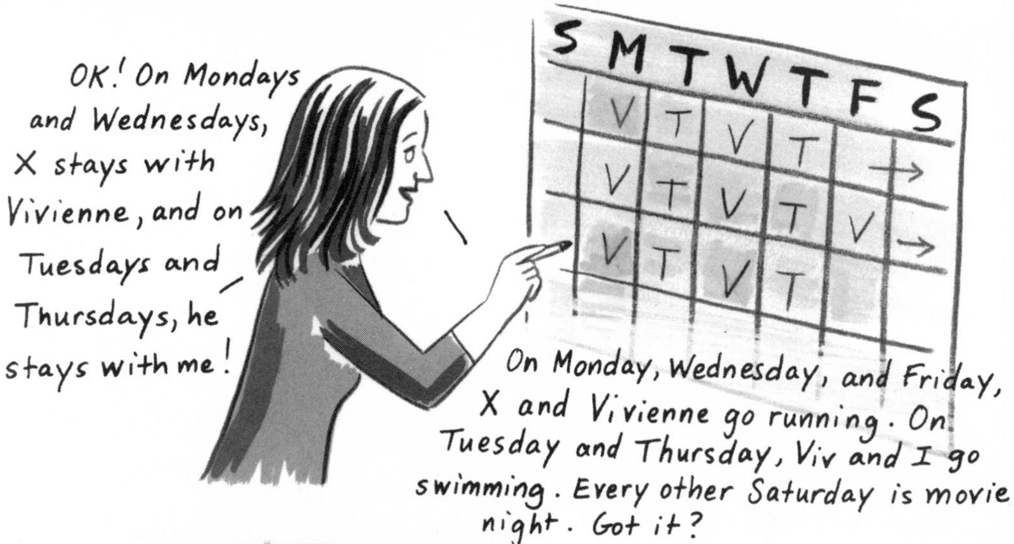
OK! On Mondays and Wednesdays, X stays with Vivienne, and on Tuesdays and Thursdays, he stays with me!
S M T W T F S
On Monday, Wednesday, and Friday, X and Vivienne go running. On Tuesday and Thursday, Viv and I go swimming. Every other Saturday is movie night. Got it?

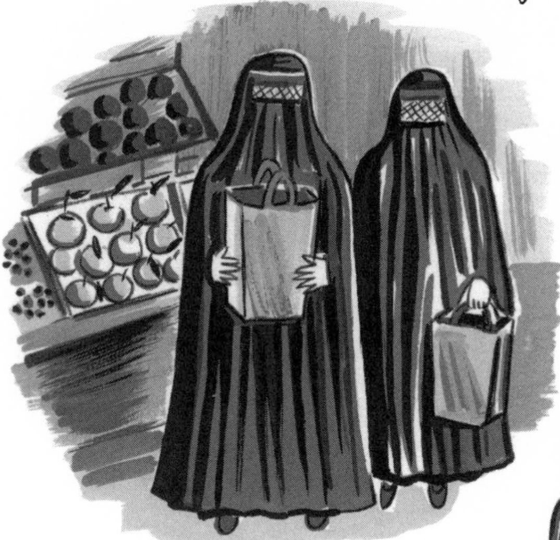

DESPITE THE TRANQUILITY OF OUR HOME LIFE, VIVIENNE AND I ARE NOT THAT KEEN TO BE SEEN TOGETHER IN PUBLIC.

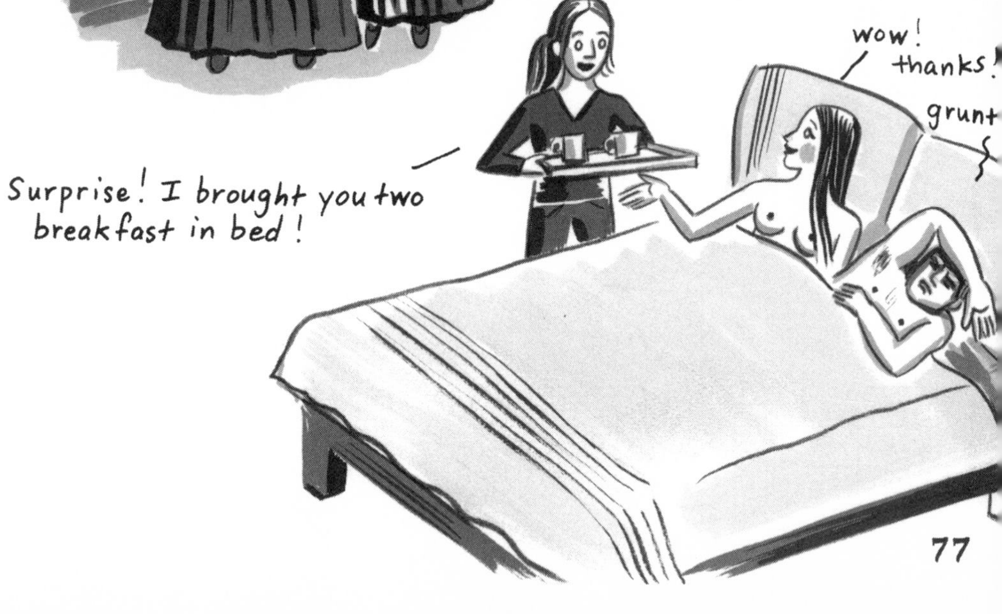
Surprise! I brought you two breakfast in bed!
wow! thanks!
grunt

THE CHORUS

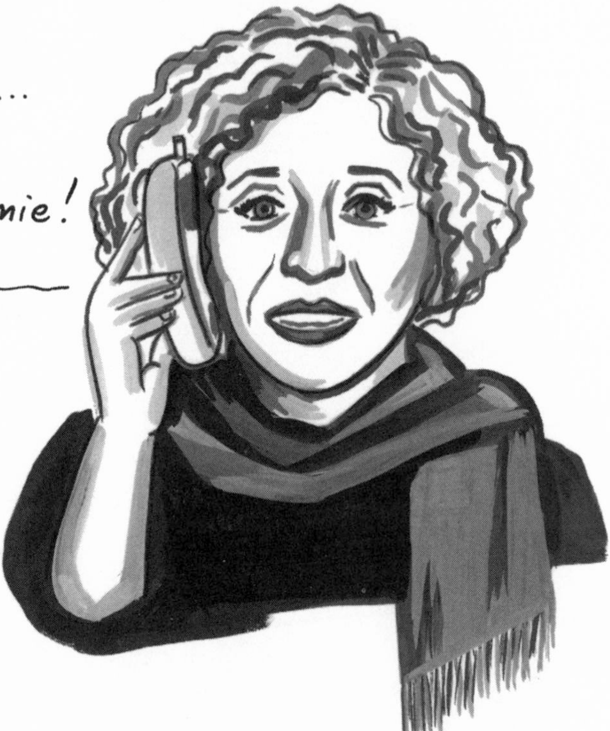
Mais ma chérie...
All men have the
dream of la polygamie!

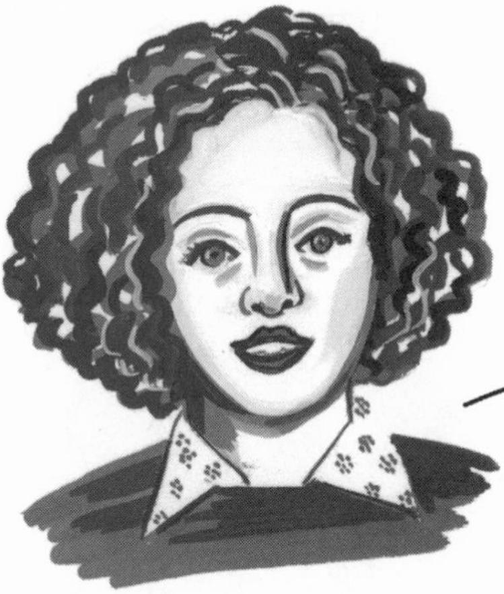
of course he blames you!
The best defense is a
good offense!

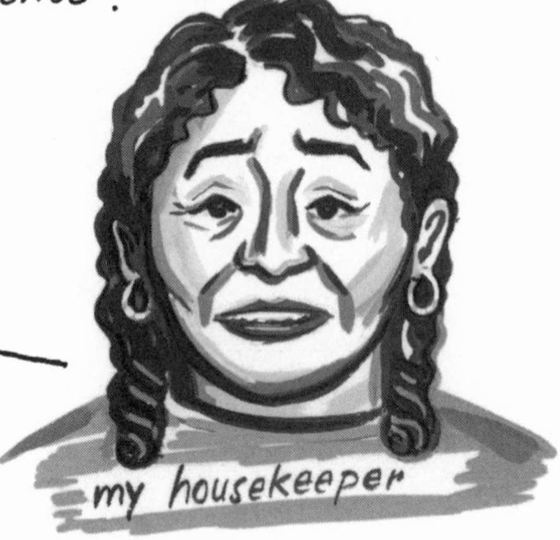
¡Oyé Thorina!
¿Porqué? ¡Los hombres
están muy locos!
my housekeeper

You're better off without him. He's a cantankerous old man trapped in — the body of a sexy photographer but soon he'll be a cantankerous old man trapped in the body of a cantankerous old man.

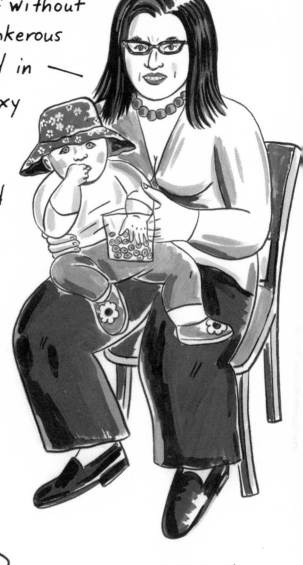

We've always had a little spark for each other, right?

79

I KNOW EVERYTHING ABOUT THIS MAN.

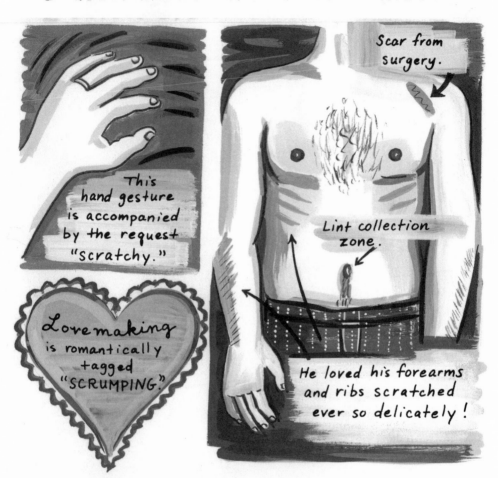

Scar from surgery.

This hand gesture is accompanied by the request "scratchy."

Lovemaking is romantically tagged "SCRUMPING."

Lint collection zone.

He loved his forearms and ribs scratched ever so delicately!

HIS DESPISED FOOD PRODUCTS INCLUDE:

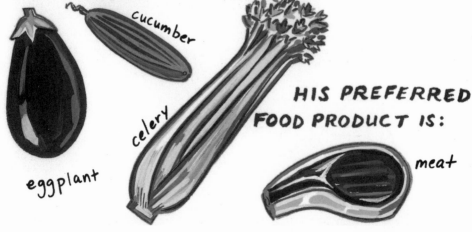

cucumber

celery

eggplant

HIS PREFERRED FOOD PRODUCT IS:

meat

WE WERE ENORMOUSLY AFFECTIONATE!

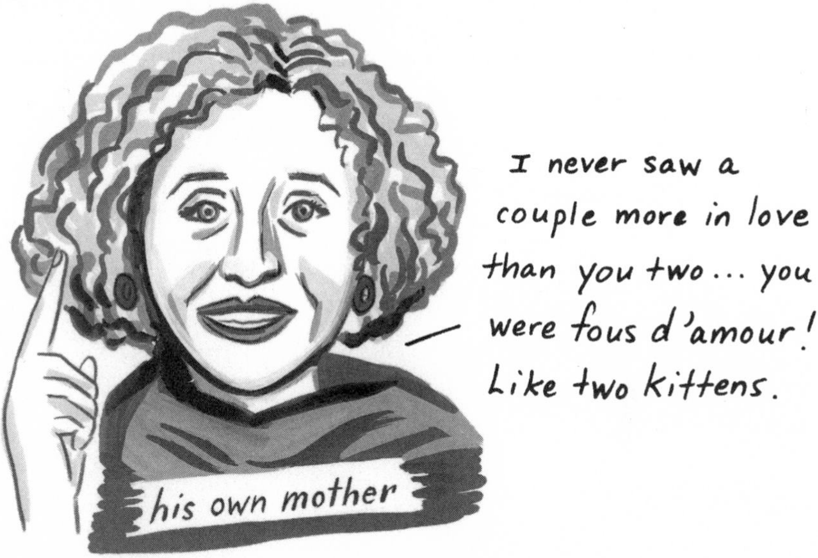
I never saw a couple more in love than you two... you were fous d'amour! Like two kittens.
his own mother

HE USED TO TICKLE ME UNTIL I WAS BREATHLESS!

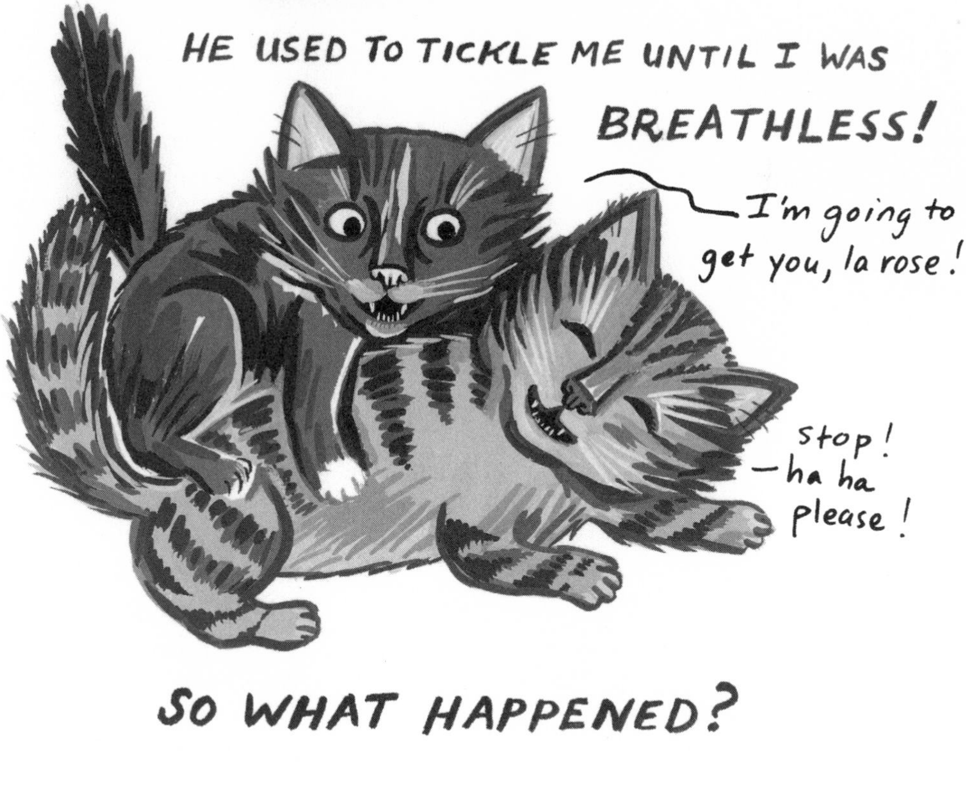
I'm going to get you, la rose!
stop! —ha ha please!

SO WHAT HAPPENED?

PERHAPS THIS IS THE MOMENT TO LOOK BACK. WHAT DREW THIS COUPLE TOGETHER AND WHAT WAS IT LIKE BEFORE IT ALL WENT KAPUT?

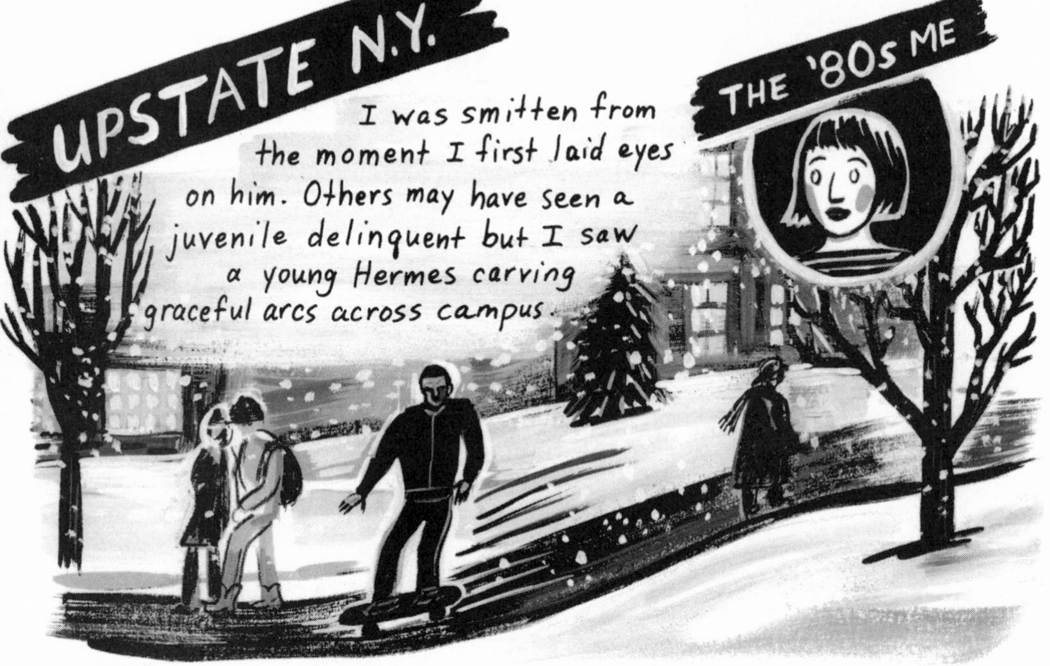
UPSTATE N.Y.
THE '80s ME
I was smitten from the moment I first laid eyes on him. Others may have seen a juvenile delinquent but I saw a young Hermes carving graceful arcs across campus.

What young woman wouldn't be seduced by the full sensuous lips, piercing green eyes, and wacko Gallic sense of humor?

I knew he liked me when he brought cookies to the studio at midnight.

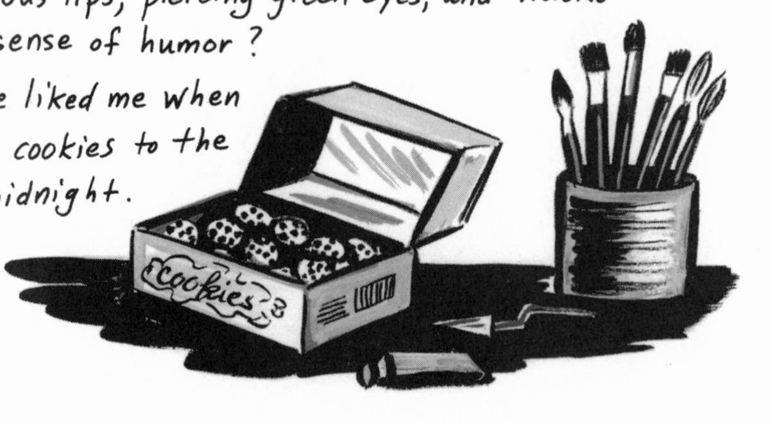
cookies

THAT FIRST SUMMER I FOLLOWED X TO PARIS, WHERE WE SPENT THE MONTH OF JUNE IN HIS BROTHER'S 7th ARRONDISSEMENT PIED-À-TERRE.

TO GAIN PRIVACY FROM THE MED-SCHOOL BROTHER, WE DECAMPED TO THE BATHROOM, WHICH IN ITS **PERFECT BLACKNESS** RECALLED FOR ME THE STORY OF **EROS** and **PSYCHE**.

In the story, Psyche doesn't know if her mysterious lover is a beautiful man, or as her sisters warn, a frightful monster.

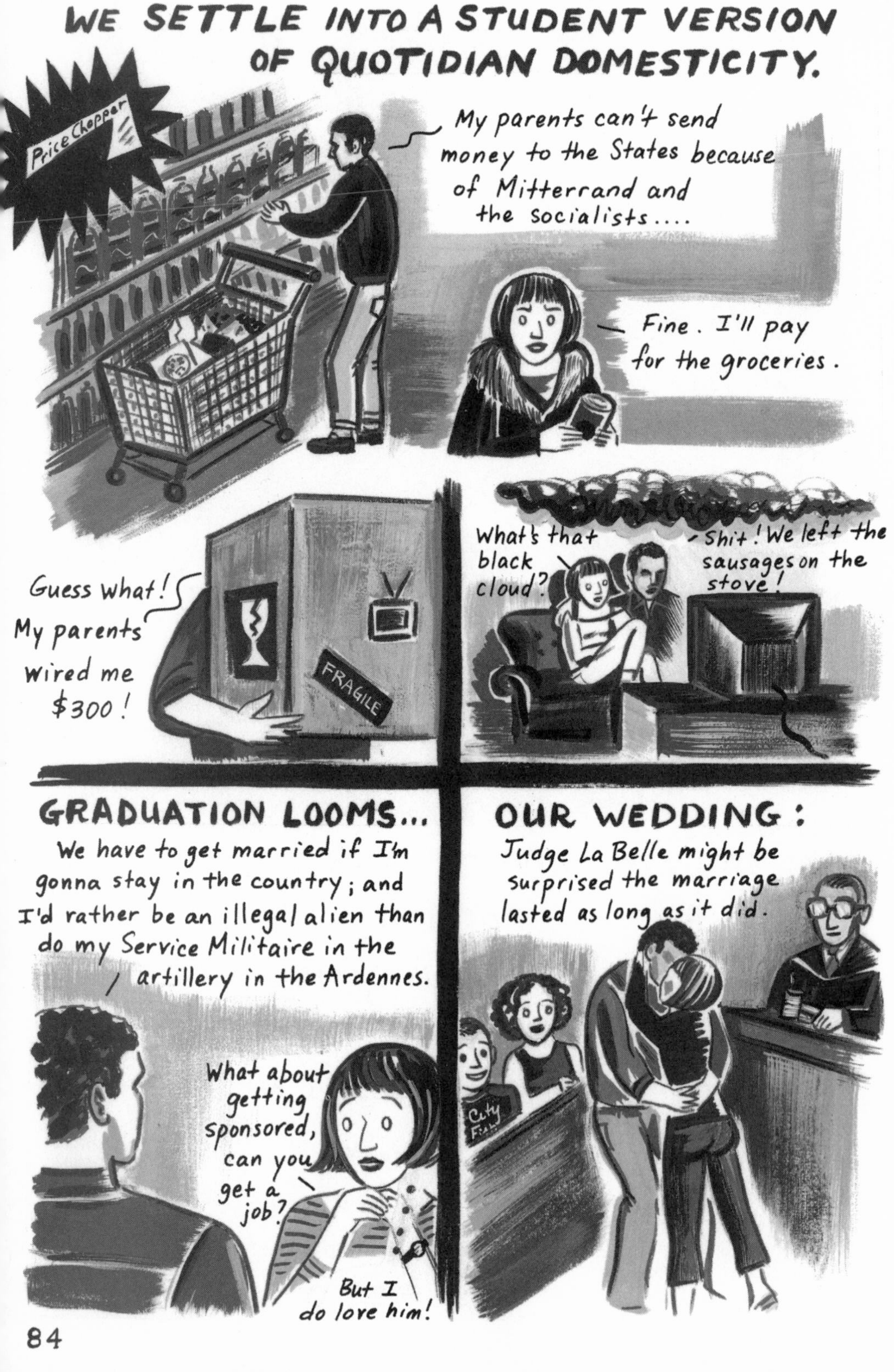
WE SETTLE INTO A STUDENT VERSION OF QUOTIDIAN DOMESTICITY.
Price Chopper
My parents can't send money to the States because of Mitterrand and the socialists....
Fine. I'll pay for the groceries.
FRAGILE
Guess what! My parents wired me $300!
What's that black cloud?
Shit! We left the sausages on the stove!
GRADUATION LOOMS...
We have to get married if I'm gonna stay in the country; and I'd rather be an illegal alien than do my Service Militaire in the artillery in the Ardennes.
What about getting sponsored, can you get a job?
But I do love him!
OUR WEDDING:
Judge La Belle might be surprised the marriage lasted as long as it did.

IT'S ROMANTIC, BUT THE RISK OF MARRYING YOUNG IS YOU'VE MET SOMEONE IN THE **LARVAL STAGE.**

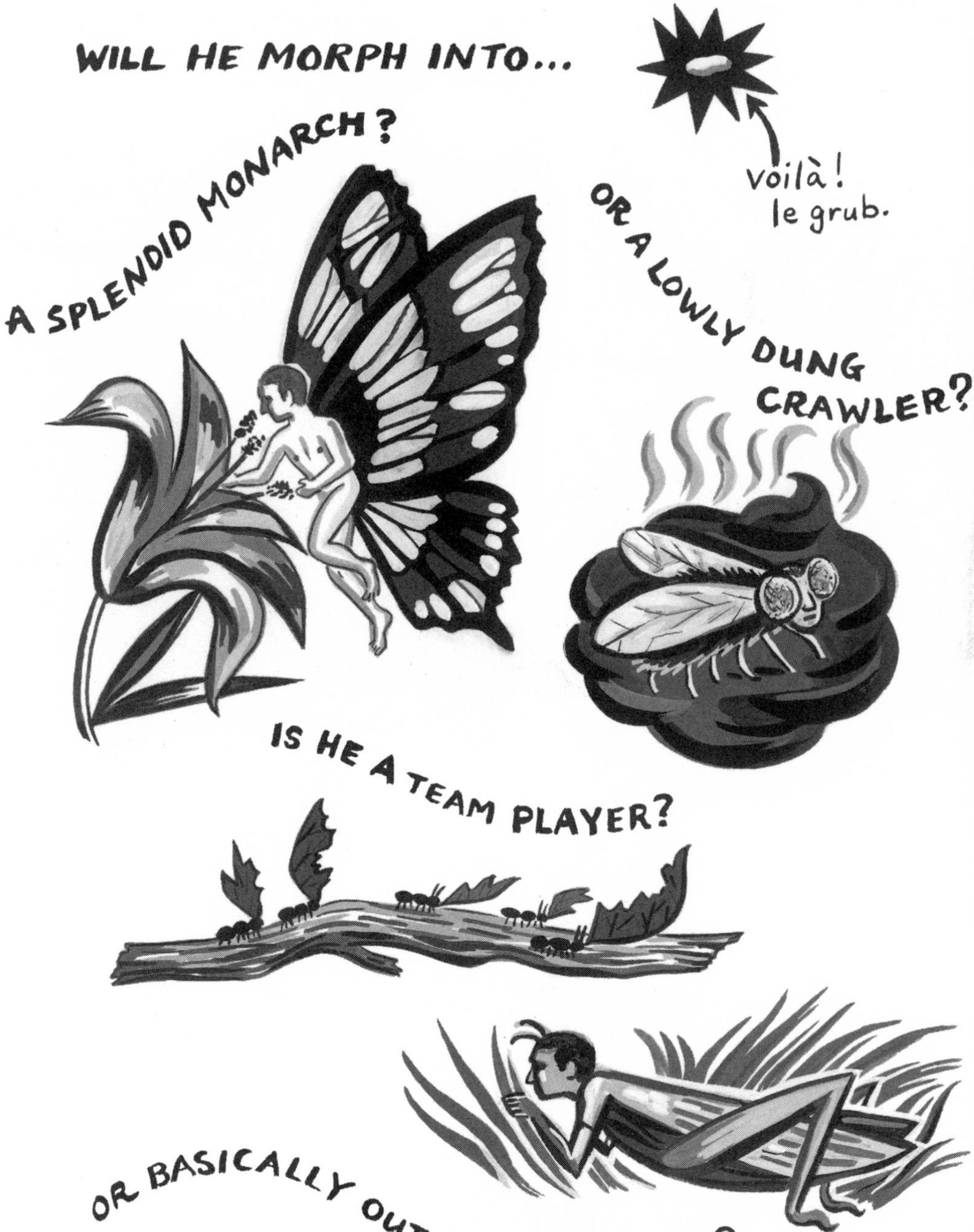
WILL HE MORPH INTO...
voilà!
le grub.
A SPLENDID MONARCH?
OR A LOWLY DUNG CRAWLER?
IS HE A TEAM PLAYER?
OR BASICALLY OUT FOR HIMSELF?

AFTER GRADUATION, WE MOVED TO NEW YORK CITY. BETWEEN THE DUMPSTER FULL OF ROTTING CRAB CARAPACES BELOW AND THE TOXIC FUMES FROM ABOVE, THE PAD HAD CERTAIN OLFACTORY DISADVANTAGES.

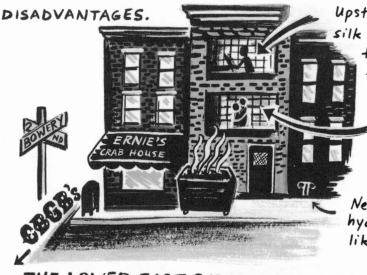

2ND
BOWERY
ERNIE'S
CRAB HOUSE
CBGB's
Upstairs neighbor silk screening t-shirts for the RAMONES.
Us in our love nest.
New York hydrants look like E.T.

THE LOWER EAST SIDE IN THE 1980s WAS PRETTY SKETCHY.

crack vials

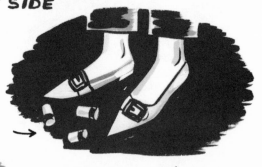

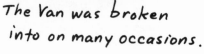

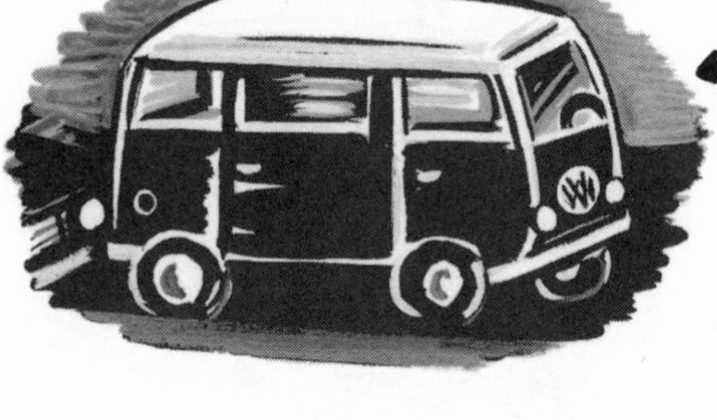

The Van was broken into on many occasions.

DESPITE THE GRITTINESS, I LOVED NEW YORK!
(He hated it.)

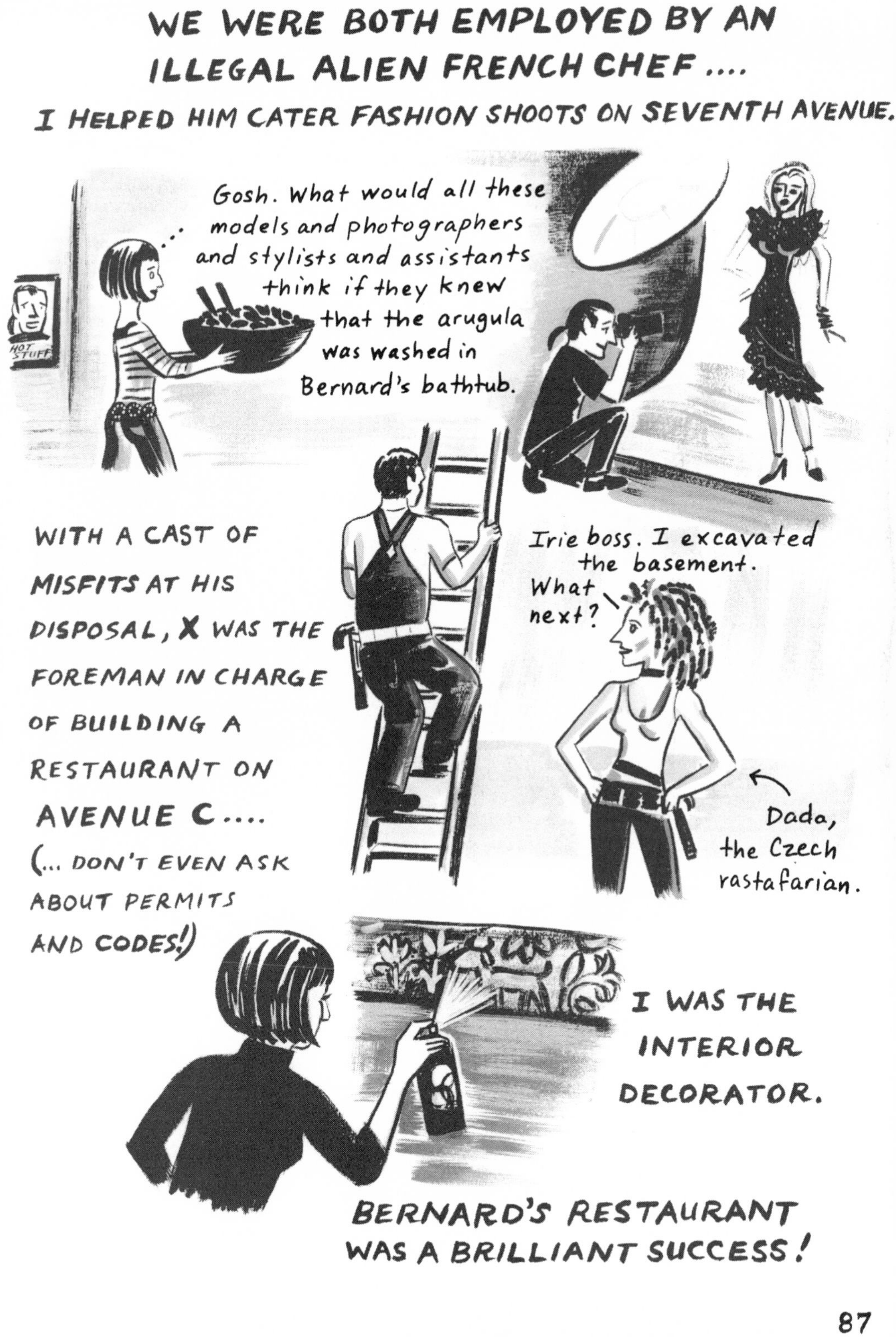
WE WERE BOTH EMPLOYED BY AN ILLEGAL ALIEN FRENCH CHEF....
I HELPED HIM CATER FASHION SHOOTS ON SEVENTH AVENUE.
HOT STUFF
...
Gosh. What would all these models and photographers and stylists and assistants think if they knew that the arugula was washed in Bernard's bathtub.
WITH A CAST OF MISFITS AT HIS DISPOSAL, X WAS THE FOREMAN IN CHARGE OF BUILDING A RESTAURANT ON AVENUE C....
(... DON'T EVEN ASK ABOUT PERMITS AND CODES!)
Irie boss. I excavated the basement. What next?
Dada, the Czech rastafarian.
I WAS THE INTERIOR DECORATOR.
BERNARD'S RESTAURANT WAS A BRILLIANT SUCCESS!

AFTER TWO YEARS IN NEW YORK,

WE EMBARK ON A TOUR DU MONDE.

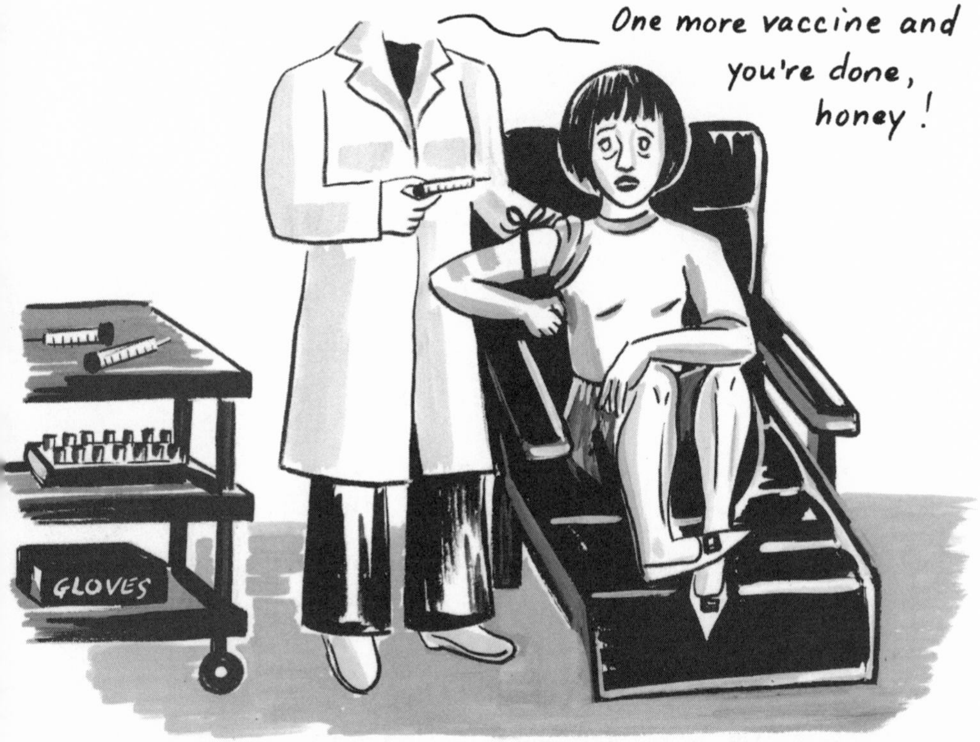
One more vaccine and you're done, honey!
GLOVES

SO, WITH LITTLE MONEY, NO ITINERARY,

AND A TICKET TO ASIA .... WE'RE OFF!

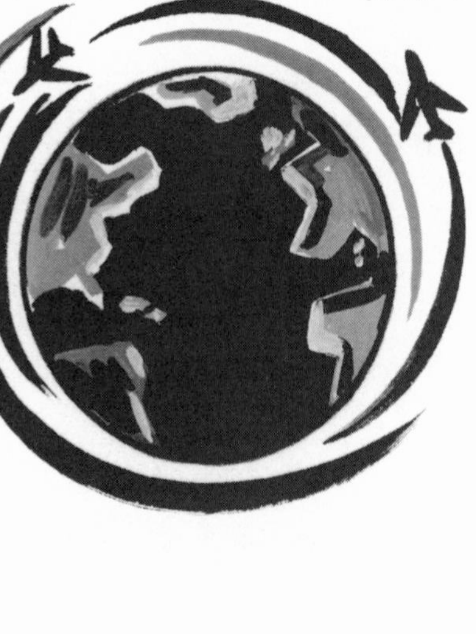

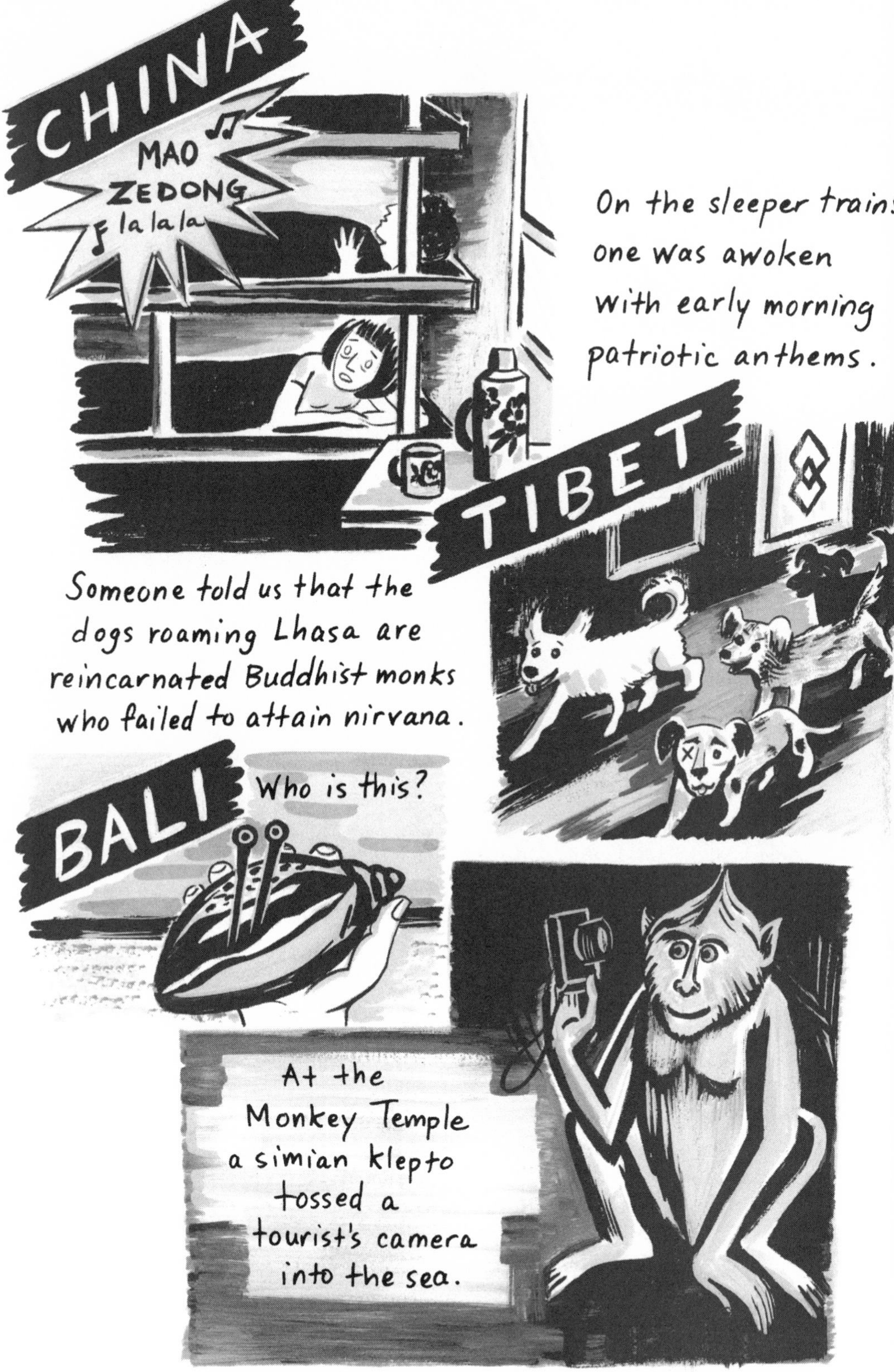
CHINA
MAO ZEDONG la la la
On the sleeper train: one was awoken with early morning patriotic anthems.
TIBET
Someone told us that the dogs roaming Lhasa are reincarnated Buddhist monks who failed to attain nirvana.
BALI
Who is this?
At the Monkey Temple a simian klepto tossed a tourist's camera into the sea.

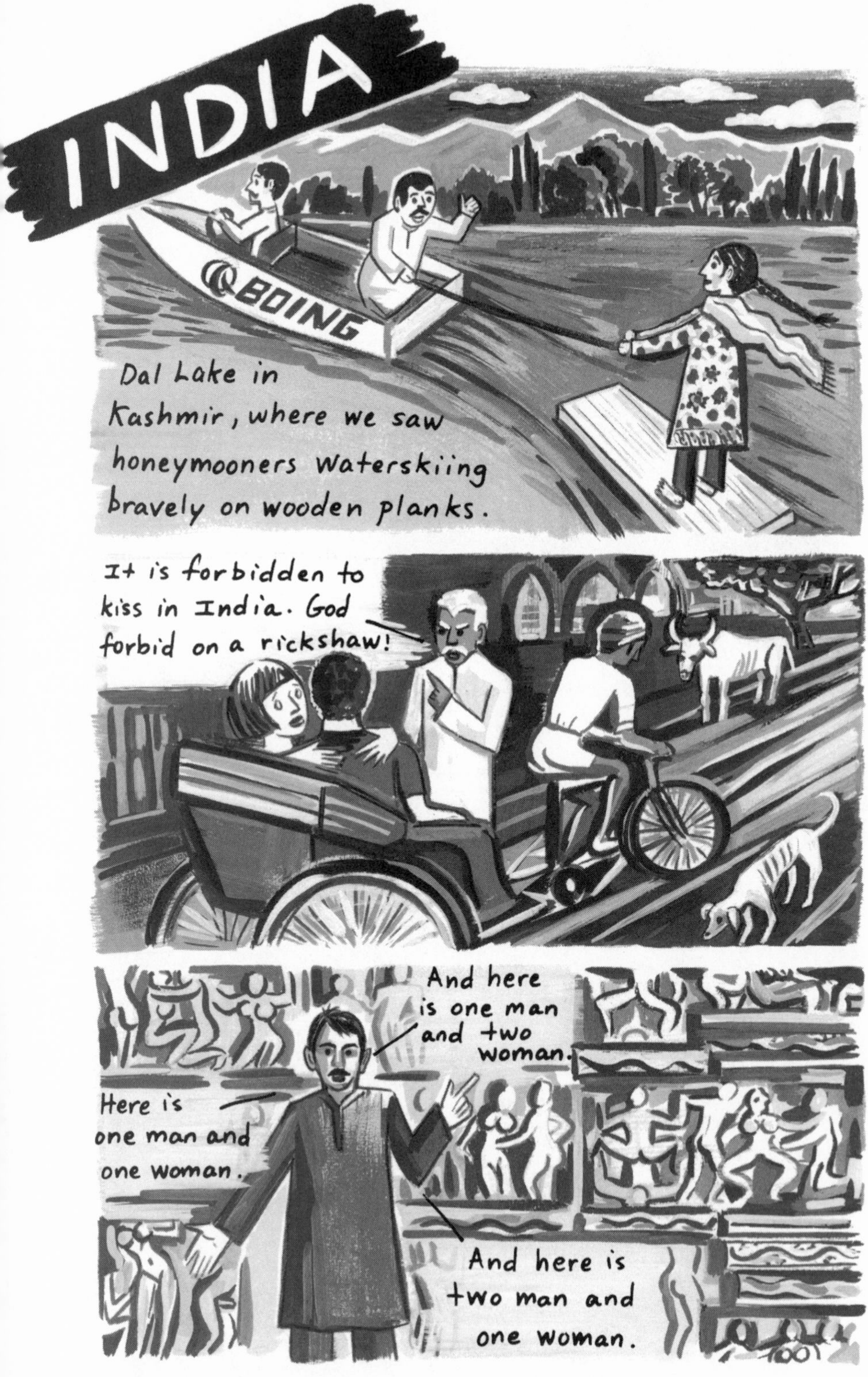
INDIA
BOING
Dal Lake in Kashmir, where we saw honeymooners waterskiing bravely on wooden planks.
It is forbidden to kiss in India. God forbid on a rickshaw!
Here is one man and one woman.
And here is one man and two woman.
And here is two man and one woman.

WE WIND UP OUR GLOBETROTTING IN TIME TO BE IN PARIS FOR CHRISTMAS. WE'D MAILED BOXES OF GOODIES FROM EVERY COUNTRY WE VISITED....

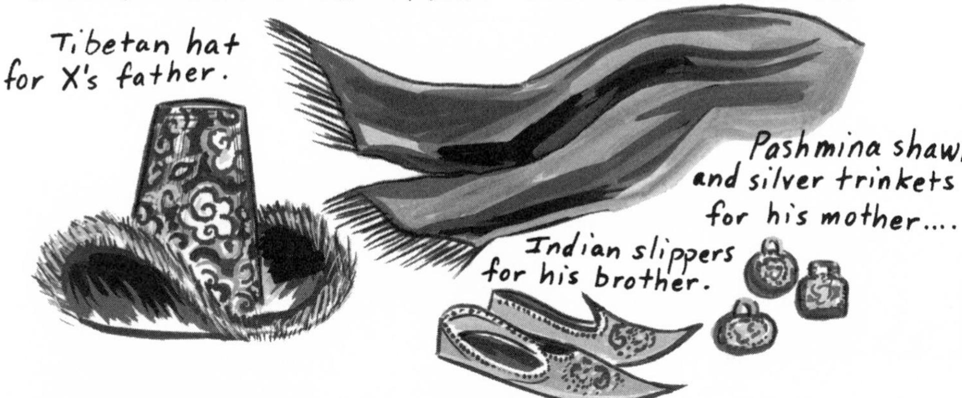
Tibetan hat for X's father.
Pashmina shawl and silver trinkets for his mother....
Indian slippers for his brother.

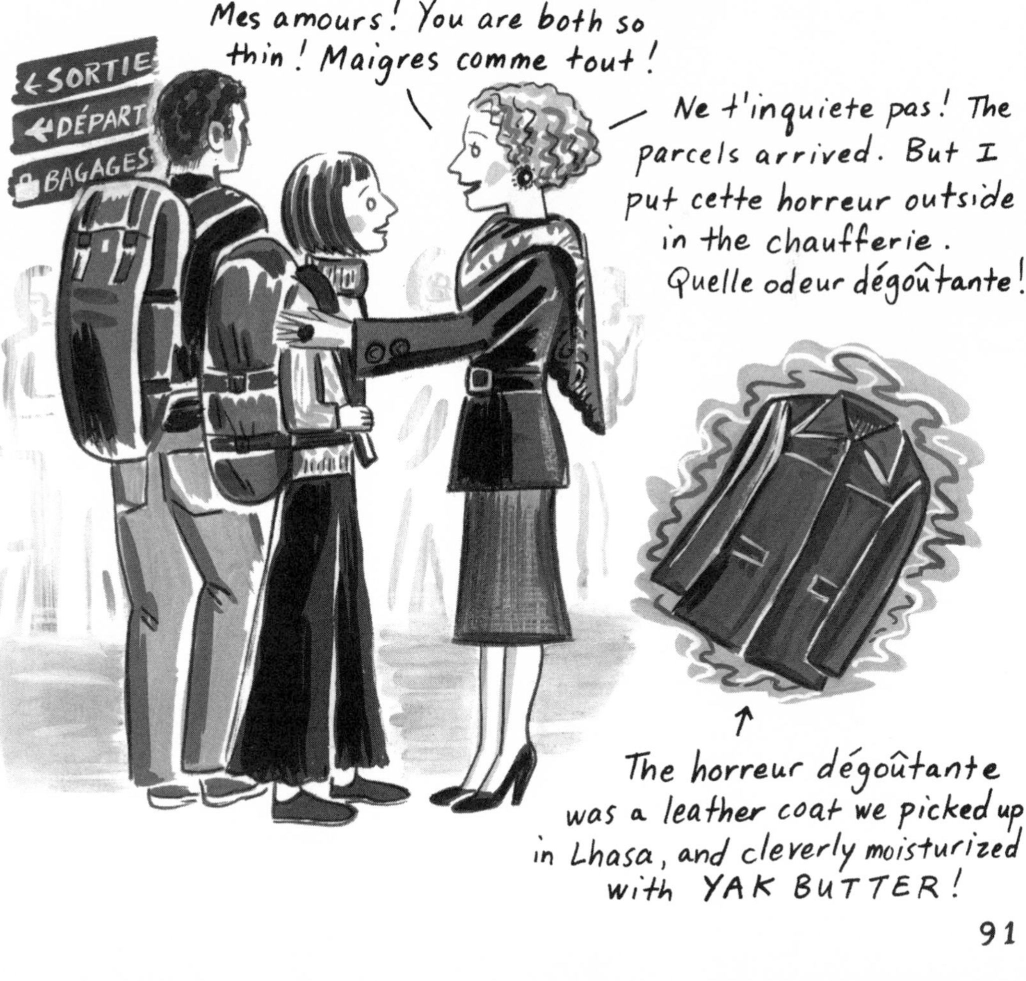
← SORTIE
← DÉPART
BAGAGES
Mes amours! You are both so thin! Maigres comme tout!
Ne t'inquiete pas! The parcels arrived. But I put cette horreur outside in the chaufferie. Quelle odeur dégoûtante!
The horreur dégoûtante was a leather coat we picked up in Lhasa, and cleverly moisturized with YAK BUTTER!

DUE TO A VISA MALFUNCTION WE SPEND NINE MONTHS IN FRANCE. I TOOK CLASSES AT THE SORBONNE, AND X WENT TO THE CINÉMA. IT WAS ENLIGHTENING TO HAVE A WINDOW INTO HIS **FAMILY DYNAMIC.**

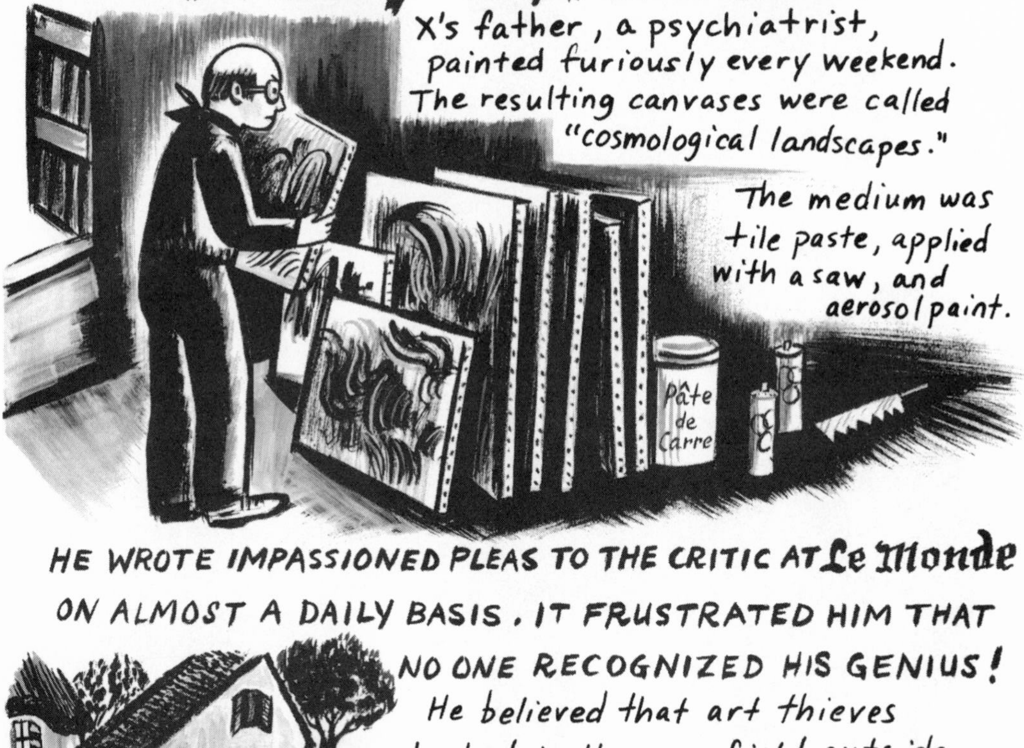
Pâte
de
Carre

X's father, a psychiatrist, painted furiously every weekend. The resulting canvases were called "cosmological landscapes."

The medium was tile paste, applied with a saw, and aerosol paint.

HE WROTE IMPASSIONED PLEAS TO THE CRITIC AT Le Monde ON ALMOST A DAILY BASIS. IT FRUSTRATED HIM THAT NO ONE RECOGNIZED HIS GENIUS!

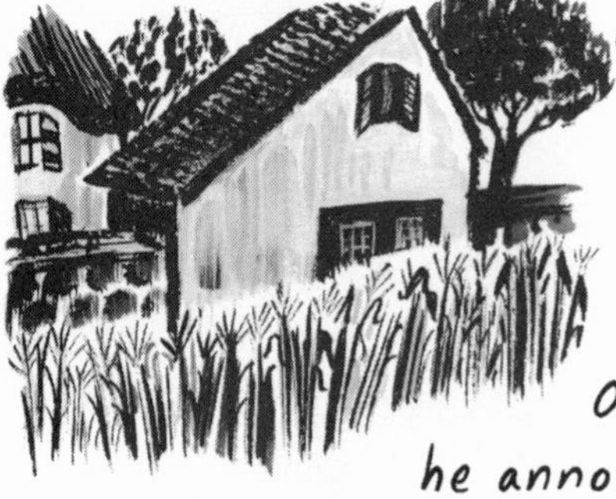

He believed that art thieves lurked in the cornfield outside his atelier.

One afternoon, he announced he would convert an old bamboo lounge into a satellite dish!

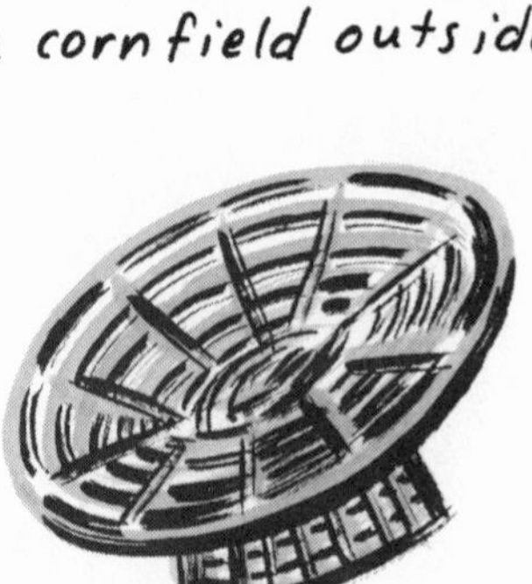

EVERY MORNING MY FATHER-IN-LAW CRUNCHED A SAUCER FULL OF "VITAMINS" WITH HIS MORNING TEA.

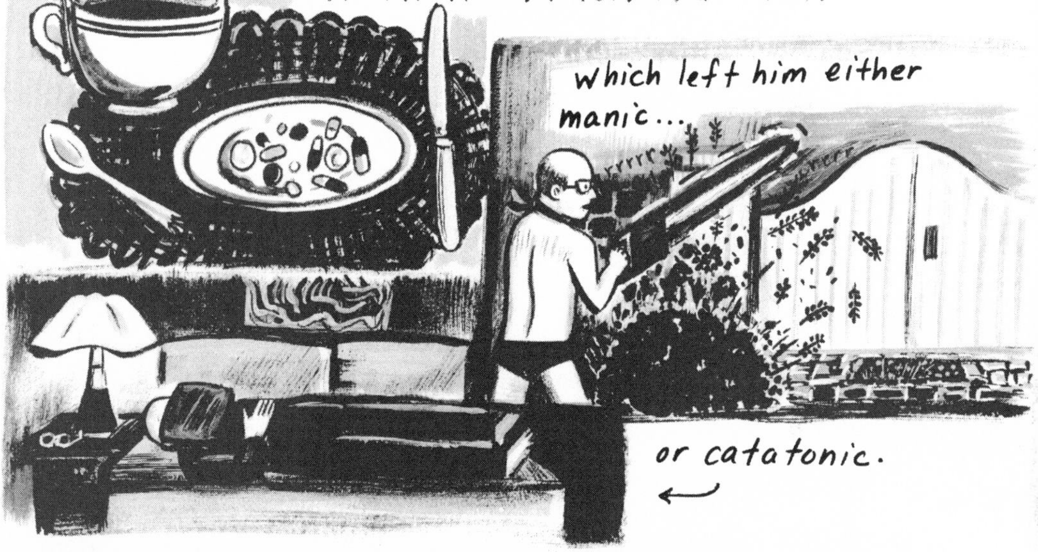
which left him either manic...
rrrrr
rrrrr
or catatonic.

AND YET MY MOTHER-IN-LAW DOTED ON HIM.

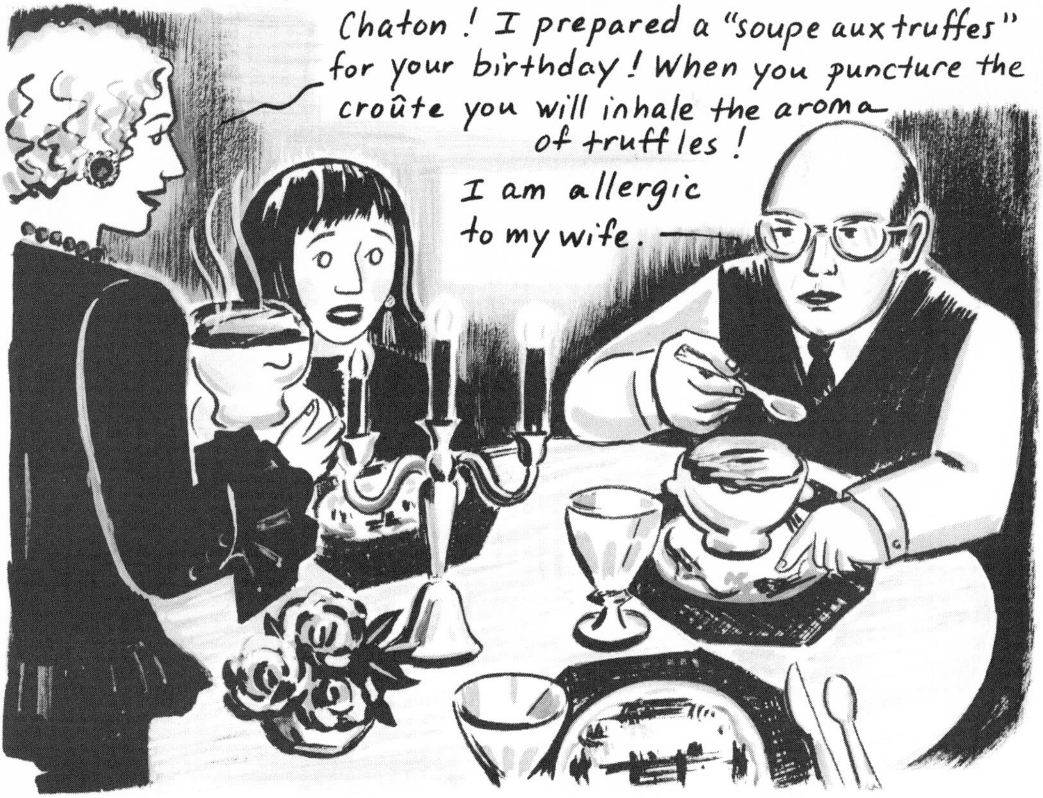
Chaton! I prepared a "soupe aux truffes" for your birthday! When you puncture the croûte you will inhale the aroma of truffles!
I am allergic to my wife.

MY FRENCH IMPROVED DRAMATICALLY AS I STRUGGLED TO UNDERSTAND WHY SHE PUT UP WITH HIM!

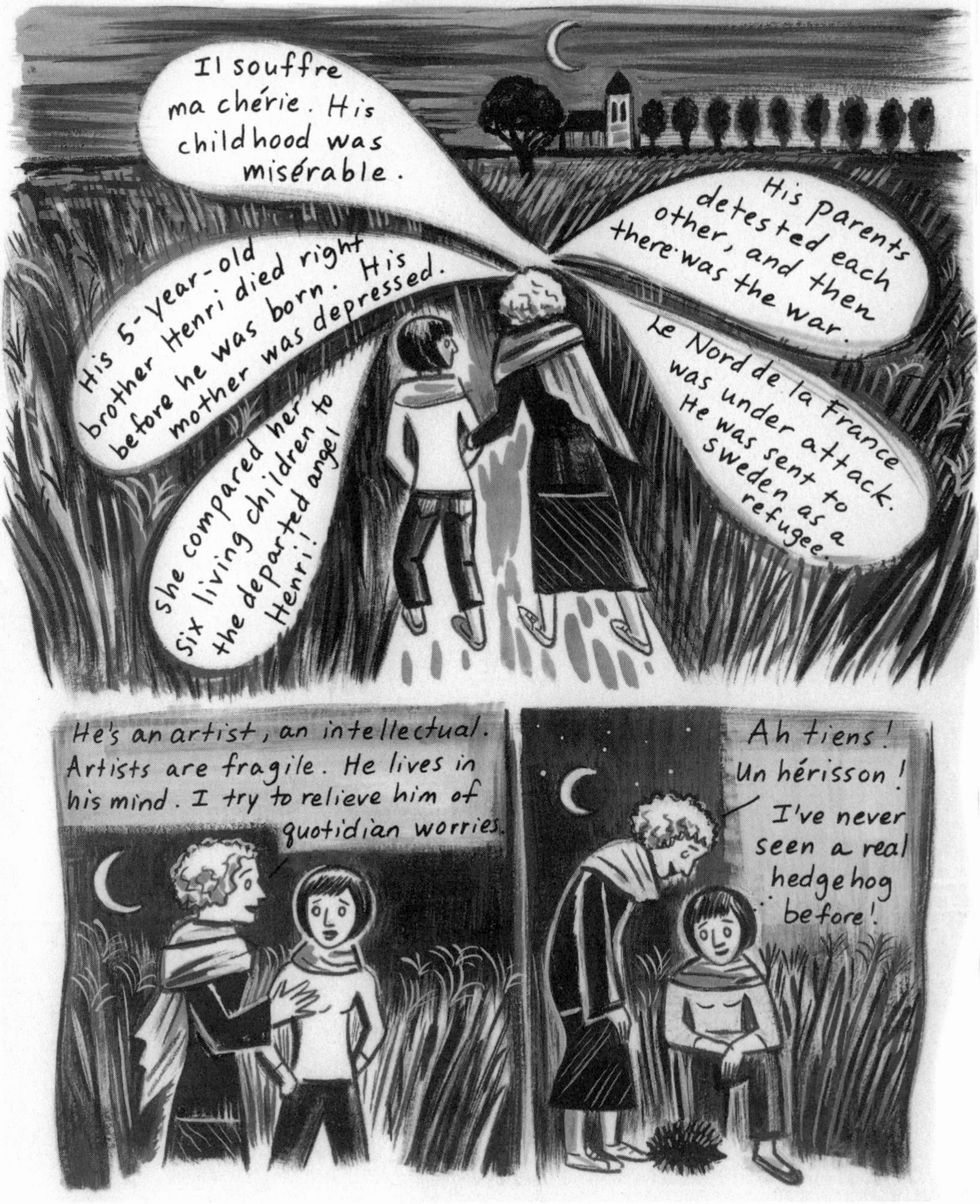
Il souffre ma chérie. His childhood was misérable.
His parents detested each other, and then there was the war.
His 5-year-old brother Henri died right before he was born. His mother was depressed.
Le Nord de la France was under attack. He was sent to Sweden as a refugee.
She compared her six living children to the departed angel Henri!
He's an artist, an intellectual. Artists are fragile. He lives in his mind. I try to relieve him of quotidian worries.
Ah tiens! Un hérisson!
I've never seen a real hedgehog before!

MAYBE THE ONLY WAY TO SURVIVE
BEING MARRIED TO SUCH A PERSON
IS TO ERASE YOURSELF — MUCH AS
SOMEONE SUFFERING FROM
STOCKHOLM SYNDROME
IS SYMPATHETIC TO, AND ADOPTS,
THE VIEWS OF THEIR CAPTOR!

BEFORE YOU KNOW IT,
YOU'RE WEARING A BERET AND
CARRYING A MACHINE GUN!

UPON RETURNING TO THE STATES IT BECOMES CLEAR THAT THE DAYS OF POSTGRADUATE SLACKING ARE OVER. WHAT ARE WE GOING TO DO WITH OUR LIVES? WE MOVE TO SAN FRANCISCO....

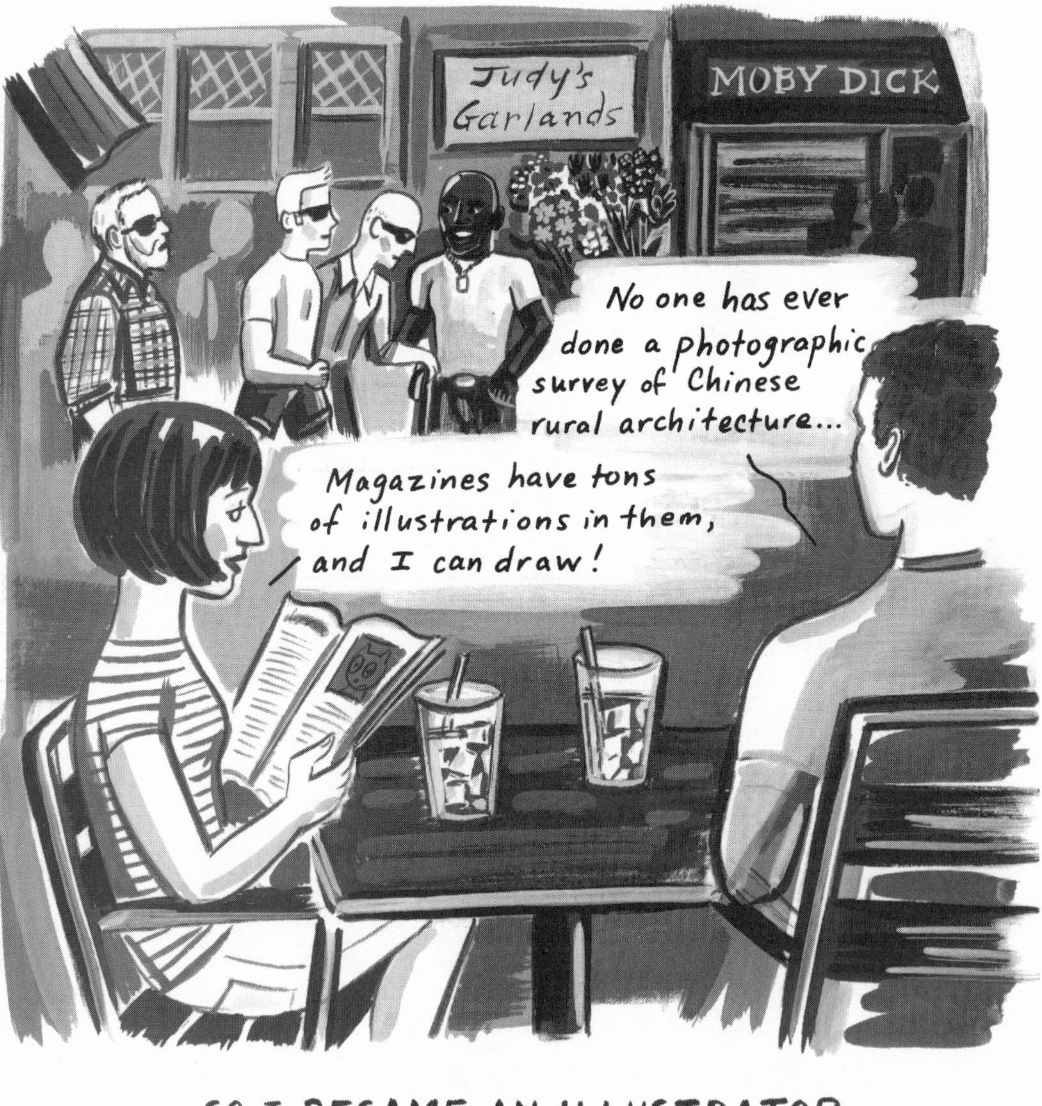
Judy's Garlands
MOBY DICK
No one has ever done a photographic survey of Chinese rural architecture...
Magazines have tons of illustrations in them, and I can draw!

SO I BECAME AN ILLUSTRATOR, AND HE BECAME A PHOTOGRAPHER.

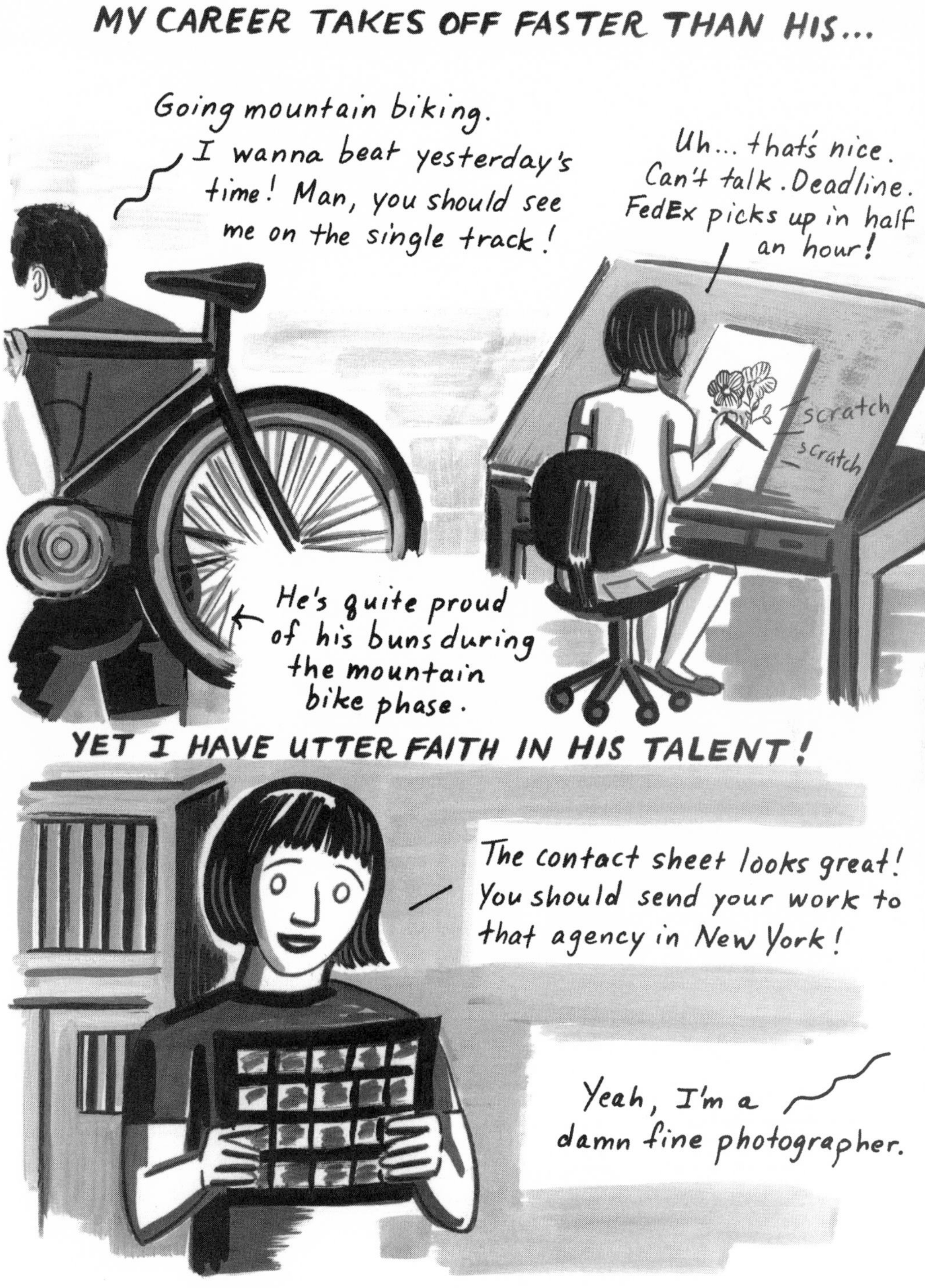
MY CAREER TAKES OFF FASTER THAN HIS...
Going mountain biking. I wanna beat yesterday's time! Man, you should see me on the single track!
Uh... that's nice. Can't talk. Deadline. FedEx picks up in half an hour!
scratch
scratch
He's quite proud of his buns during the mountain bike phase.
YET I HAVE UTTER FAITH IN HIS TALENT!
The contact sheet looks great! You should send your work to that agency in New York!
Yeah, I'm a damn fine photographer.

I NEVER HAD MUCH INTEREST IN CHILDREN, SO, MUCH TO MY ASTONISHMENT, I DISCOVER MY BIOLOGICAL CLOCK IS TICKING!

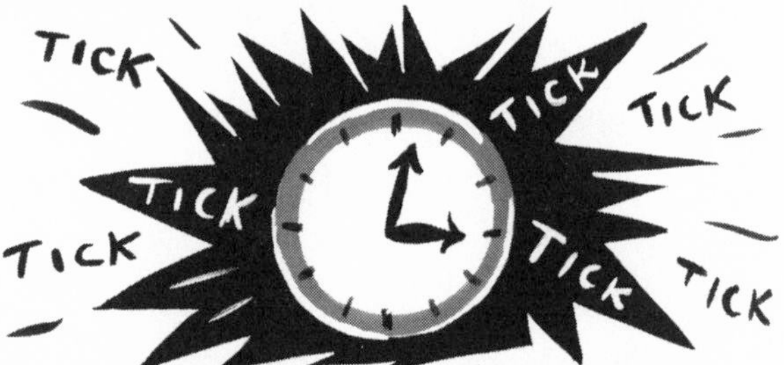

TICK
TICK
TICK
TICK
TICK
TICK
TICK

THOSE ANNOYING CREATURES (i.e., my friends' offspring) SUDDENLY SEEM LESS ANNOYING.

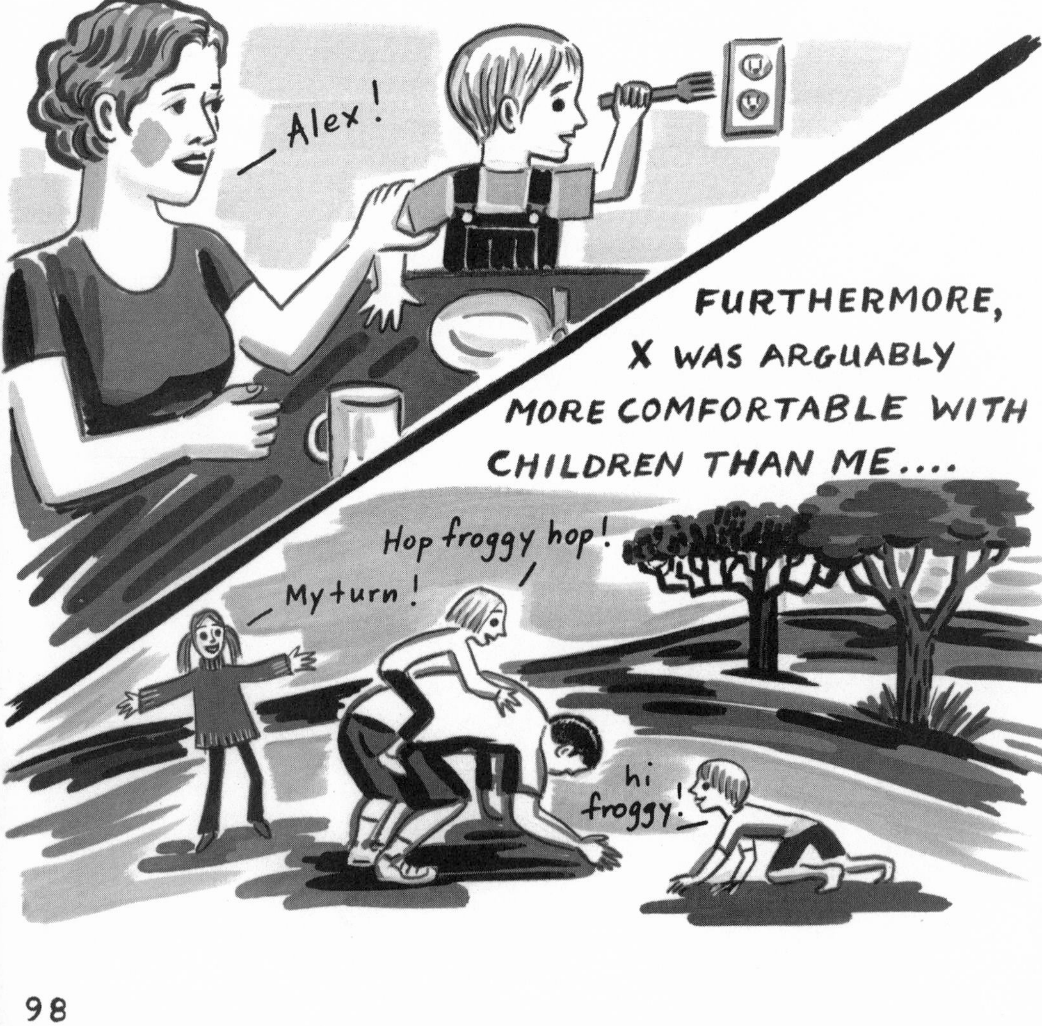

Alex!
FURTHERMORE, X WAS ARGUABLY MORE COMFORTABLE WITH CHILDREN THAN ME....
Hop froggy hop!
My turn!
hi froggy!

AND YET HE TOLD ME HE WASN'T READY.

I know it's a big decision, but I am 32. I don't want to be an OLD mother! If we wait till you're 35, I'll be 37! We don't even know if I can get pregnant at 37!

FINALLY, TWO EVENTS SWAY HIM:

He is smitten with his newborn niece!

AND HE RETURNS FROM A PARTY ONE EVENING RECOUNTING....

I saw a woman with her kid. Jeez, she coulda been its grandmother!

CONCEPTION IS AN IMMEDIATE BULL'S-EYE!

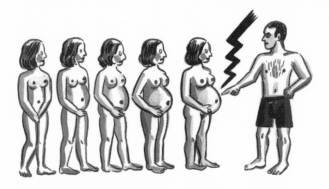

X IS PROUD TO HAVE INSTIGATED MY TRANSMOGRIFICATION.

The night before the birth of my first son, I dreamt vividly of a goldfish trying desperately to escape his confinement.

We meet the little creature (he's so alert!) with a mixture of curiosity and relief. Rare tears of joy shine in my husband's eyes.

LIFE IS TRANSFORMED BY THE PHYSICAL REQUIREMENTS OF MOTHERHOOD. I RECALL MY 6th GRADE BIOLOGY LESSONS.

Mammal (mam′el), *n*

1) Having hair. 2) Any vertebrate that feeds its young with milk from the female mammary glands.

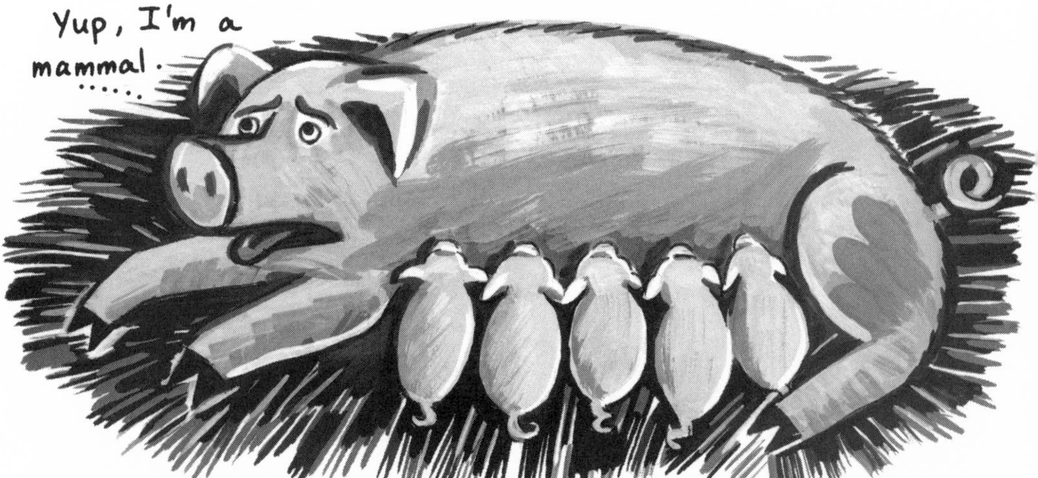
Yup, I'm a mammal. ......

THE WORD "MAMMAL" INCIDENTALLY IS DERIVED FROM INFANTS' UNIVERSAL CRY FOR MILK.

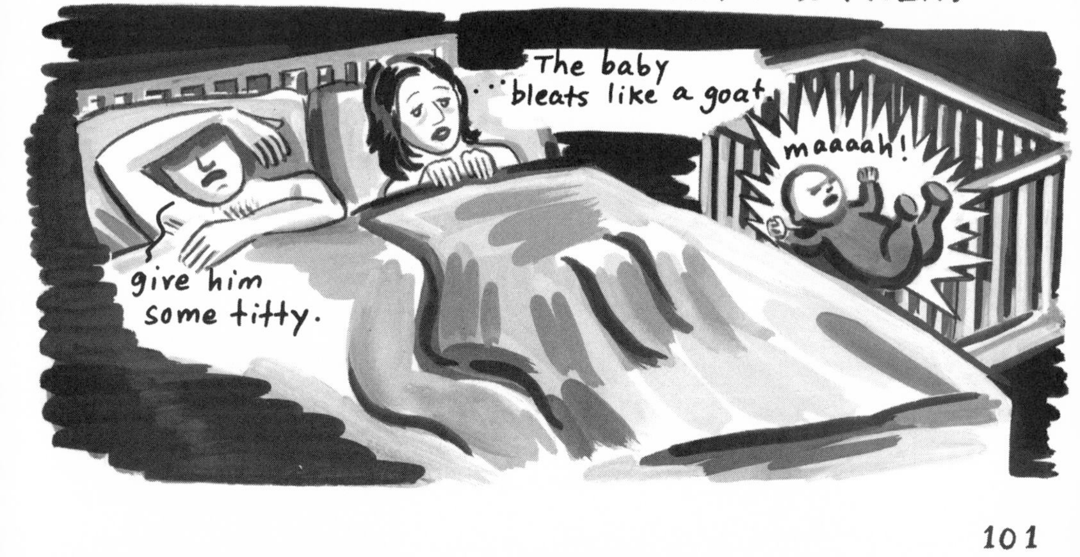
give him some titty.
...The baby bleats like a goat.
maaaah!

THE BABY IS LIKE ANOTHER APPENDAGE. I HAVE
NEVER SPENT SO MUCH TIME WITH ANOTHER BEING.

I SPEND HOURS
GAZING INTO A FACE THE
SIZE OF A GRAPEFRUIT.

Meanwhile OXYTOCIN,
the warm, fuzzy,
falling-in-love hormone,
surges through my body,
bonding mother
and infant.

AS A NEW MOTHER, I AM SO IN LOVE AND
ABSORBED I HAVE NO INTEREST IN ANYTHING ELSE.

The nursing baby
stimulates the
hormone PROLACTIN,
which is linked
hypothetically to
LACTATIONAL
AGGRESSION,
a trait that makes
Mama want to
protect her baby!

102

SUDDENLY! INTO THIS MYOPIC UNIVERSE BLUNDERS A DISPROPORTIONALLY LARGE, HIRSUTE CREATURE....

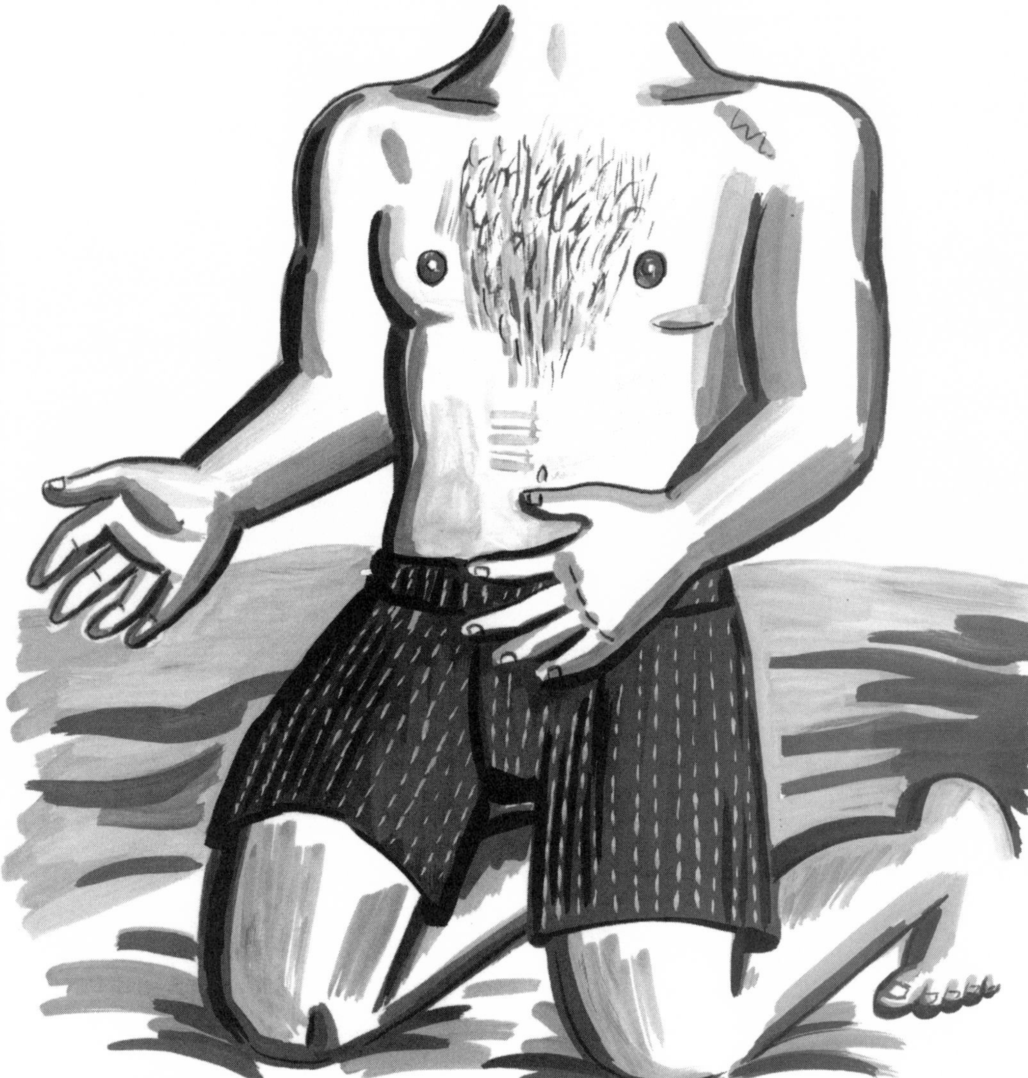

AND THE CREATURE IS DEMANDING MY ATTENTION! HE WANTS ME TO TOUCH HIM!

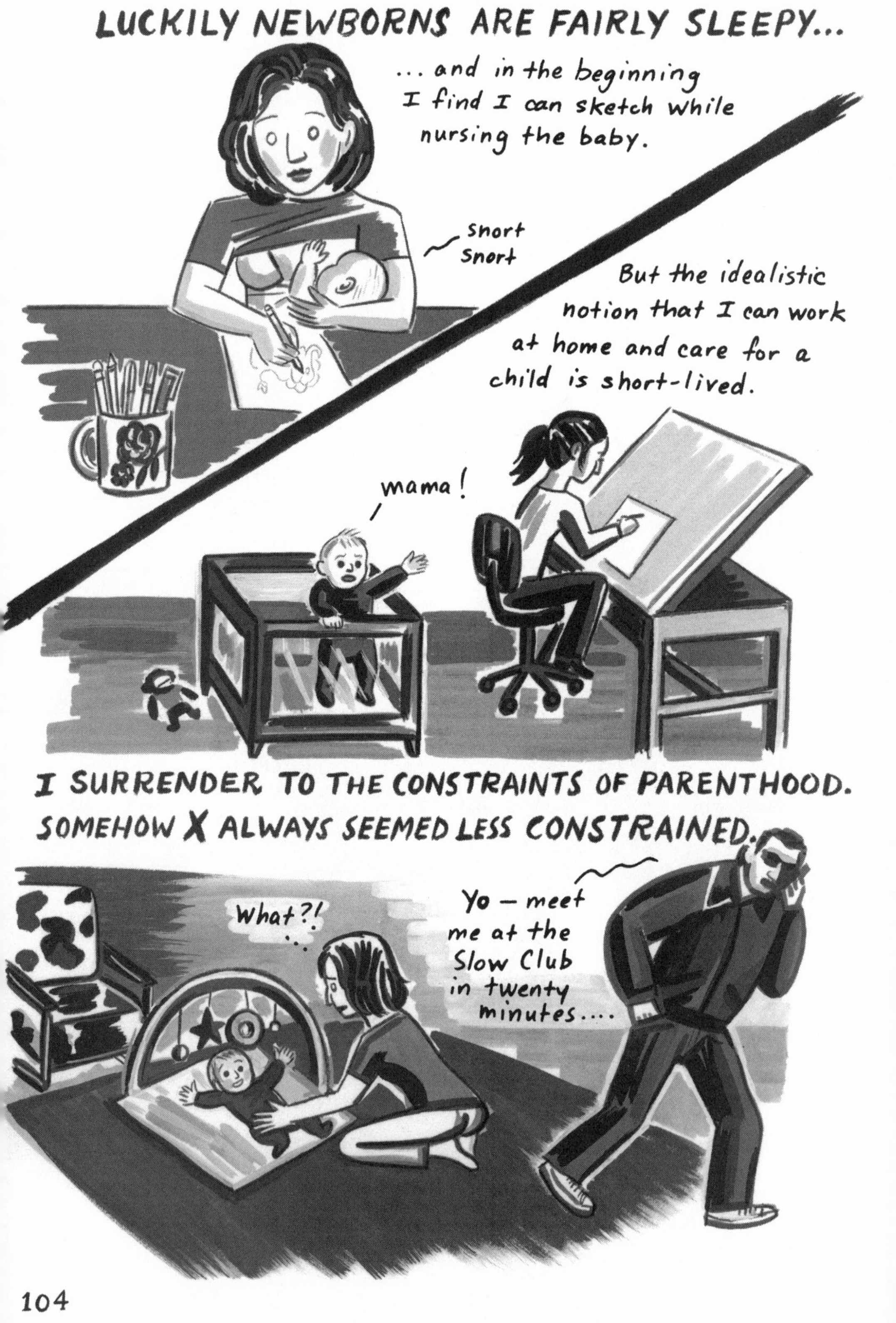
LUCKILY NEWBORNS ARE FAIRLY SLEEPY...
... and in the beginning I find I can sketch while nursing the baby.
snort snort
But the idealistic notion that I can work at home and care for a child is short-lived.
mama!
I SURRENDER TO THE CONSTRAINTS OF PARENTHOOD.
SOMEHOW X ALWAYS SEEMED LESS CONSTRAINED.
What?!
Yo — meet me at the Slow Club in twenty minutes....

MEANWHILE, OUR CITY IS BEING TRANSFORMED BEFORE OUR VERY EYES. IT'S THE DAWN OF A NEW ERA; A SECOND GOLD RUSH IS UNDERWAY. X QUICKLY GRASPS THE IMPLICATIONS.

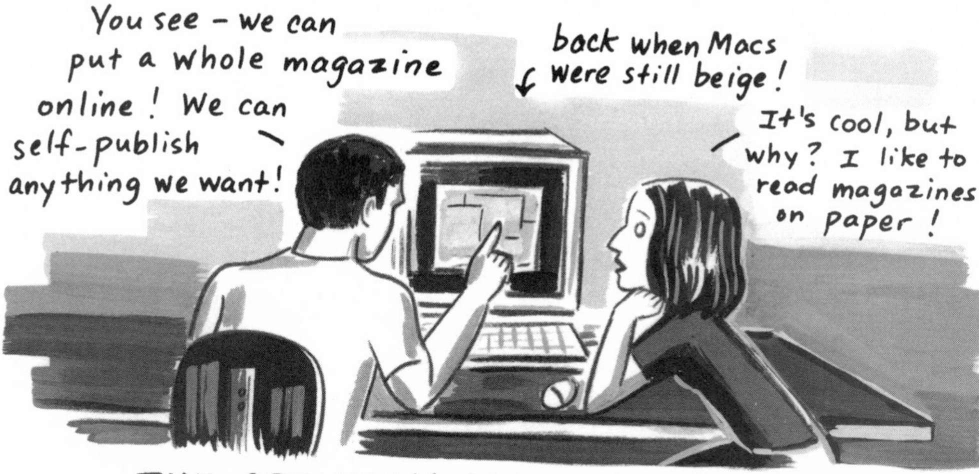

You see – we can put a whole magazine online! We can self-publish anything we want!
back when Macs were still beige!
It's cool, but why? I like to read magazines on paper!

THE OPTIMISM AND PIONEERING SPIRIT IS EVIDENT ALL AROUND US. THE MASTERS OF THE UNIVERSE LOOK LIKE THIS:

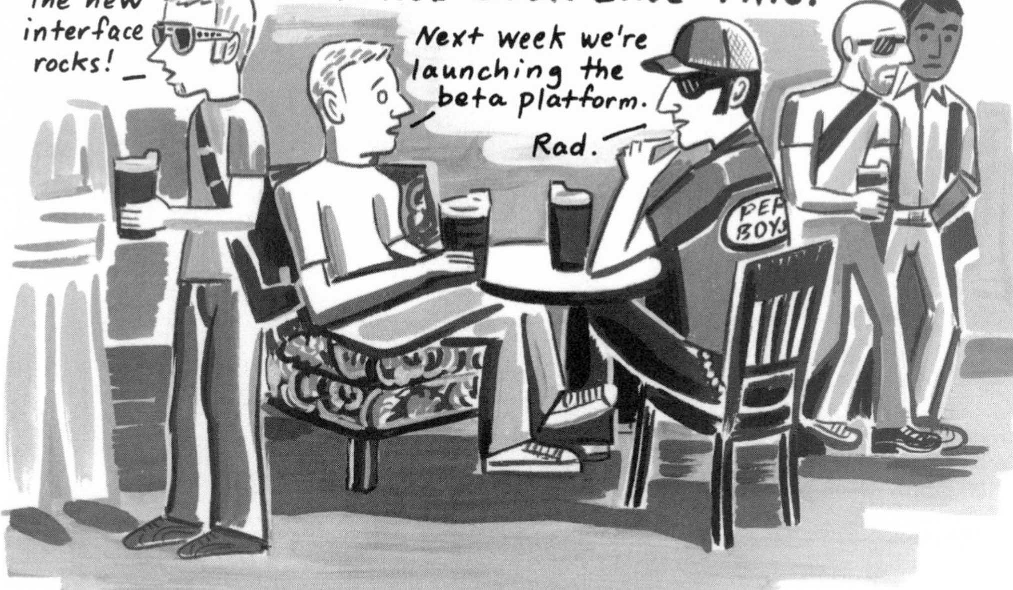

The new interface rocks!
Next week we're launching the beta platform.
Rad.
PEP BOYS

THE ECONOMY INSPIRES CONFIDENCE, WE BUY A FIXER-UPPER. AND BABY #2 IS CONCEIVED.

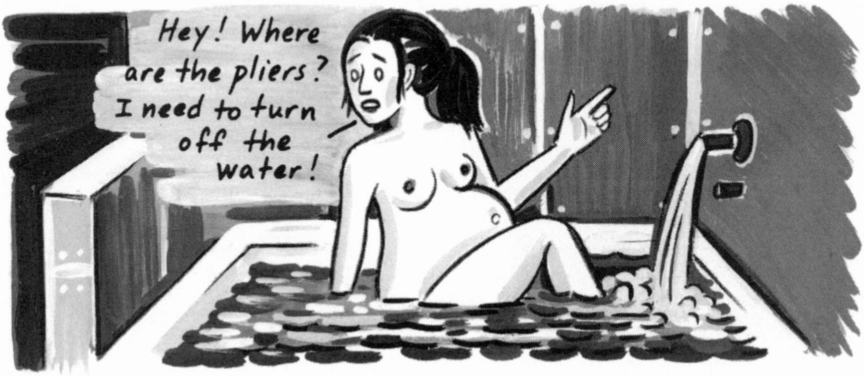
Hey! Where are the pliers? I need to turn off the water!

WE'RE STILL LIVING IN A CONSTRUCTION ZONE WHEN WE BRING HIM HOME FROM THE HOSPITAL.

Maybe that's why he cried so much!

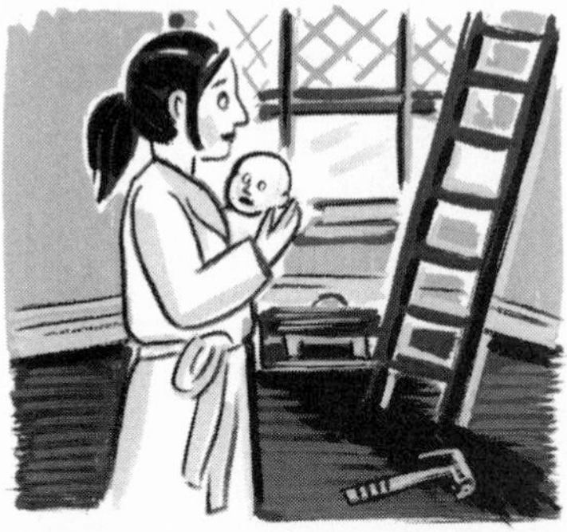

X WORKED ON THE HOUSE EVERY WEEKEND WHILE I MANAGED INFANT AND TODDLER.

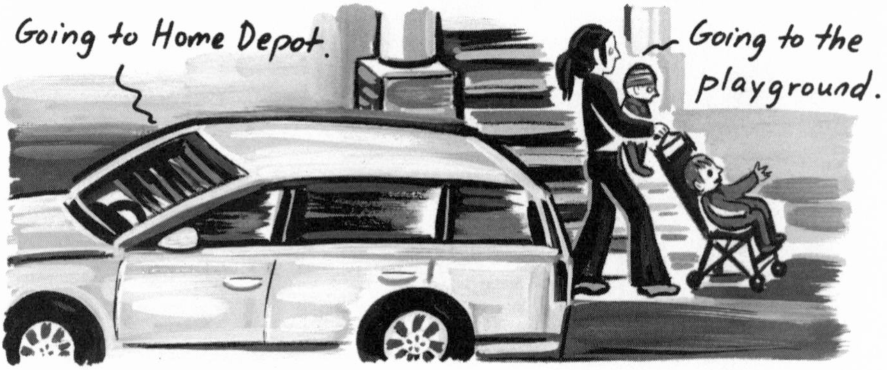
Going to Home Depot.
Going to the playground.

FATHERHOOD BROUGHT OUT THE PLAYFUL SIDE OF MY HUSBAND. HE DEVISED A SERIES OF **X-TREME** BABY SPORTS!

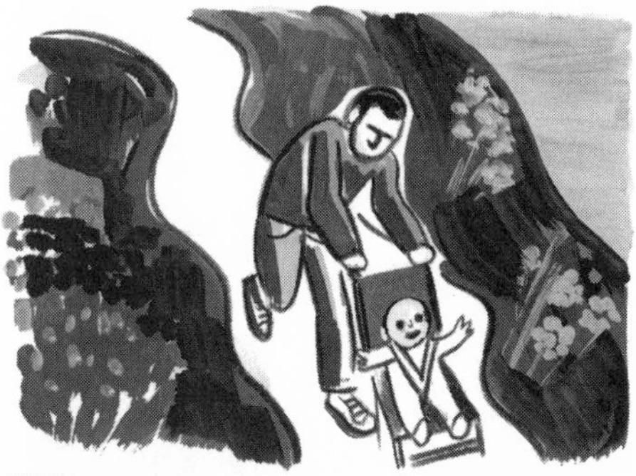

THE DOWNHILL RACER

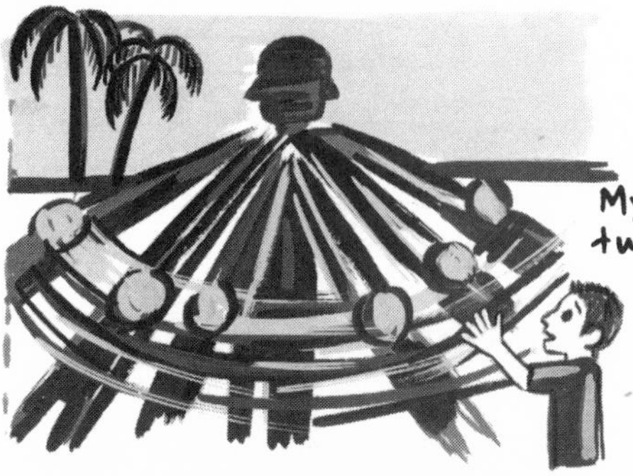
My turn.

THE HELICOPTER

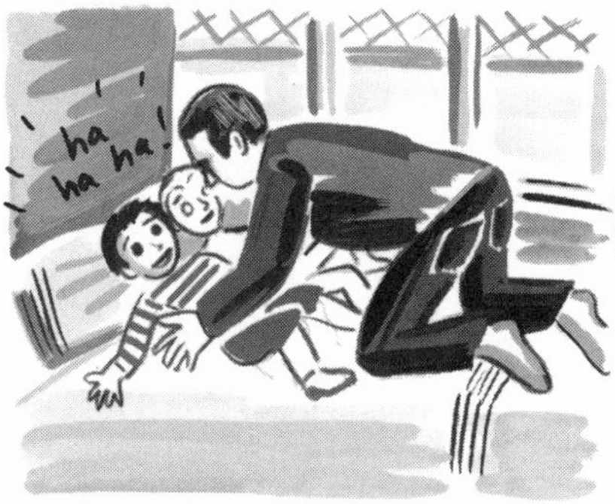
ha ha ha!

TICKLE MONSTER

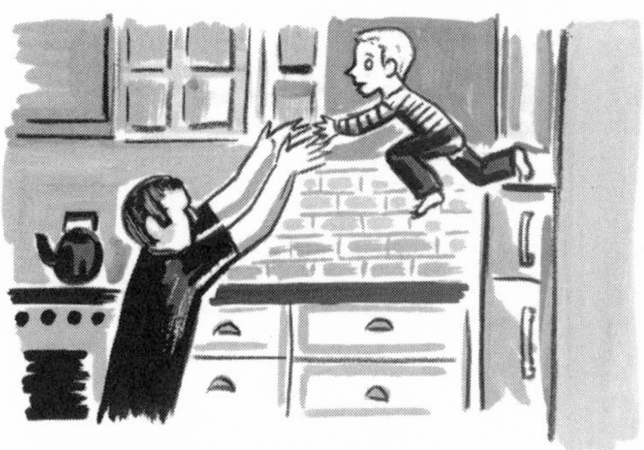

REFRIGERATOR DIVING

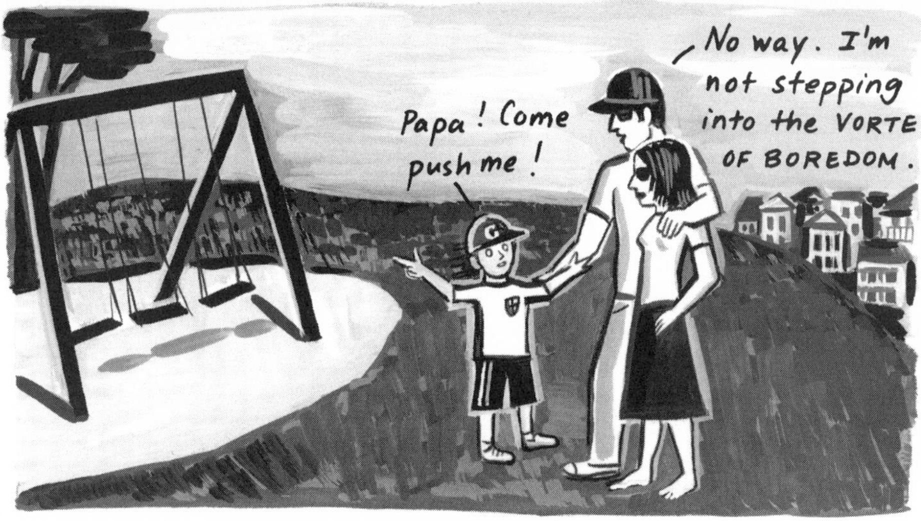
Papa! Come push me!
No way. I'm not stepping into the VORTEX OF BOREDOM.

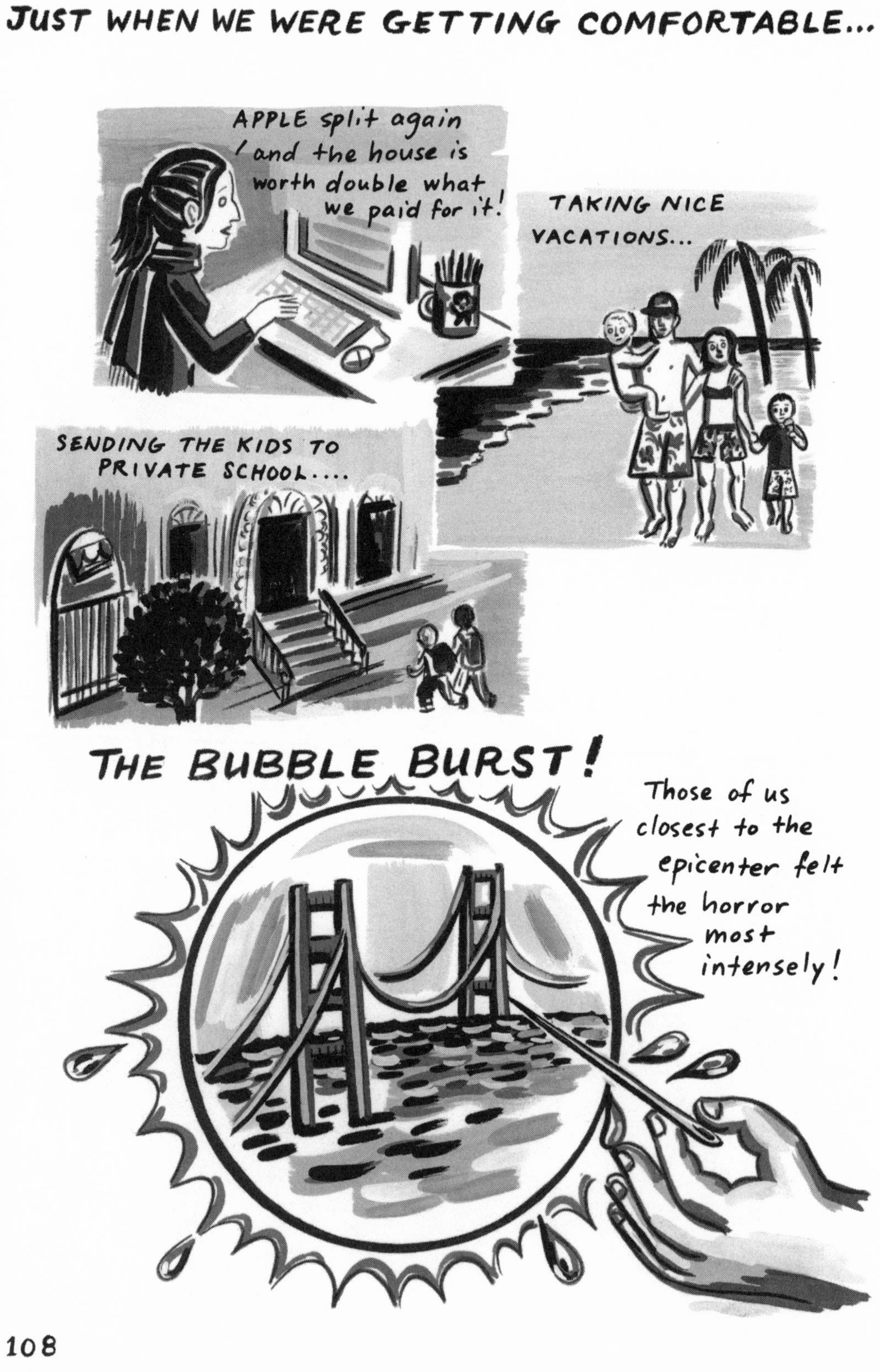
JUST WHEN WE WERE GETTING COMFORTABLE...
APPLE split again and the house is worth double what we paid for it!
TAKING NICE VACATIONS...
SENDING THE KIDS TO PRIVATE SCHOOL....
THE BUBBLE BURST!
Those of us closest to the epicenter felt the horror most intensely!

AT THE SAME TIME, THE MIND-NUMBING ROUTINE OF DAILY LIFE TOOK A TOLL ON OUR MARRIAGE.

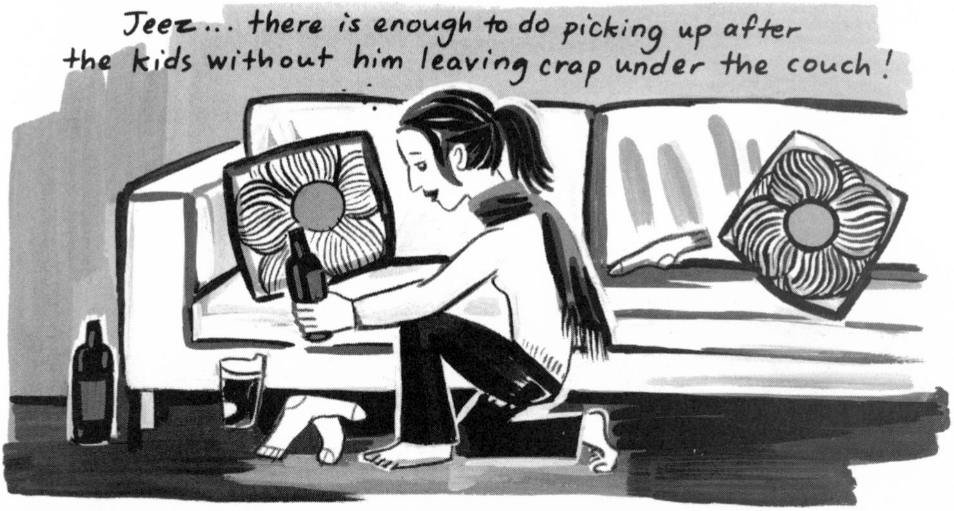
Jeez... there is enough to do picking up after the kids without him leaving crap under the couch!

IN FAMILY LIFE, IT'S IMPORTANT TO BE A TEAM AND AGREE ON A BASIC GAME PLAN!

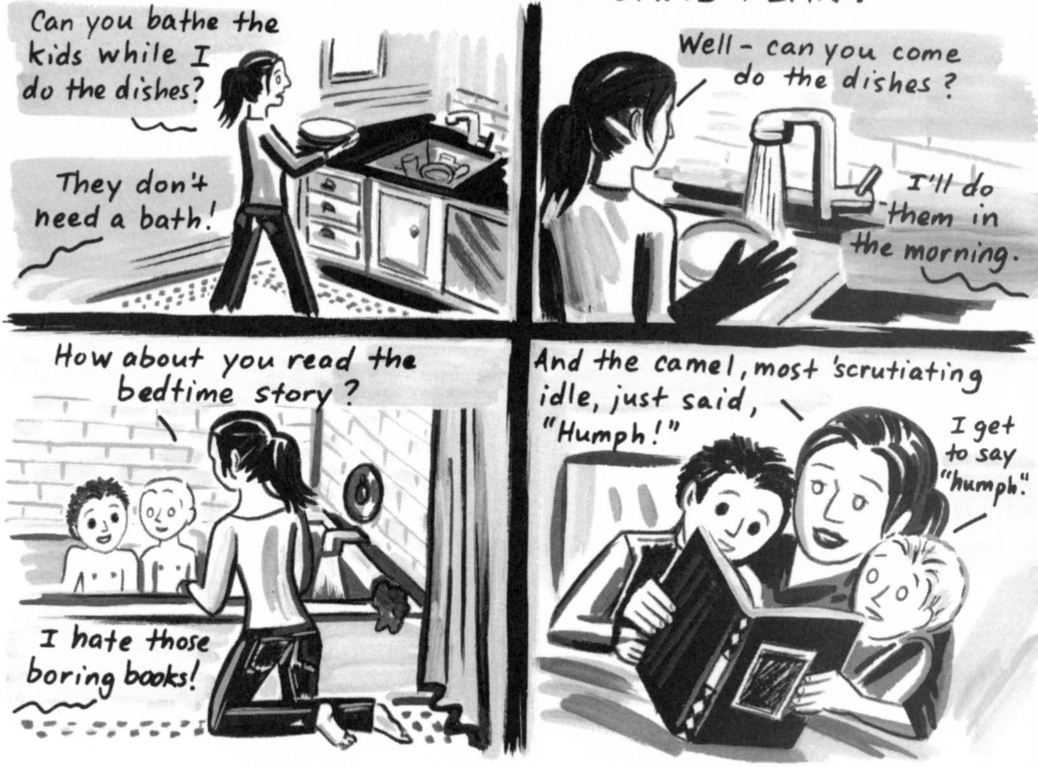
Can you bathe the kids while I do the dishes?
They don't need a bath!
Well - can you come do the dishes?
I'll do them in the morning.
How about you read the bedtime story?
I hate those boring books!
And the camel, most 'scrutiating idle, just said, "Humph!"
I get to say "humph."

FURTHERMORE, IT'S HARD TO KEEP THE FLAMES OF ADORATION LIT...

WHEN YOU'VE HEARD THE SAME DINNER PARTY PATTER A THOUSAND TIMES....

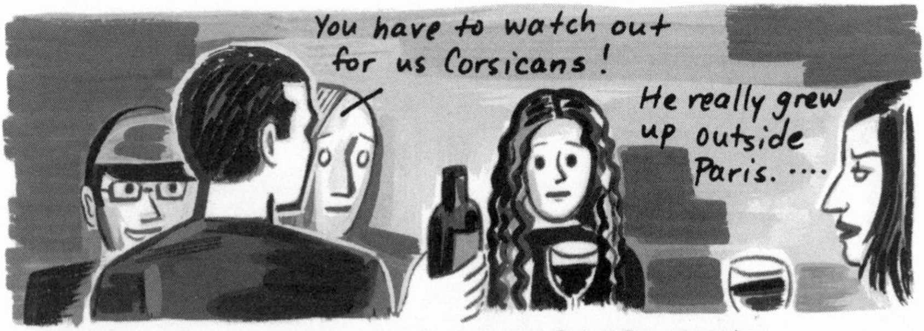
You have to watch out for us Corsicans!
He really grew up outside Paris.....

OR HE INTERRUPTS WHEN YOU ARE SPEAKING...

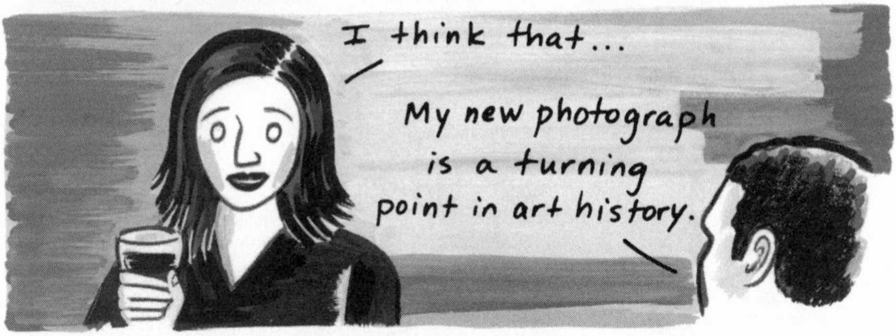
I think that...
My new photograph is a turning point in art history.

OR HE BEHAVES INAPPROPRIATELY IN PUBLIC....

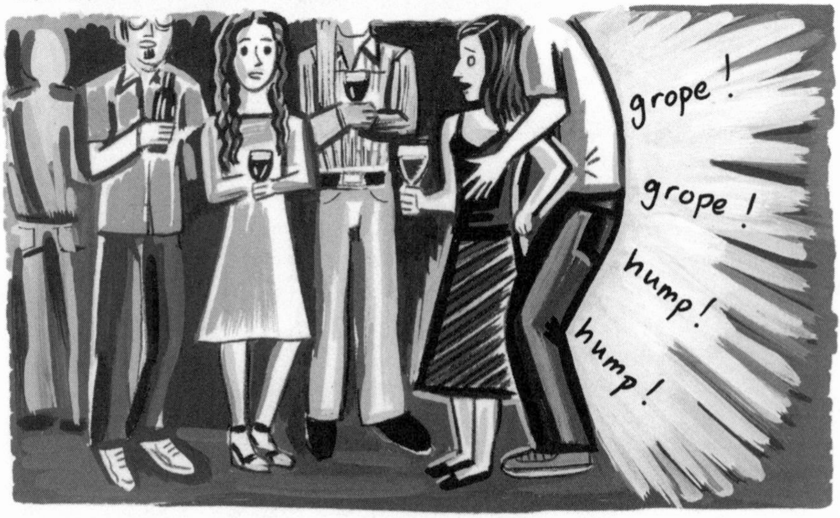
grope!
grope!
hump!
hump!

Words of Wise Women

"All marriages are happy.
It's trying to live together afterward
that causes all the problems."

Shelley Winters

A HORTICULTURIST FRIEND ONCE MENTIONED THAT YOU CANNOT GROW TWO CACTI IN ONE POT. ONE WILL THRIVE AND THE OTHER WILL WITHER. MAYBE THAT'S WHAT HAPPENED TO US?

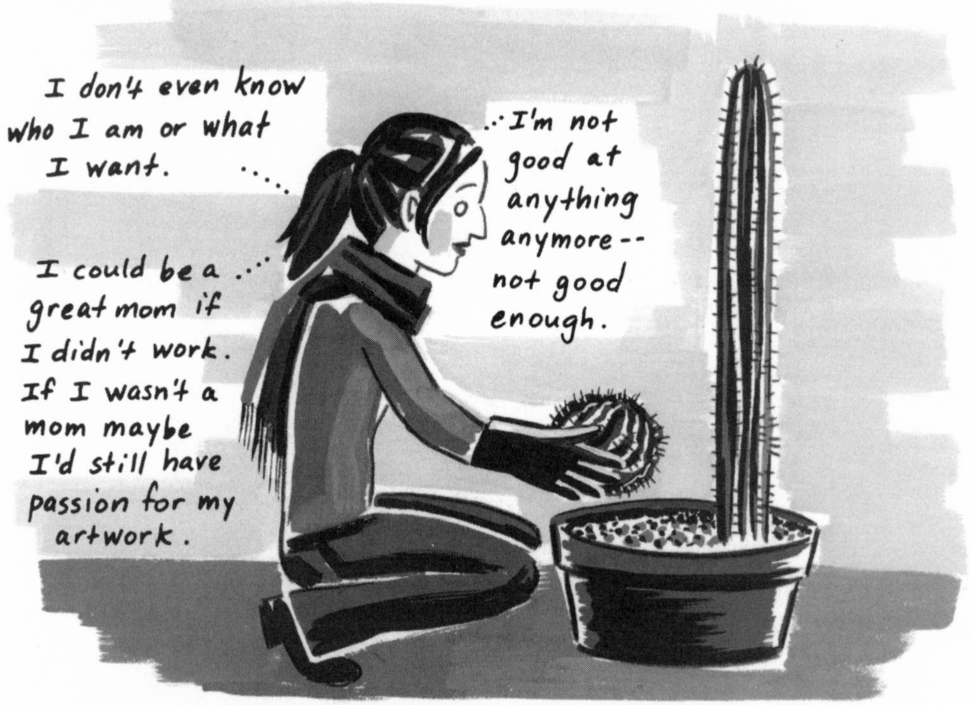

I don't even know who I am or what I want.
I could be a great mom if I didn't work. If I wasn't a mom maybe I'd still have passion for my artwork.
I'm not good at anything anymore -- not good enough.

I HAD LET X TAKE CENTER STAGE... WHILE I APPLAUDED FROM THE WINGS.

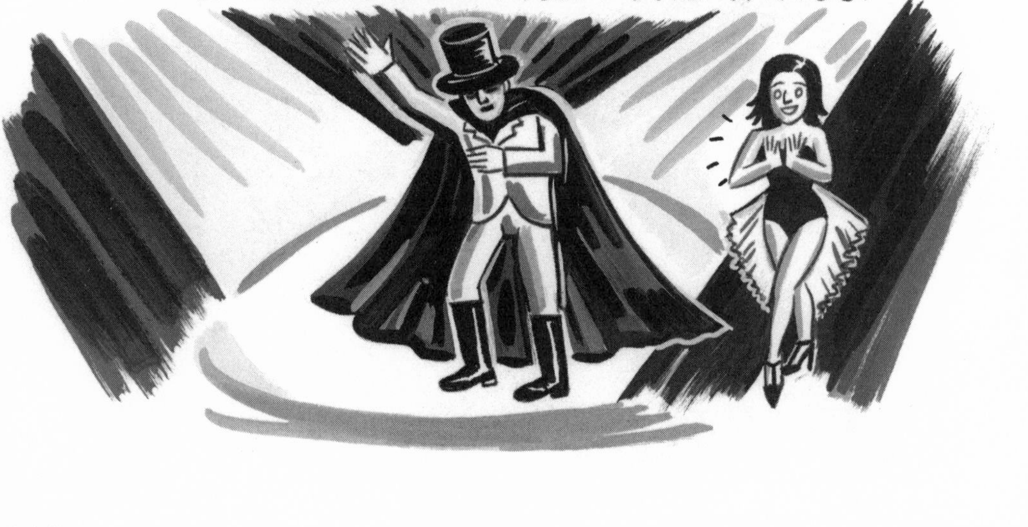

AND YET BEFORE IT WENT TO PIECES,
FAMILY LIFE COULD BE

INDESCRIBABLY SWEET!

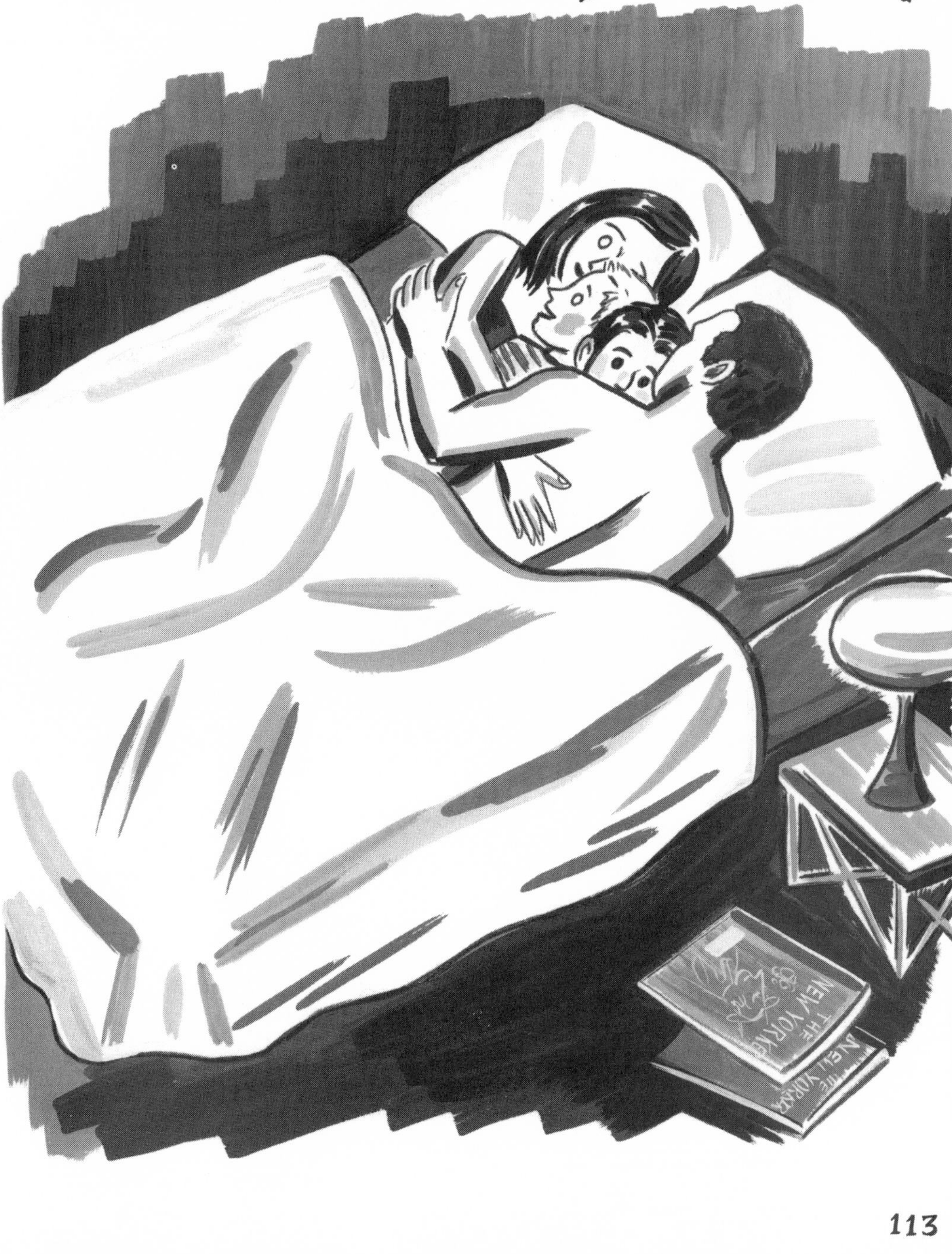
THE NEW YORKER
THE NEW YORKER

AND SO, I AM DESPERATE TO SAVE OUR FAMILY! I BEG HIM TO TRY COUPLES' COUNSELING ONE LAST TIME. UPON A FRIEND'S RECOMMENDATION, WE MEET "WILL."

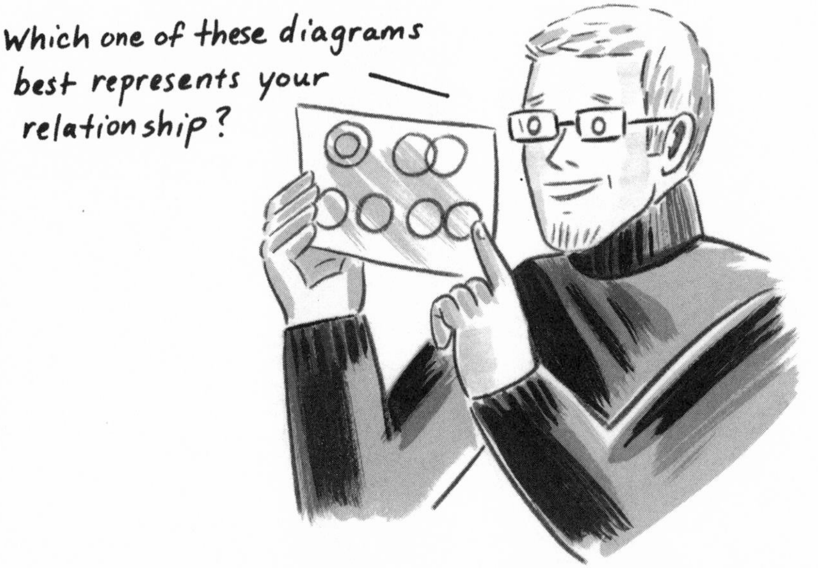
Which one of these diagrams best represents your relationship?

FROM WEEK TO WEEK THE STORY CHANGES.

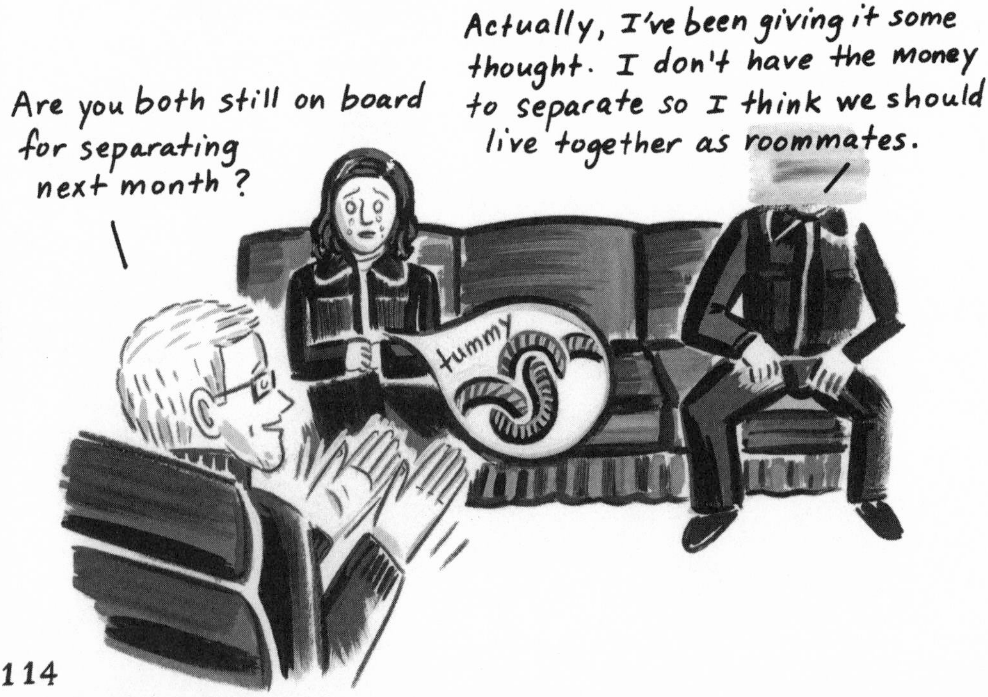
Are you both still on board for separating next month?
Actually, I've been giving it some thought. I don't have the money to separate so I think we should live together as roommates.
tummy

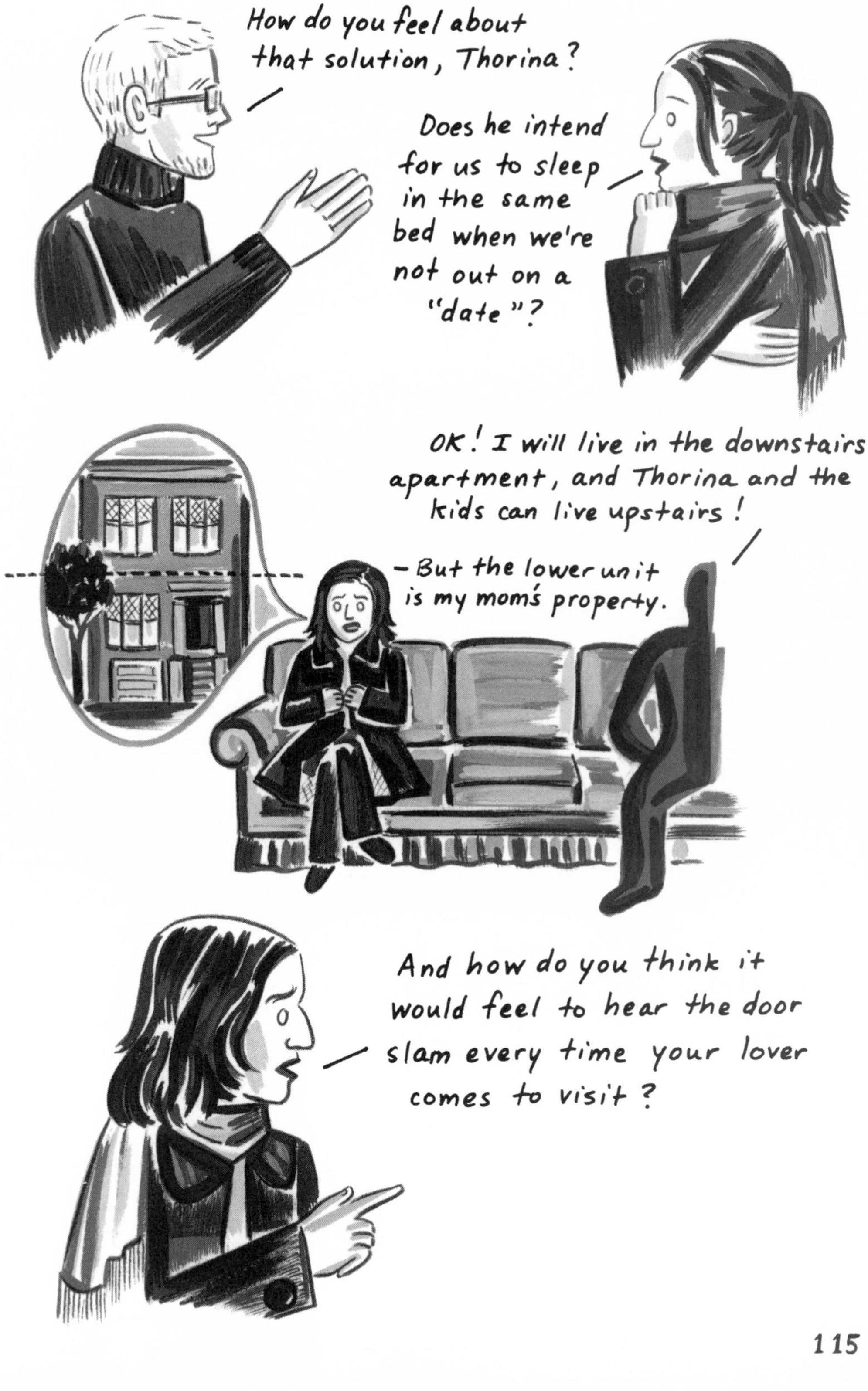
How do you feel about that solution, Thorina?
Does he intend for us to sleep in the same bed when we're not out on a "date"?
OK! I will live in the downstairs apartment, and Thorina and the kids can live upstairs!
—But the lower unit is my mom's property.
And how do you think it would feel to hear the door slam every time your lover comes to visit?

... and he talks about us having some kind of open marriage! Basically, I suppose he's only interested in being with her, but it's convenient to have me around to be the nanny and the housekeeper!

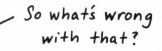

So what's wrong with that?

I've looked into it. There are over 100,000 polyamorous couples in the United States. Vivienne has been a great influence on me; I think it will be good for the kids to have her around!

This is lunacy. ......

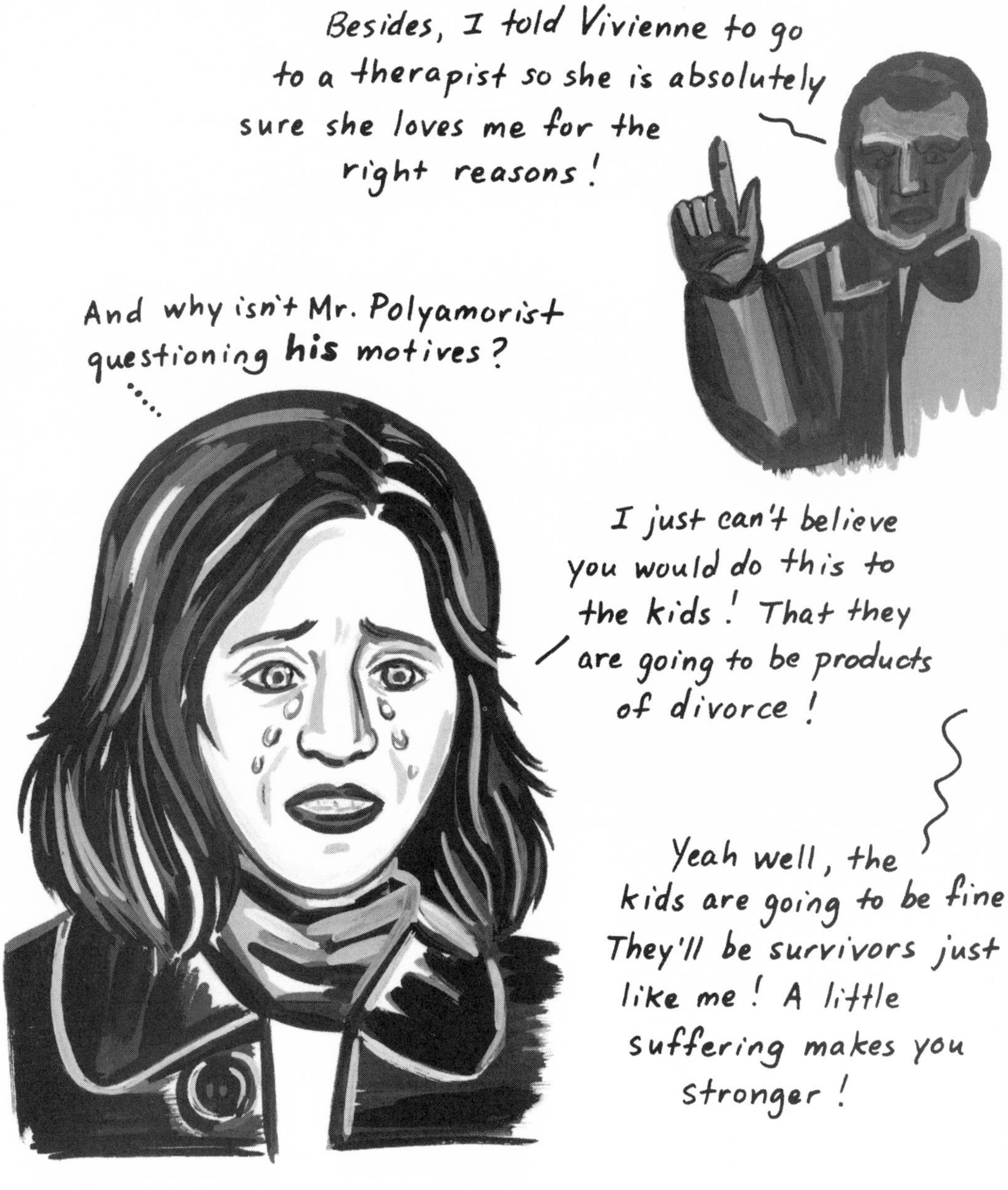
Besides, I told Vivienne to go to a therapist so she is absolutely sure she loves me for the right reasons!
And why isn't Mr. Polyamorist questioning **his** motives?
I just can't believe you would do this to the kids! That they are going to be products of divorce!
Yeah well, the kids are going to be fine They'll be survivors just like me! A little suffering makes you stronger!

ONE THING IS CERTAIN,
A FAMILY IS NOT A DEMOCRACY!
ONE PERSON OFTEN DECIDES WHAT
HAPPENS TO THE REST OF YOU!

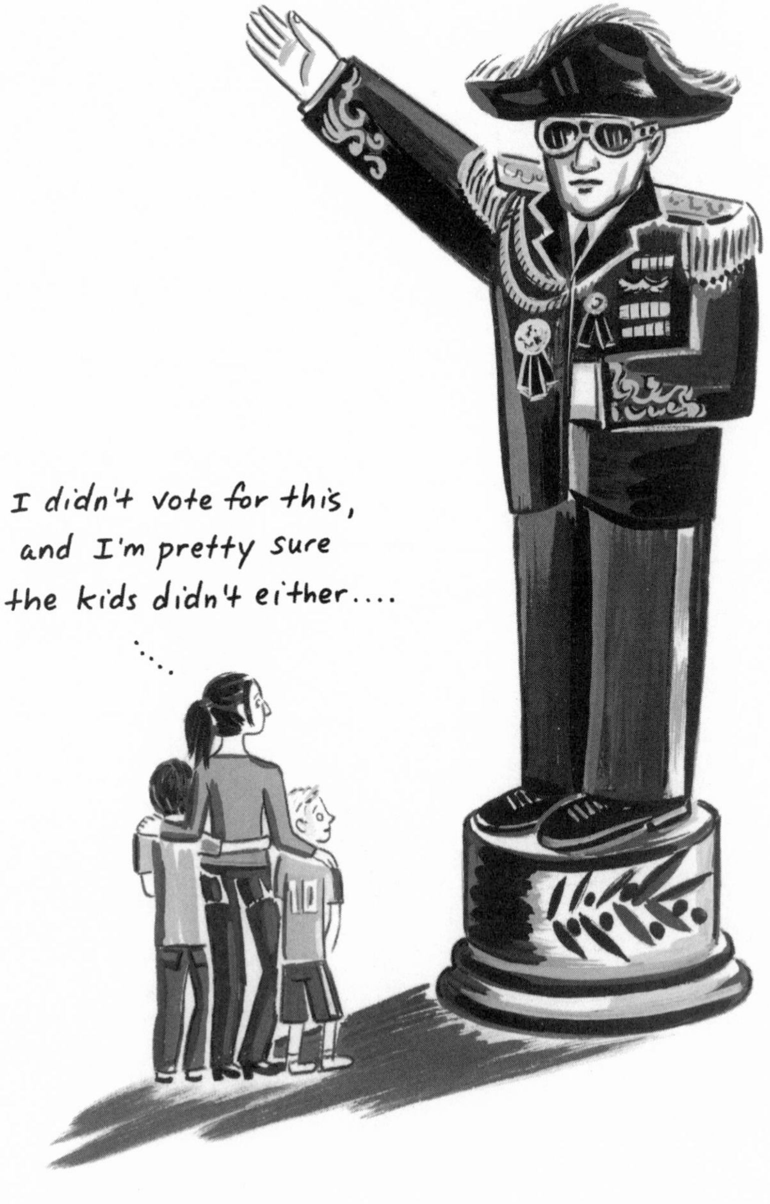
I didn't vote for this, and I'm pretty sure the kids didn't either....

AS COUPLES' COUNSELING DRAGS ON, I REALIZE THAT I NEED A LITTLE SOMETHING TO TAKE THE EDGE OFF.

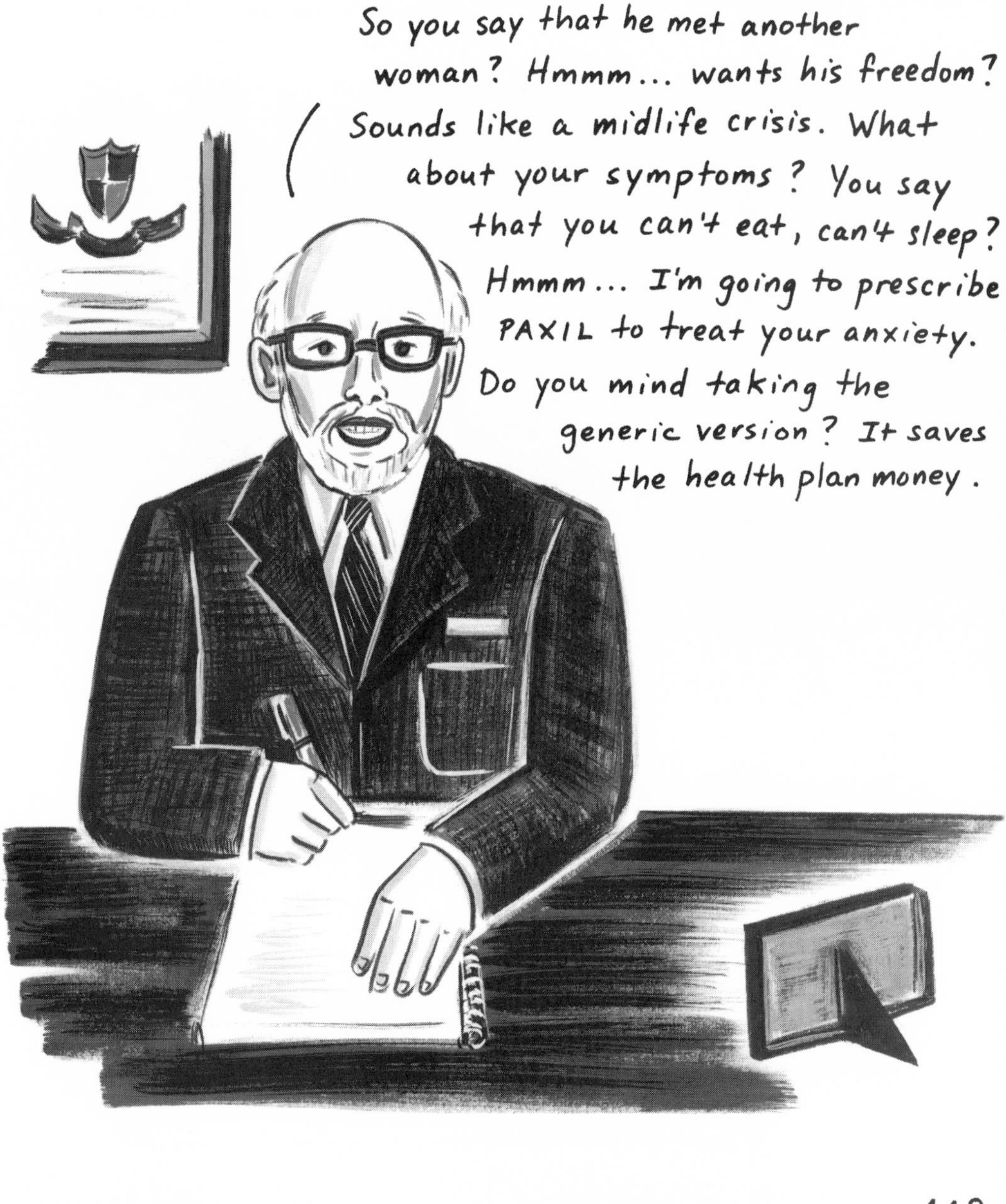
So you say that he met another woman? Hmmm... wants his freedom? Sounds like a midlife crisis. What about your symptoms? You say that you can't eat, can't sleep? Hmmm... I'm going to prescribe PAXIL to treat your anxiety. Do you mind taking the generic version? It saves the health plan money.

I'VE BEEN SEEING MYSELF THROUGH HIS EYES FOR SO LONG NOW, I NEED TO LEARN TO SEE MYSELF... UNDISTORTED.

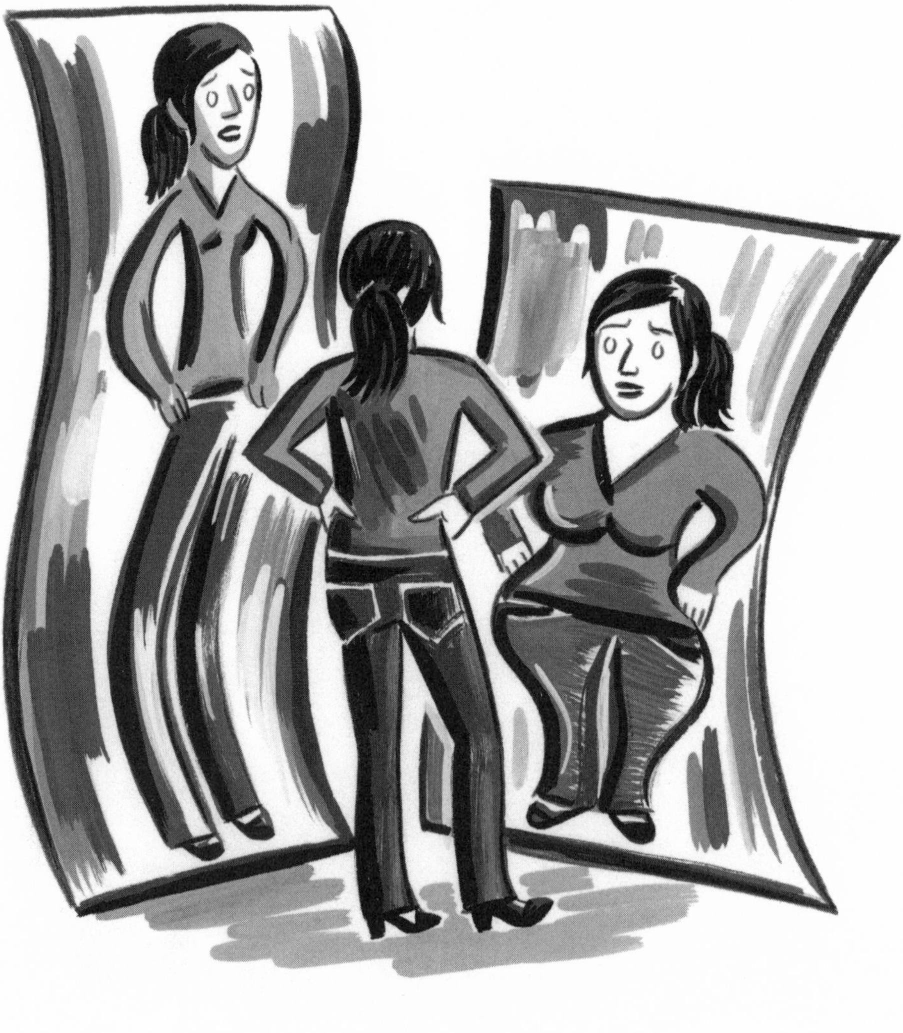

Words of Wise Women

"Falling out of love is very enlightening:
for a short while you see the world with new eyes."

Iris Murdoch

NOW THAT WE'VE SET THE DATE FOR X's DEPARTURE, SMALL THINGS IGNITE INTO MAJOR CRISES.

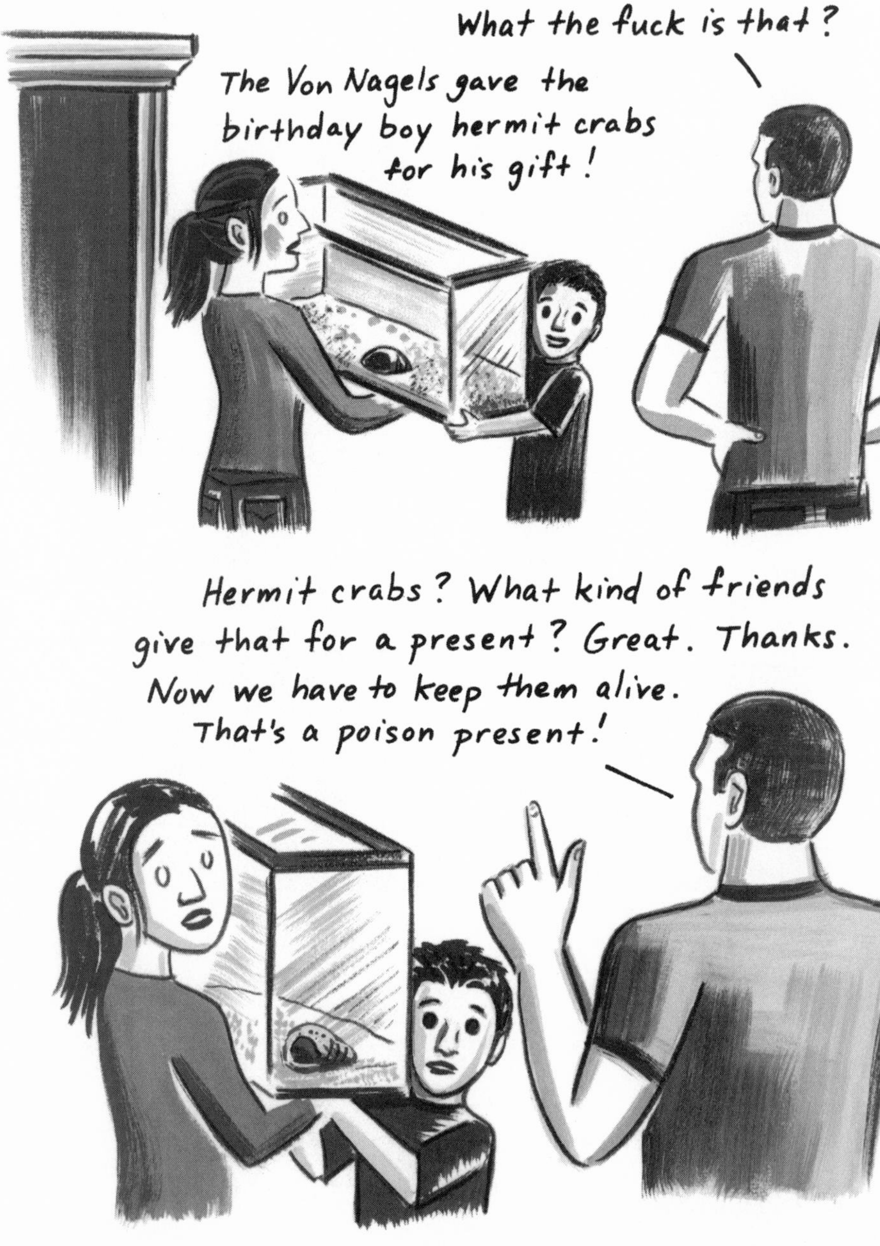
What the fuck is that?
The Von Nagels gave the birthday boy hermit crabs for his gift!
Hermit crabs? What kind of friends give that for a present? Great. Thanks. Now we have to keep them alive. That's a poison present!

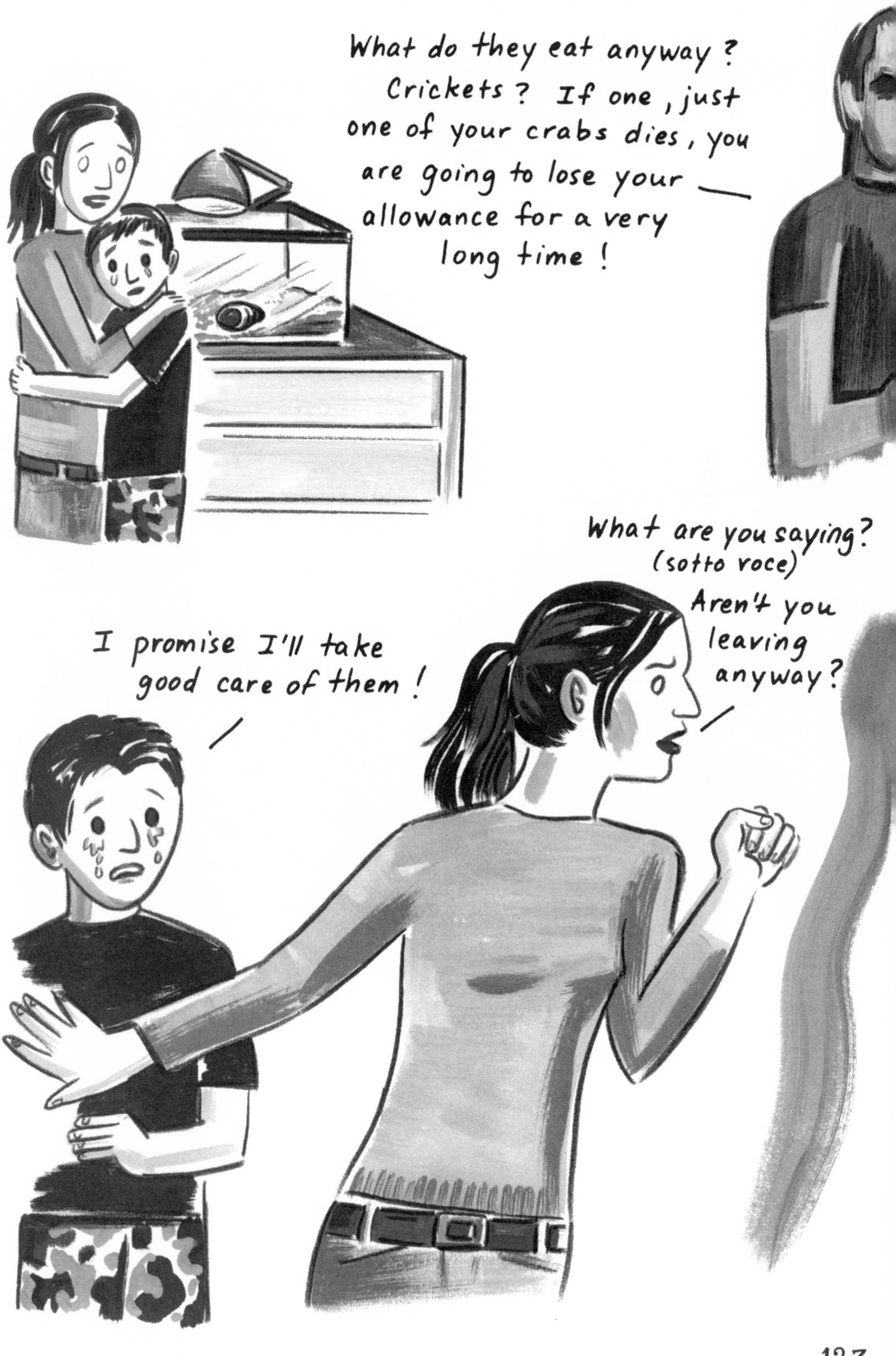
What do they eat anyway? Crickets? If one, just one of your crabs dies, you are going to lose your — allowance for a very long time!
What are you saying? (sotto voce) Aren't you leaving anyway?
I promise I'll take good care of them!

IT'S TIME FOR

THE TALK,

WHEN THE CHILDREN LEARN THEIR LIVES ARE CHANGING FOREVER.

(The kids almost seem to know what's in store.)

SEATED AT THE LITTLE TABLE, X PROCEEDS....

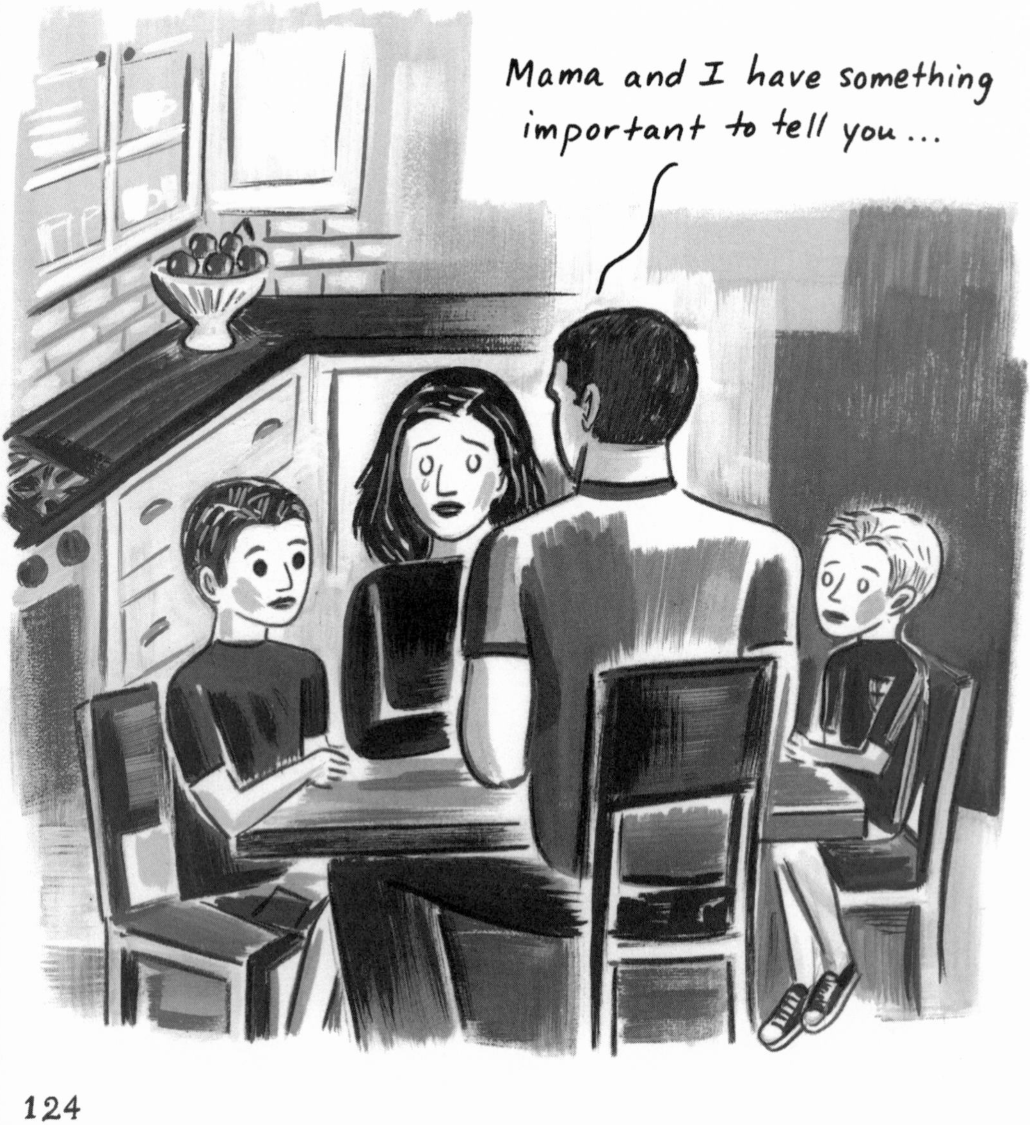
Mama and I have something important to tell you ...

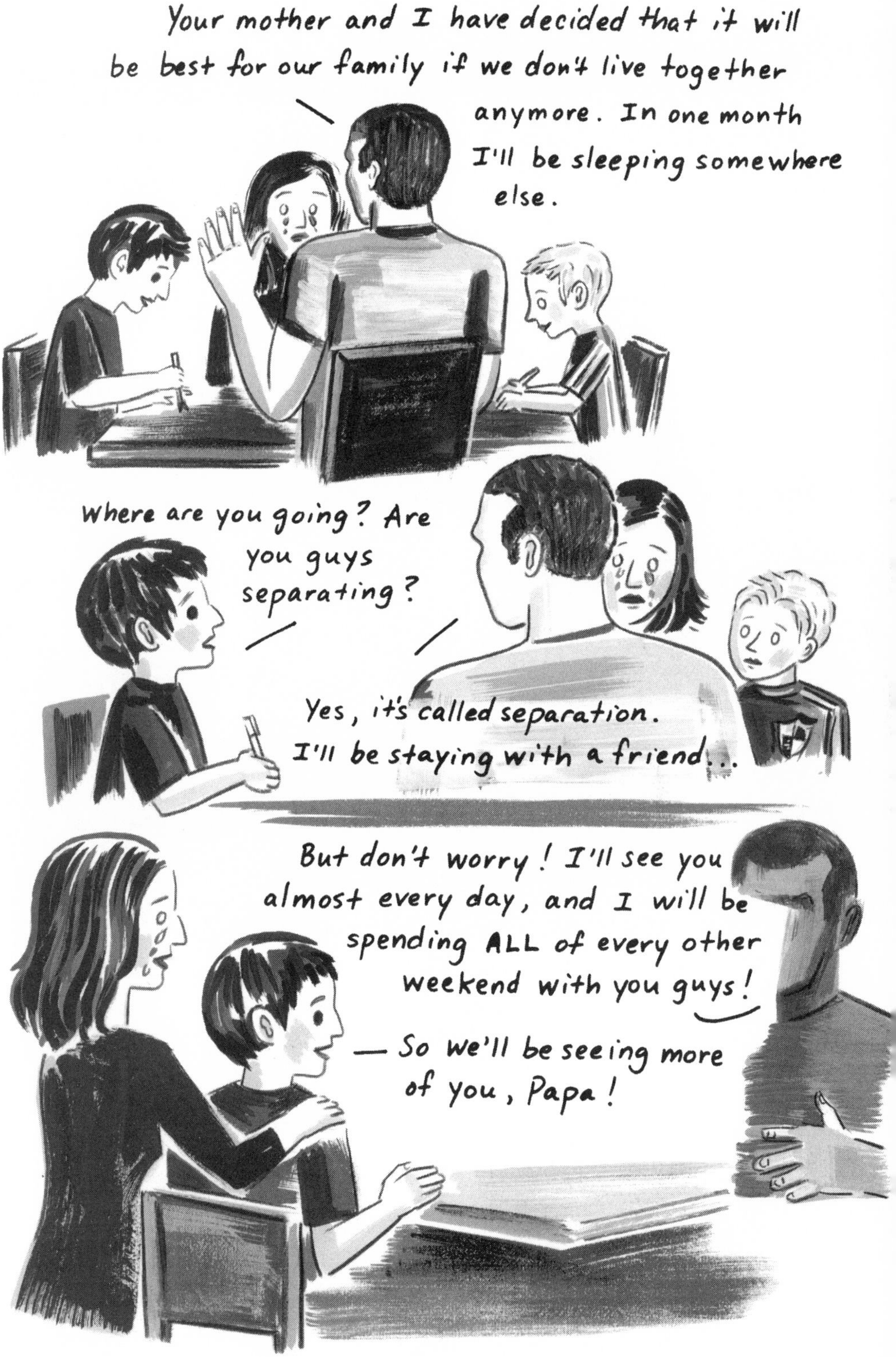
Your mother and I have decided that it will be best for our family if we don't live together anymore. In one month I'll be sleeping somewhere else.
Where are you going? Are you guys separating?
Yes, it's called separation. I'll be staying with a friend...
But don't worry! I'll see you almost every day, and I will be spending ALL of every other weekend with you guys!
— So we'll be seeing more of you, Papa!

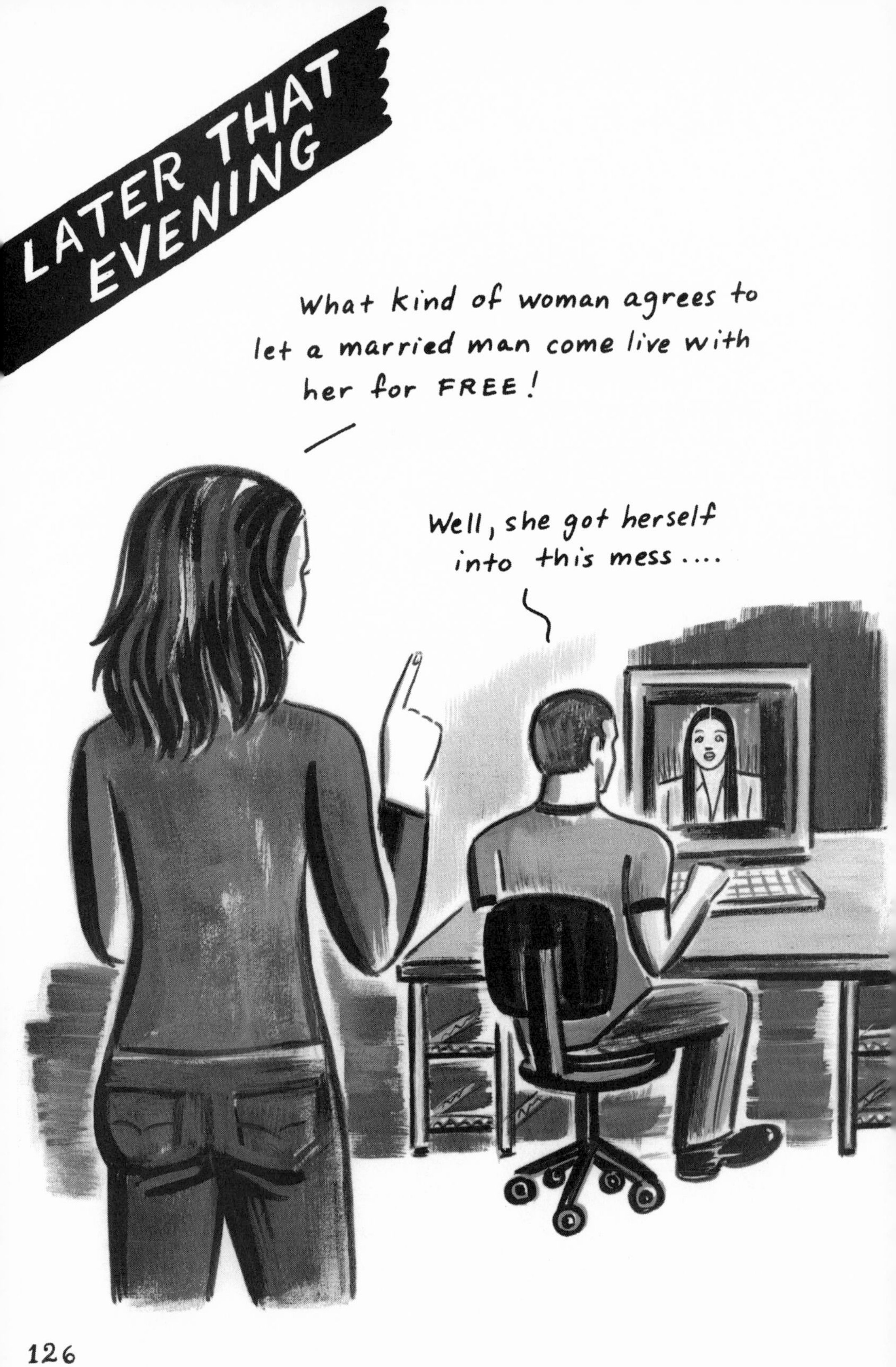
LATER THAT EVENING
What kind of woman agrees to let a married man come live with her for FREE!
Well, she got herself into this mess....

Words of Wise Women

"As long as you know men are like children, you know everything."

Coco Chanel

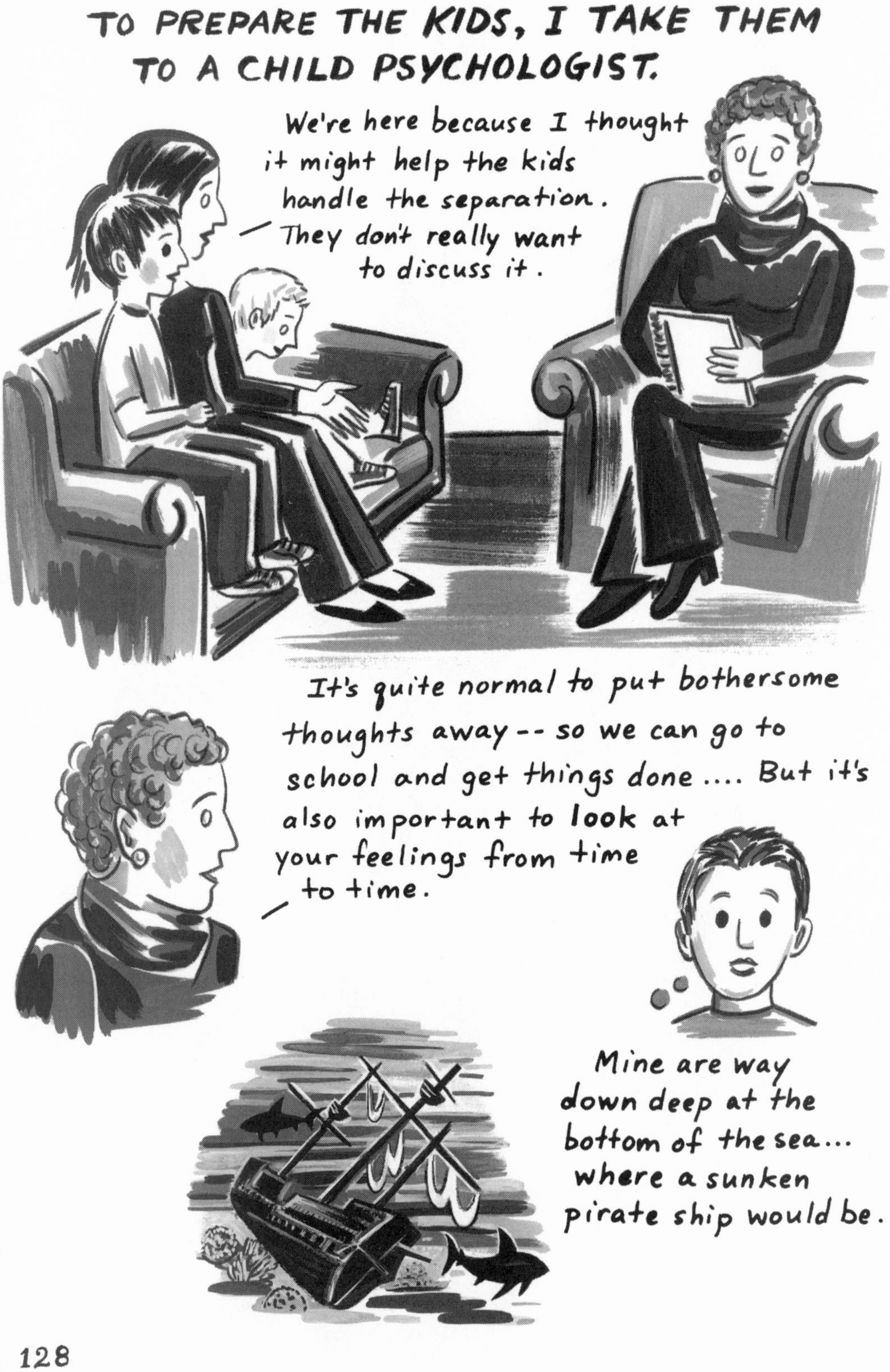
TO PREPARE THE KIDS, I TAKE THEM TO A CHILD PSYCHOLOGIST.
We're here because I thought it might help the kids handle the separation. They don't really want to discuss it.
It's quite normal to put bothersome thoughts away -- so we can go to school and get things done .... But it's also important to look at your feelings from time to time.
Mine are way down deep at the bottom of the sea... where a sunken pirate ship would be.

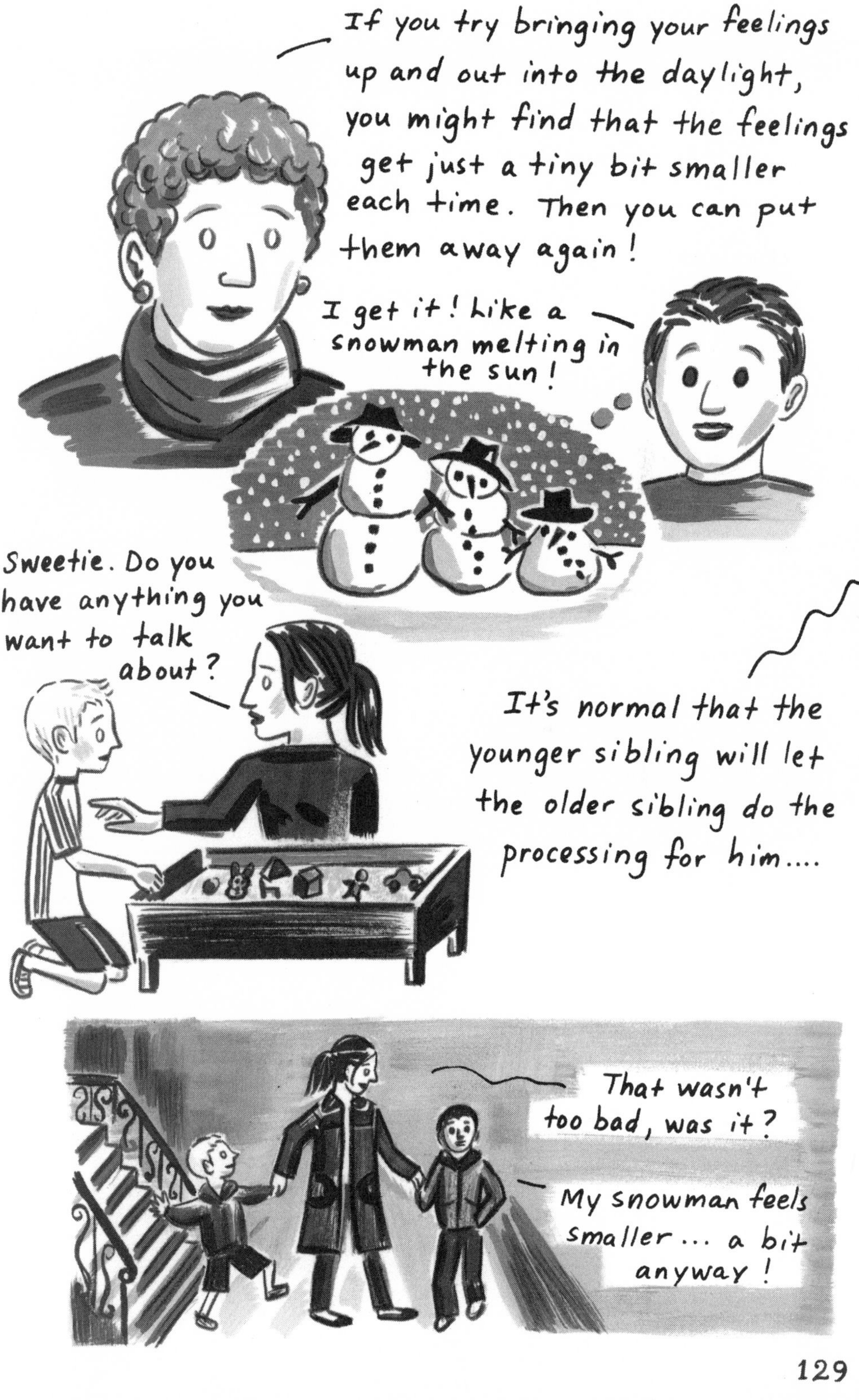
If you try bringing your feelings up and out into the daylight, you might find that the feelings get just a tiny bit smaller each time. Then you can put them away again!
I get it! Like a snowman melting in the sun!
Sweetie. Do you have anything you want to talk about?
It's normal that the younger sibling will let the older sibling do the processing for him....
That wasn't too bad, was it?
My snowman feels smaller... a bit anyway!

AND SO... THE DREADED DAY ARRIVES.

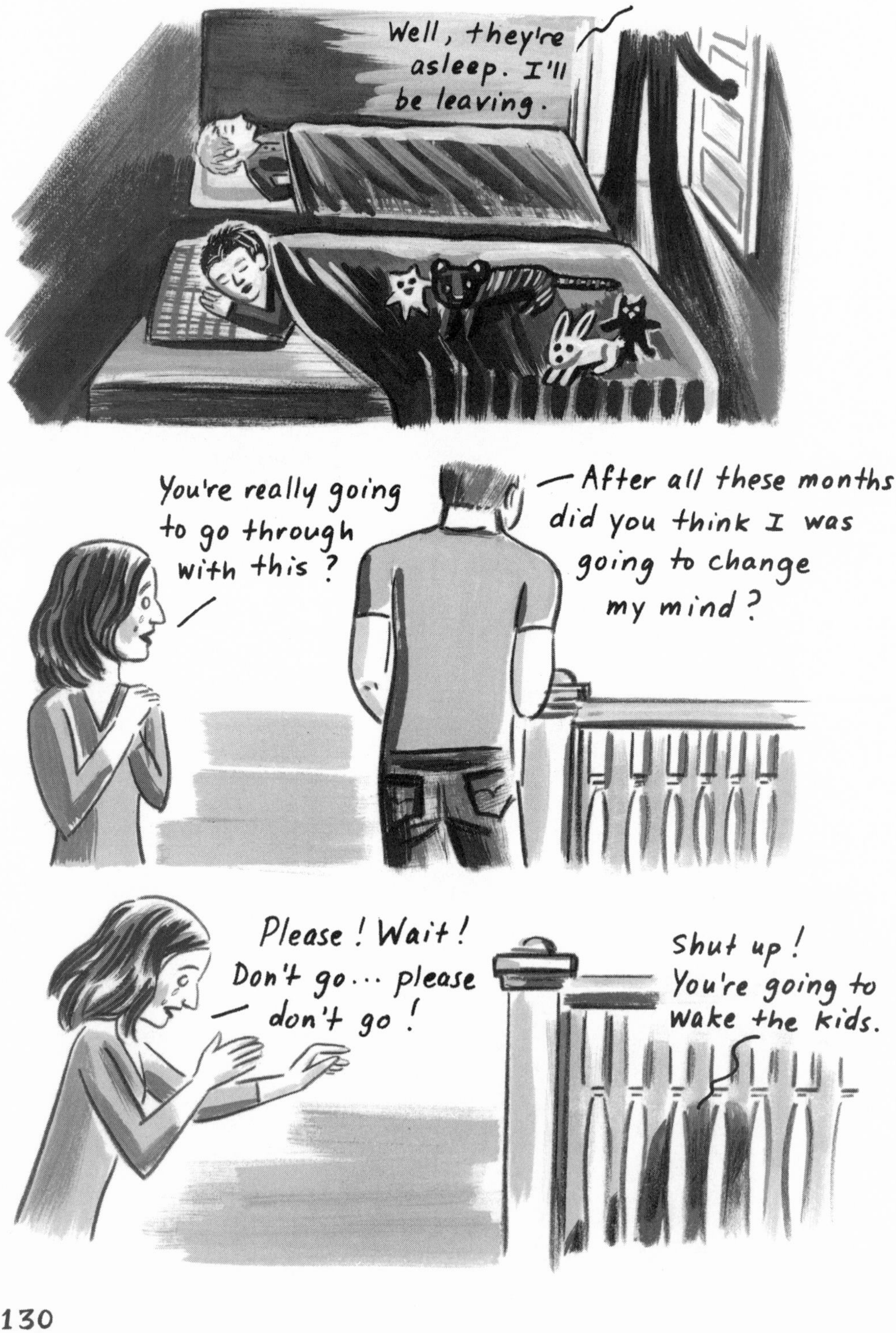
Well, they're asleep. I'll be leaving.
You're really going to go through with this?
After all these months did you think I was going to change my mind?
Please! Wait! Don't go... please don't go!
Shut up! You're going to wake the kids.

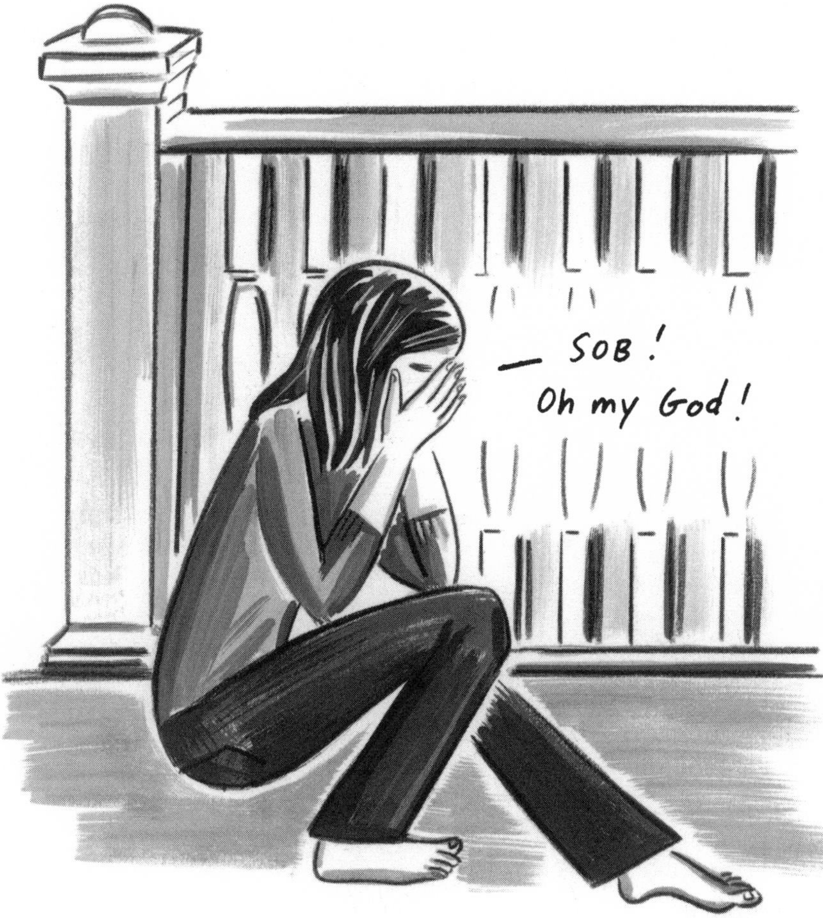
— SOB!
Oh my God!

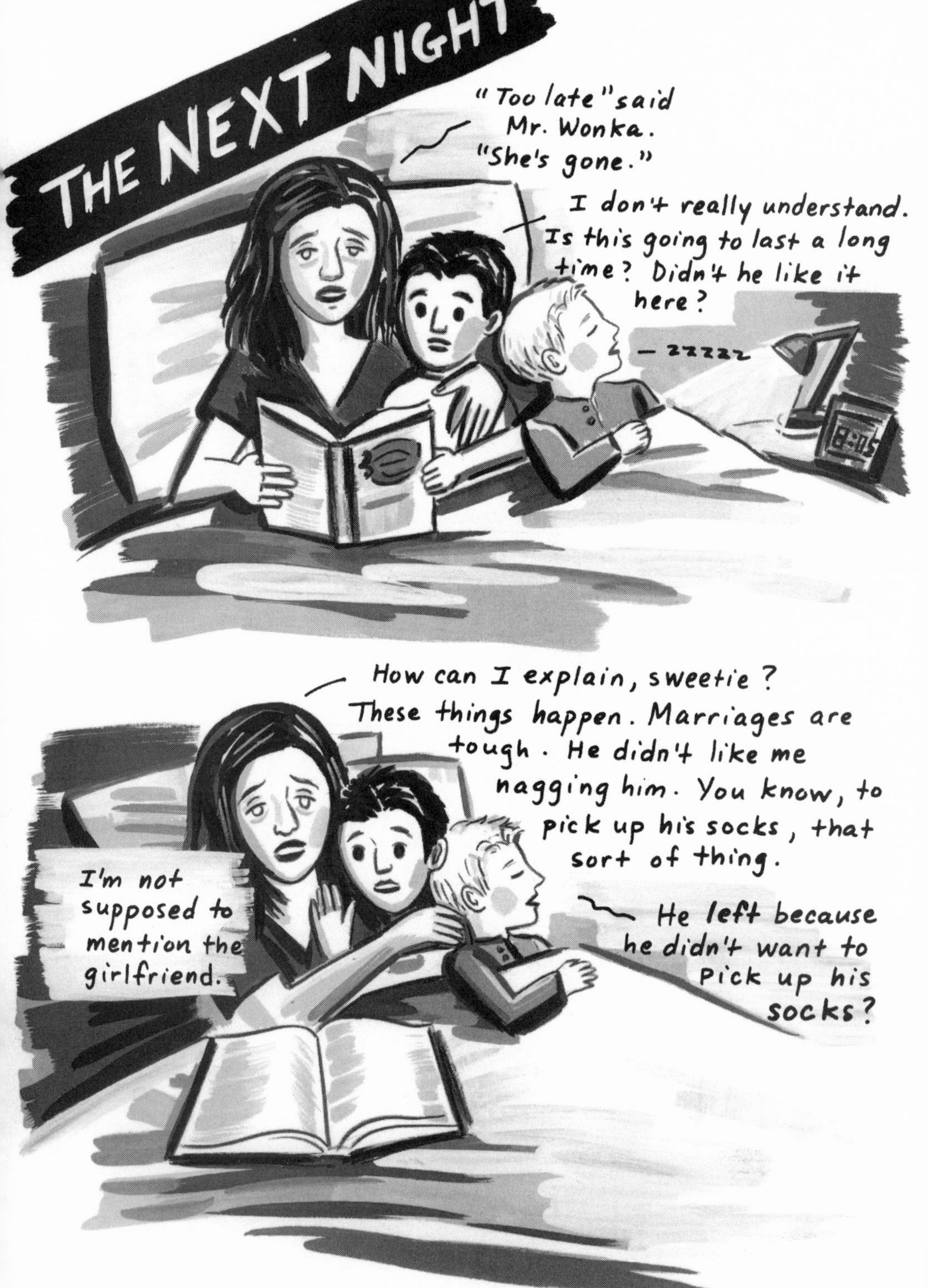
THE NEXT NIGHT
"Too late" said Mr. Wonka. "She's gone."
I don't really understand. Is this going to last a long time? Didn't he like it here?
— zzzzz
8:05
How can I explain, sweetie? These things happen. Marriages are tough. He didn't like me nagging him. You know, to pick up his socks, that sort of thing.
I'm not supposed to mention the girlfriend.
He left because he didn't want to pick up his socks?

Words of Wise Women

"I wanted a perfect ending. Now I've learned the hard way that some poems don't rhyme, and some stories don't have a clear beginning, middle, and end. Life is about not knowing, having to change, taking the moment and making the best of it without knowing what's going to happen next."

Gilda Radner

THE CHORUS

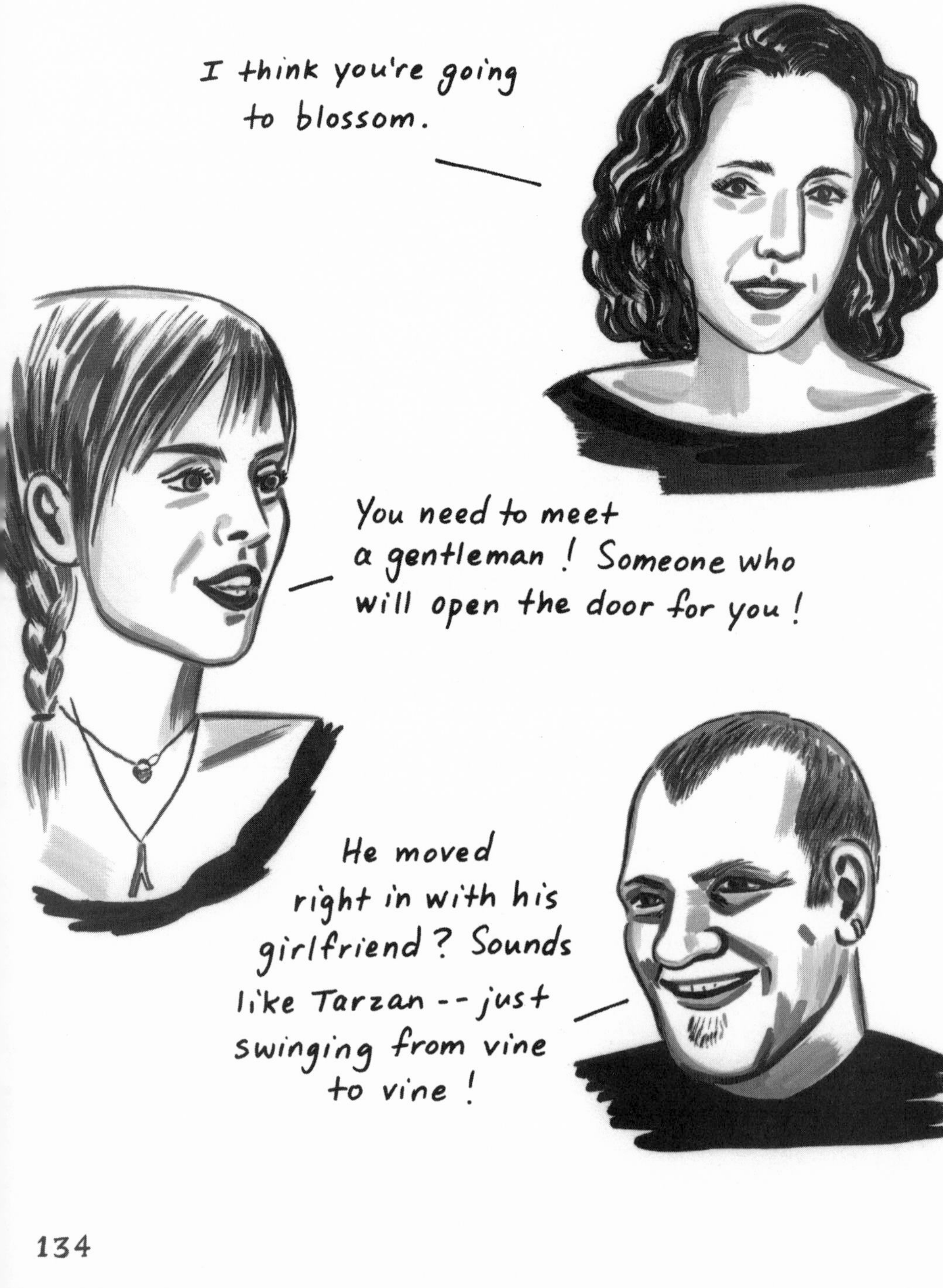

I think you're going to blossom.
You need to meet a gentleman! Someone who will open the door for you!
He moved right in with his girlfriend? Sounds like Tarzan -- just swinging from vine to vine!

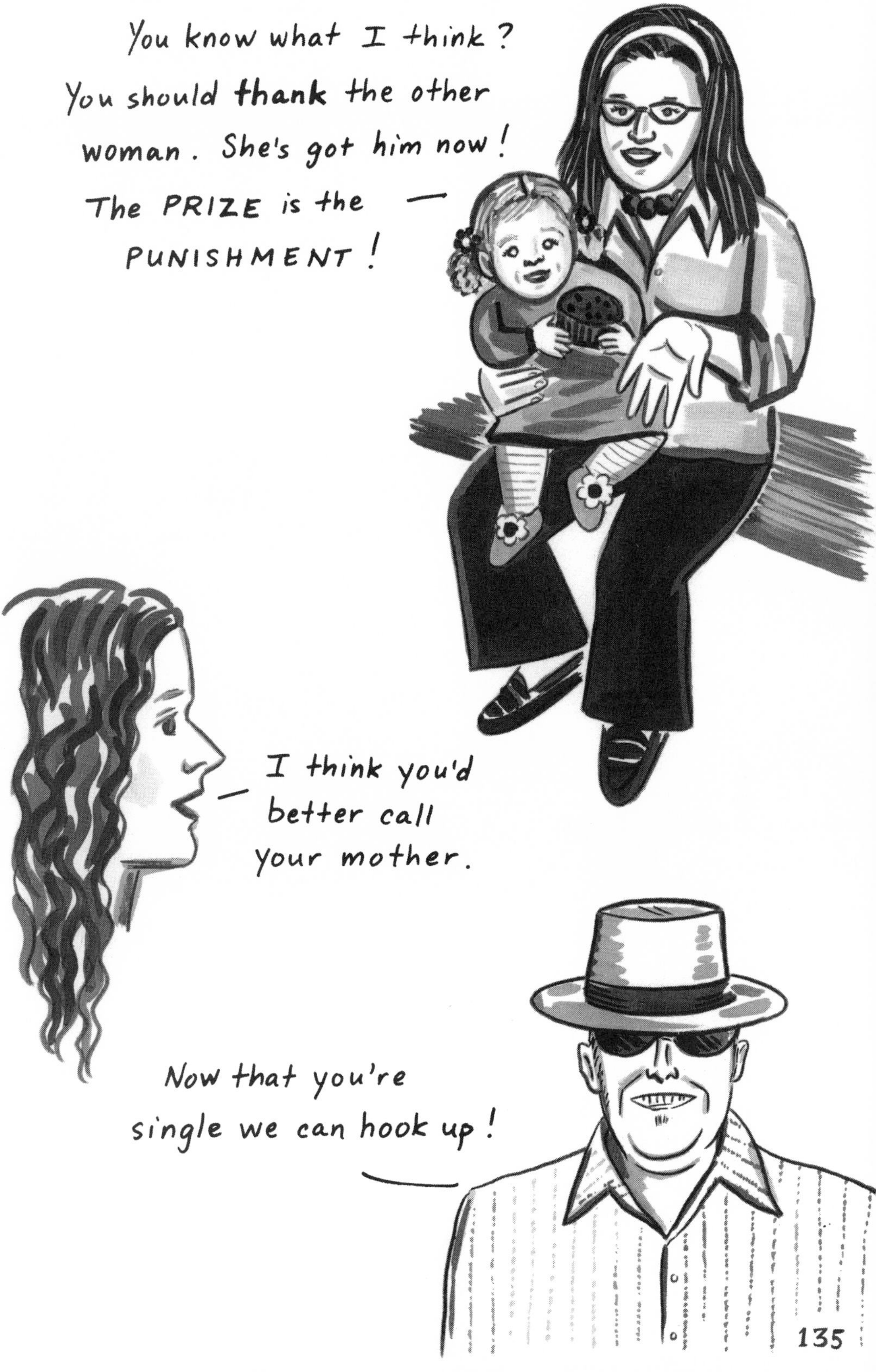
You know what I think? You should **thank** the other woman. She's got him now! The PRIZE is the PUNISHMENT!
I think you'd better call your mother.
Now that you're single we can hook up!

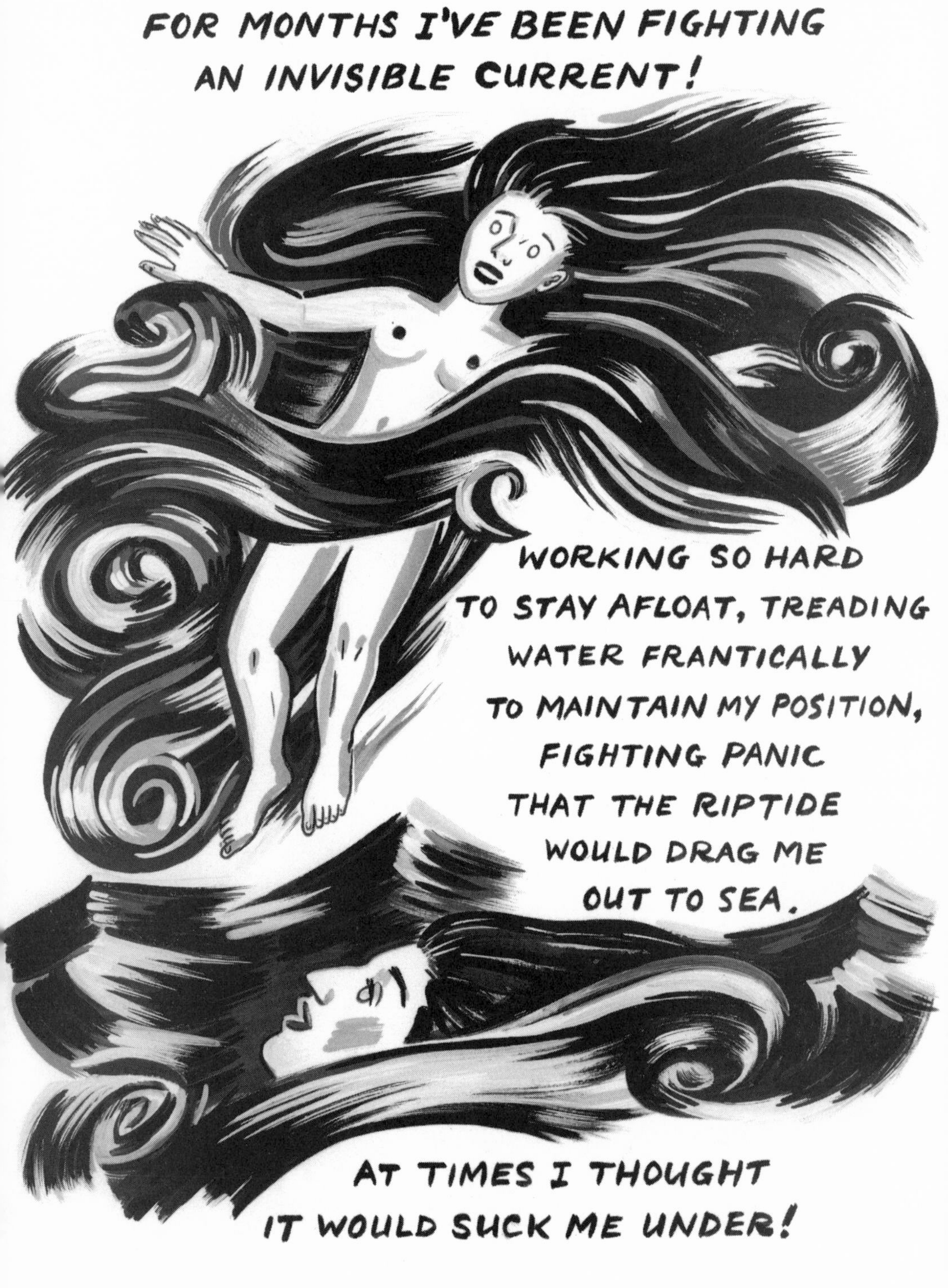
FOR MONTHS I'VE BEEN FIGHTING AN INVISIBLE CURRENT!
WORKING SO HARD TO STAY AFLOAT, TREADING WATER FRANTICALLY TO MAINTAIN MY POSITION, FIGHTING PANIC THAT THE RIPTIDE WOULD DRAG ME OUT TO SEA.
AT TIMES I THOUGHT IT WOULD SUCK ME UNDER!

BUT I AM SO EXHAUSTED NOW.

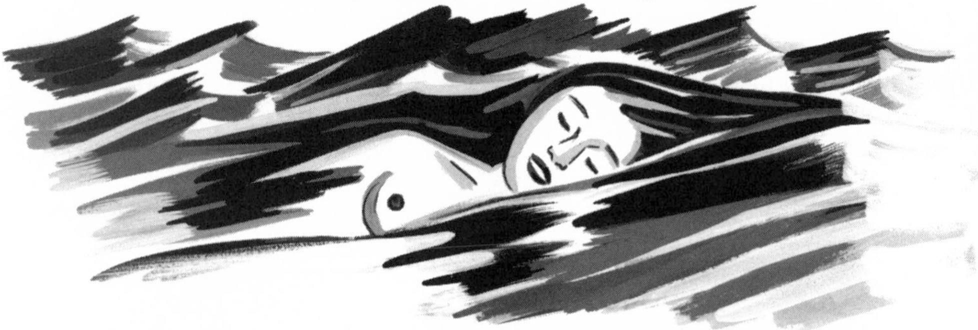

I CAN'T RESIST IT ANY LONGER...

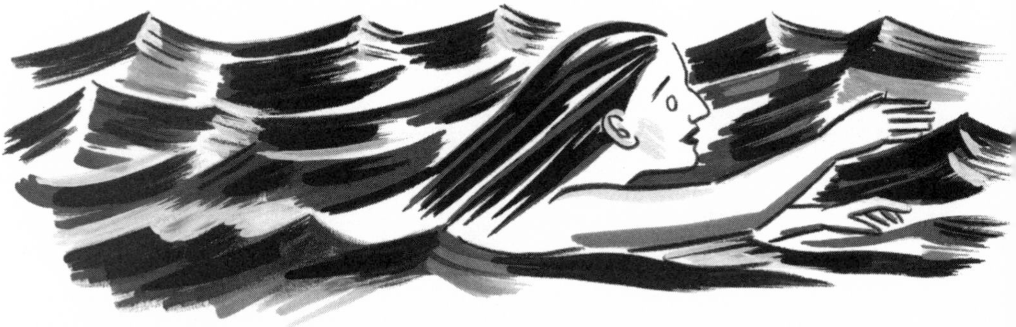

AT THIS POINT I HAVE TO GO WHERE THE CURRENT IS TAKING ME!

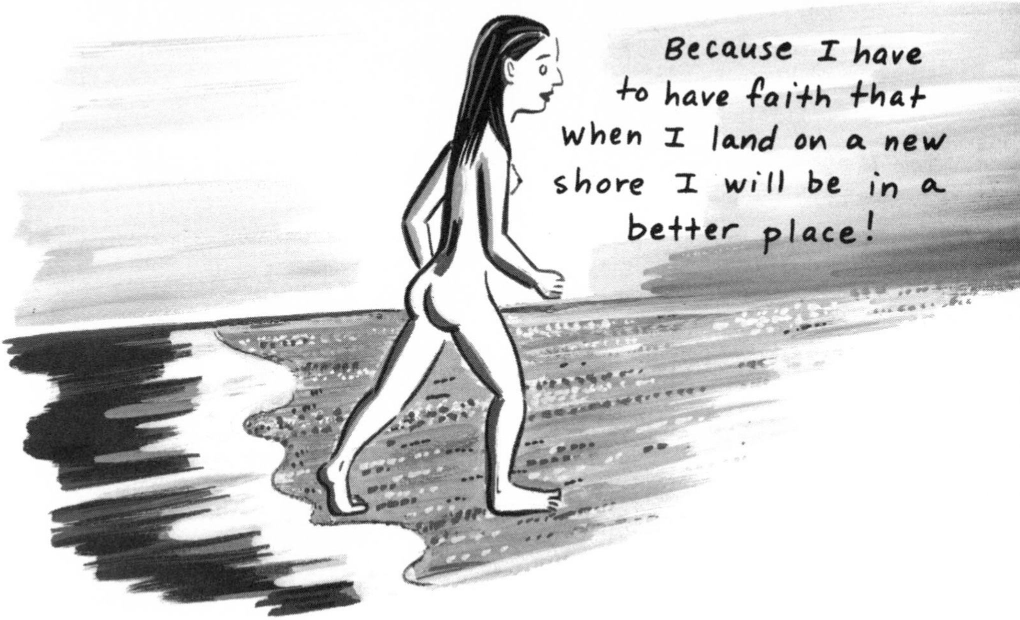
Because I have to have faith that when I land on a new shore I will be in a better place!

SO WHAT IS THE MOST LOGICAL FIRST STEP TO TAKE CHARGE OF MY LIFE?

REBUILDING MECHANISM #1 "HENRY"

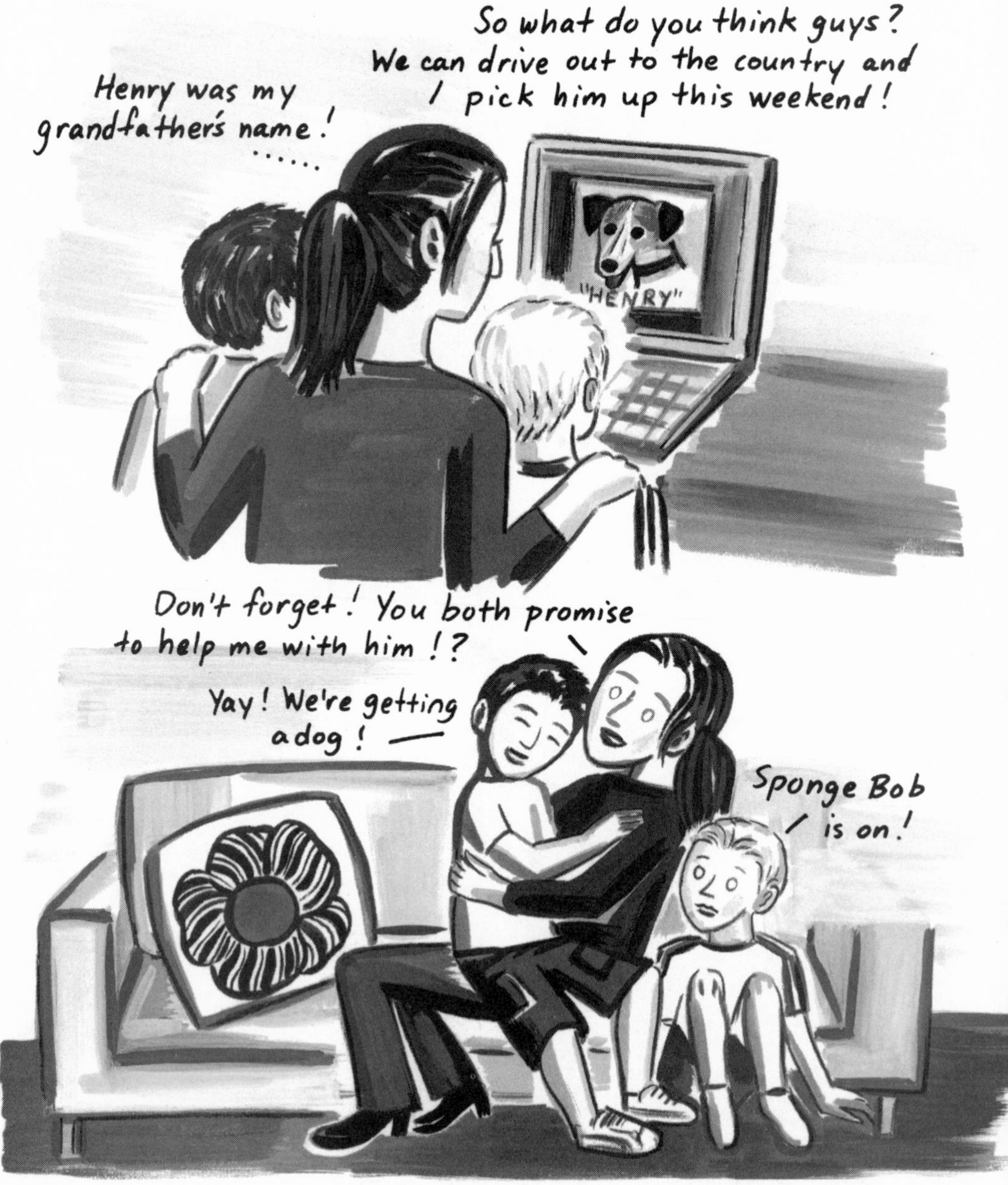

Henry was my grandfather's name! ......
So what do you think guys? We can drive out to the country and pick him up this weekend!
"HENRY"
Don't forget! You both promise to help me with him!?
Yay! We're getting a dog!
Sponge Bob is on!

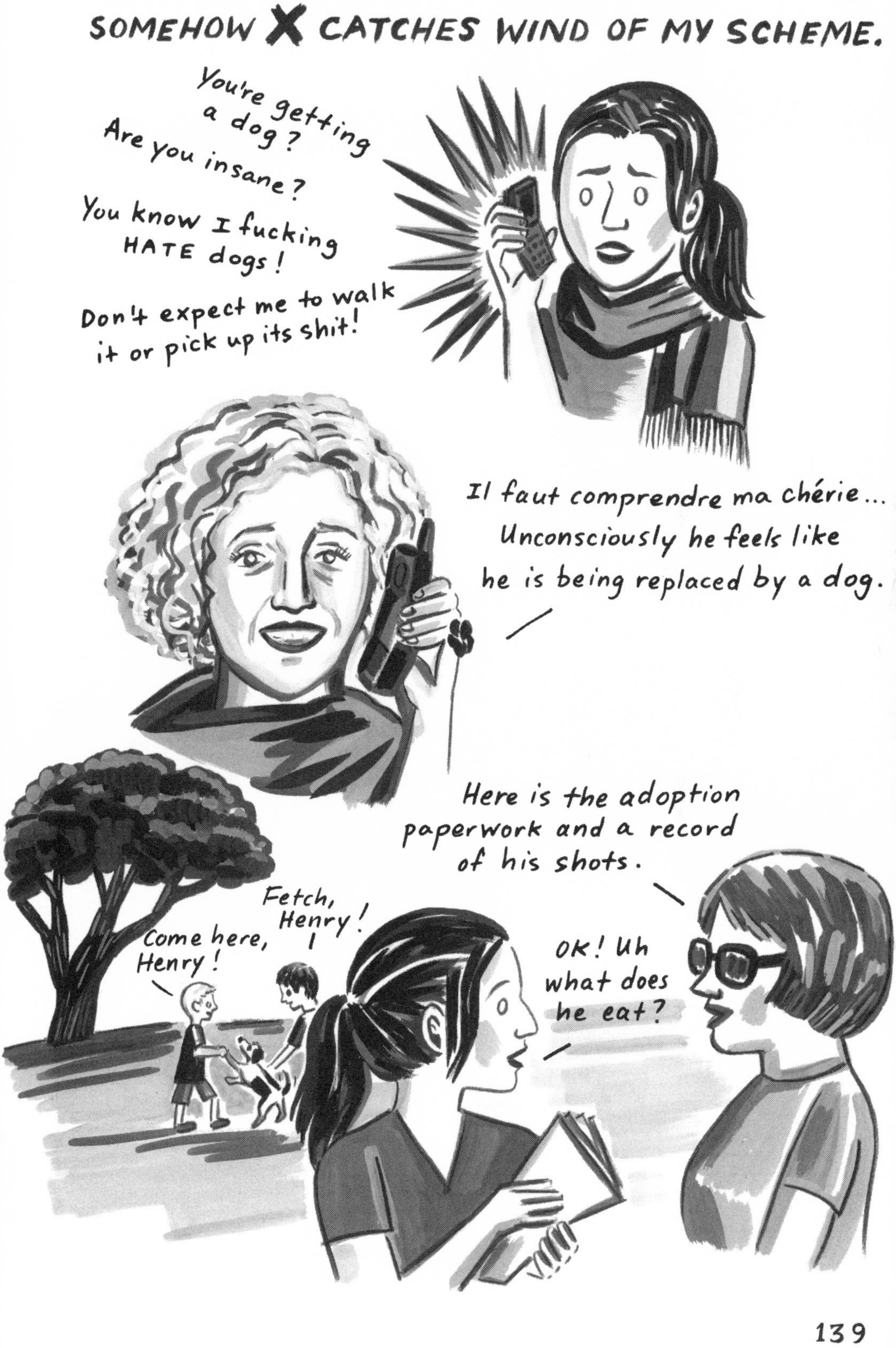
SOMEHOW X CATCHES WIND OF MY SCHEME.
You're getting a dog?
Are you insane?
You know I fucking HATE dogs!
Don't expect me to walk it or pick up its shit!
Il faut comprendre ma chérie... Unconsciously he feels like he is being replaced by a dog.
Here is the adoption paperwork and a record of his shots.
OK! Uh what does he eat?
Fetch, Henry!
Come here, Henry!

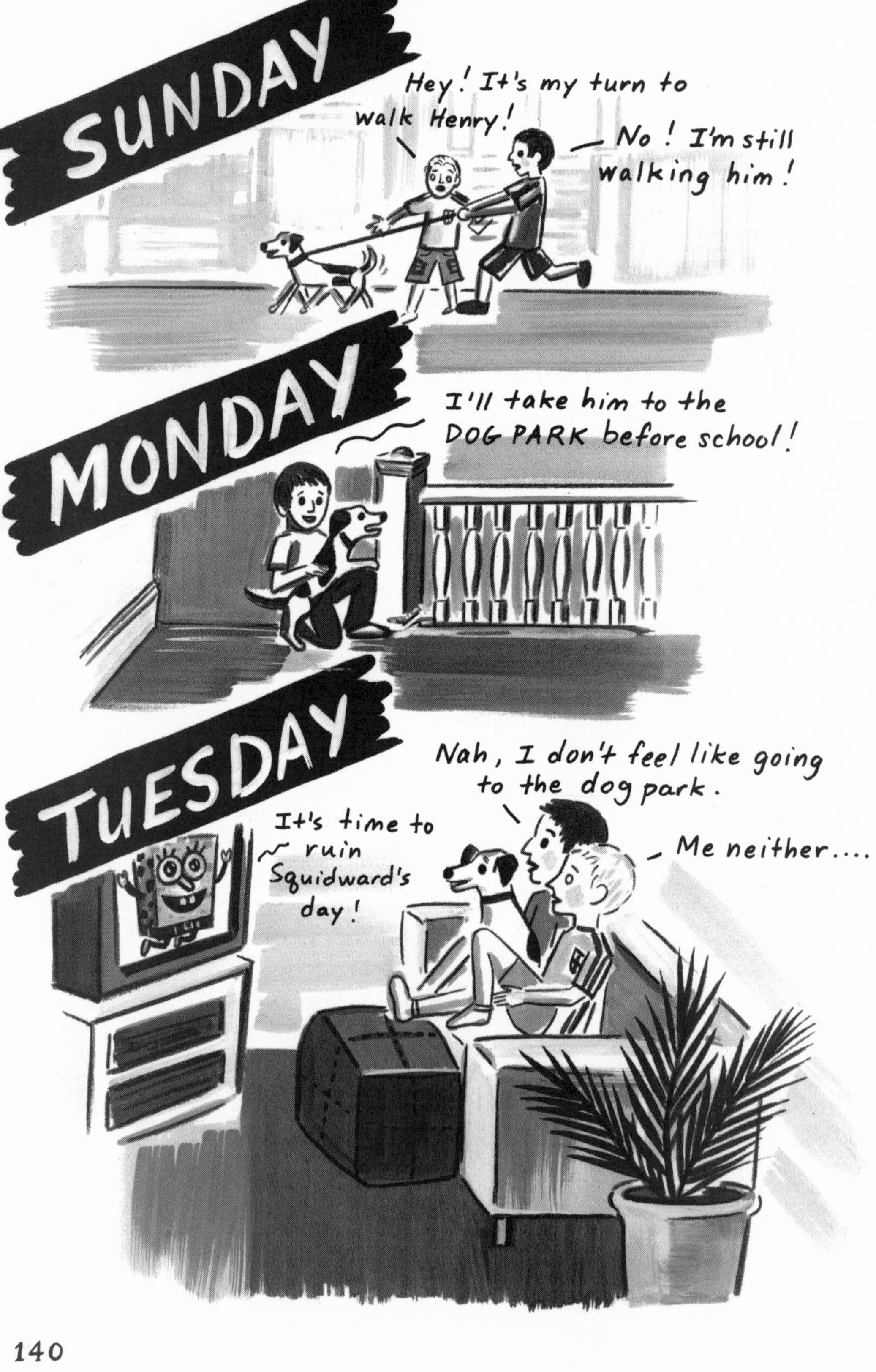
SUNDAY
Hey! It's my turn to walk Henry!
No! I'm still walking him!
MONDAY
I'll take him to the DOG PARK before school!
TUESDAY
It's time to ruin Squidward's day!
Nah, I don't feel like going to the dog park.
Me neither....

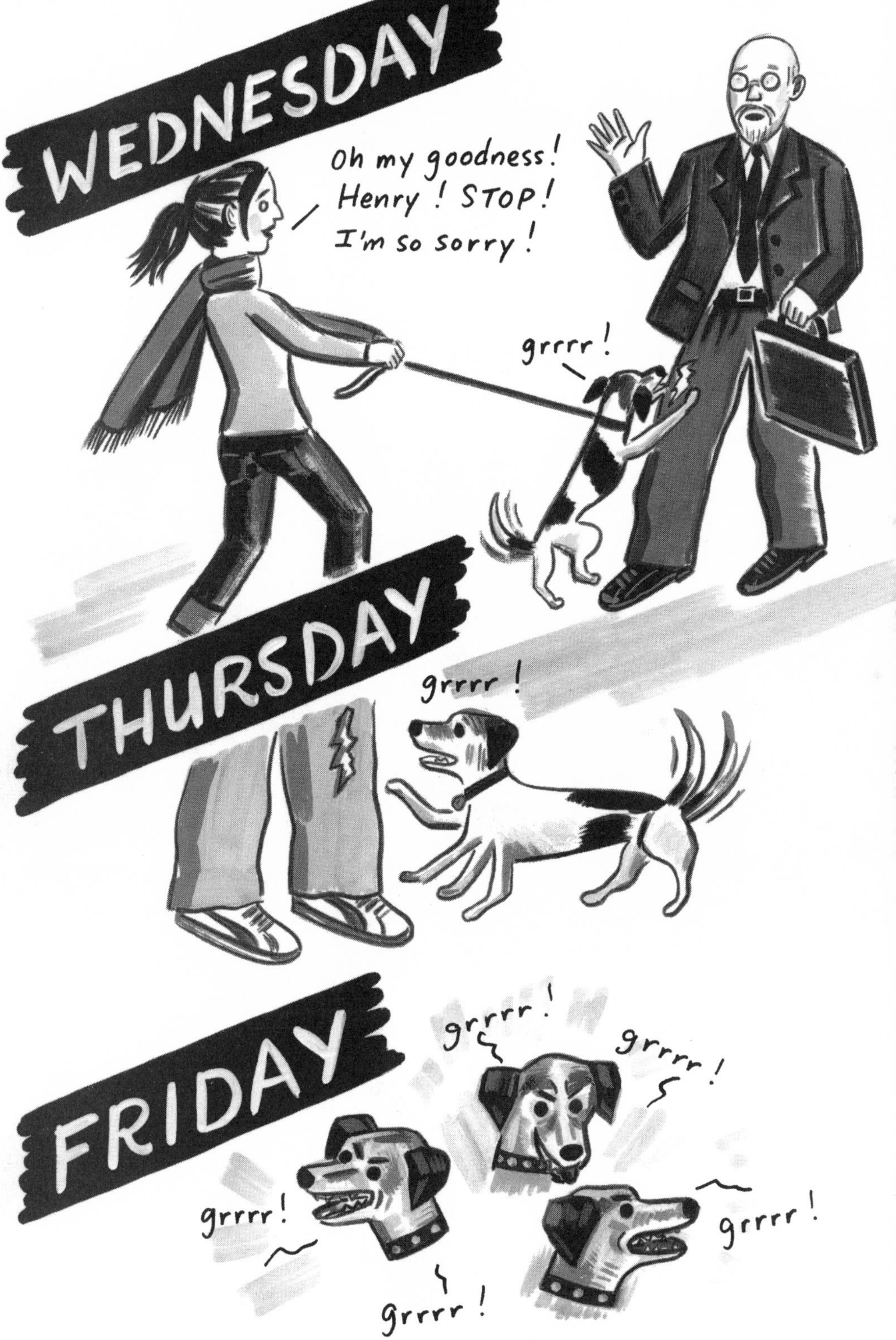
WEDNESDAY
Oh my goodness! Henry! STOP! I'm so sorry!
grrrr!
THURSDAY
grrrr!
FRIDAY
grrrr!
grrrr!
grrrr!
grrrr!
grrrr!

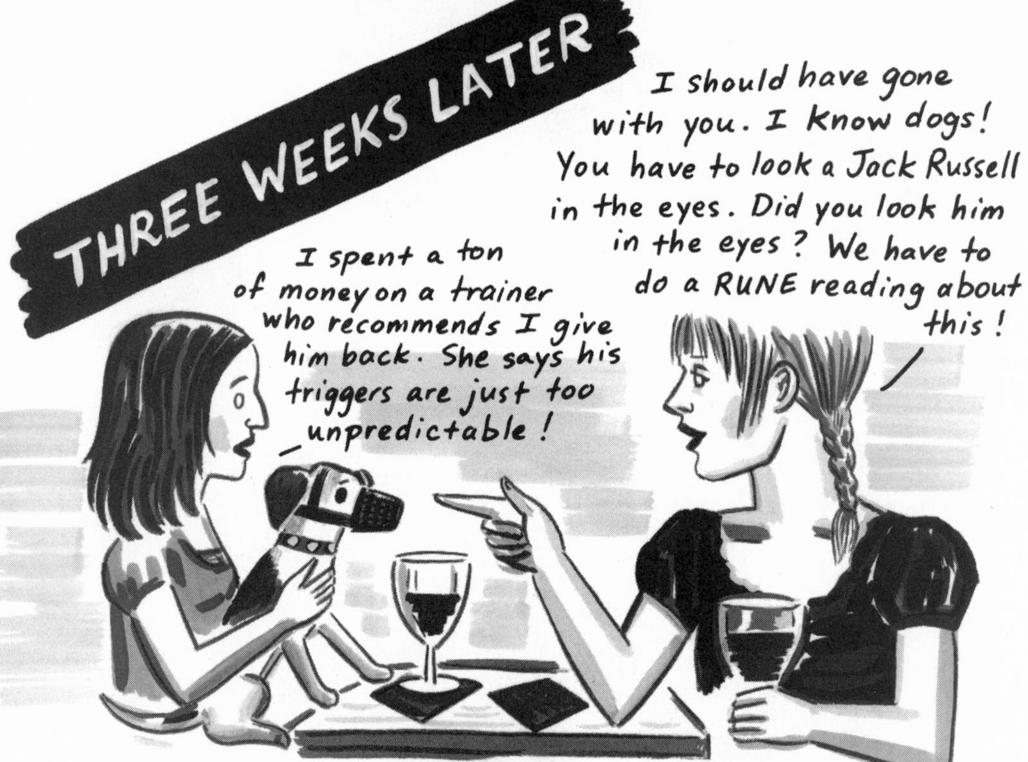
THREE WEEKS LATER
I should have gone with you. I know dogs! You have to look a Jack Russell in the eyes. Did you look him in the eyes? We have to do a RUNE reading about this!
I spent a ton of money on a trainer who recommends I give him back. She says his triggers are just too unpredictable!

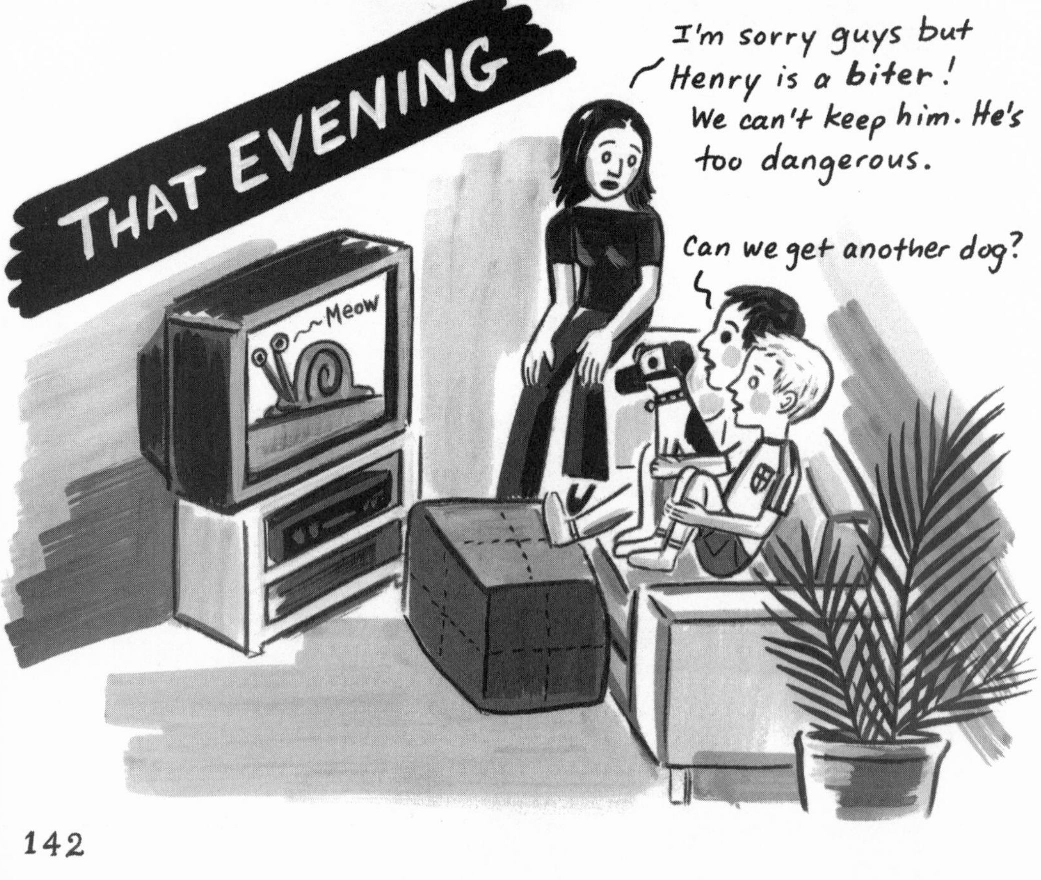
THAT EVENING
I'm sorry guys but Henry is a biter! We can't keep him. He's too dangerous.
Can we get another dog?
Meow

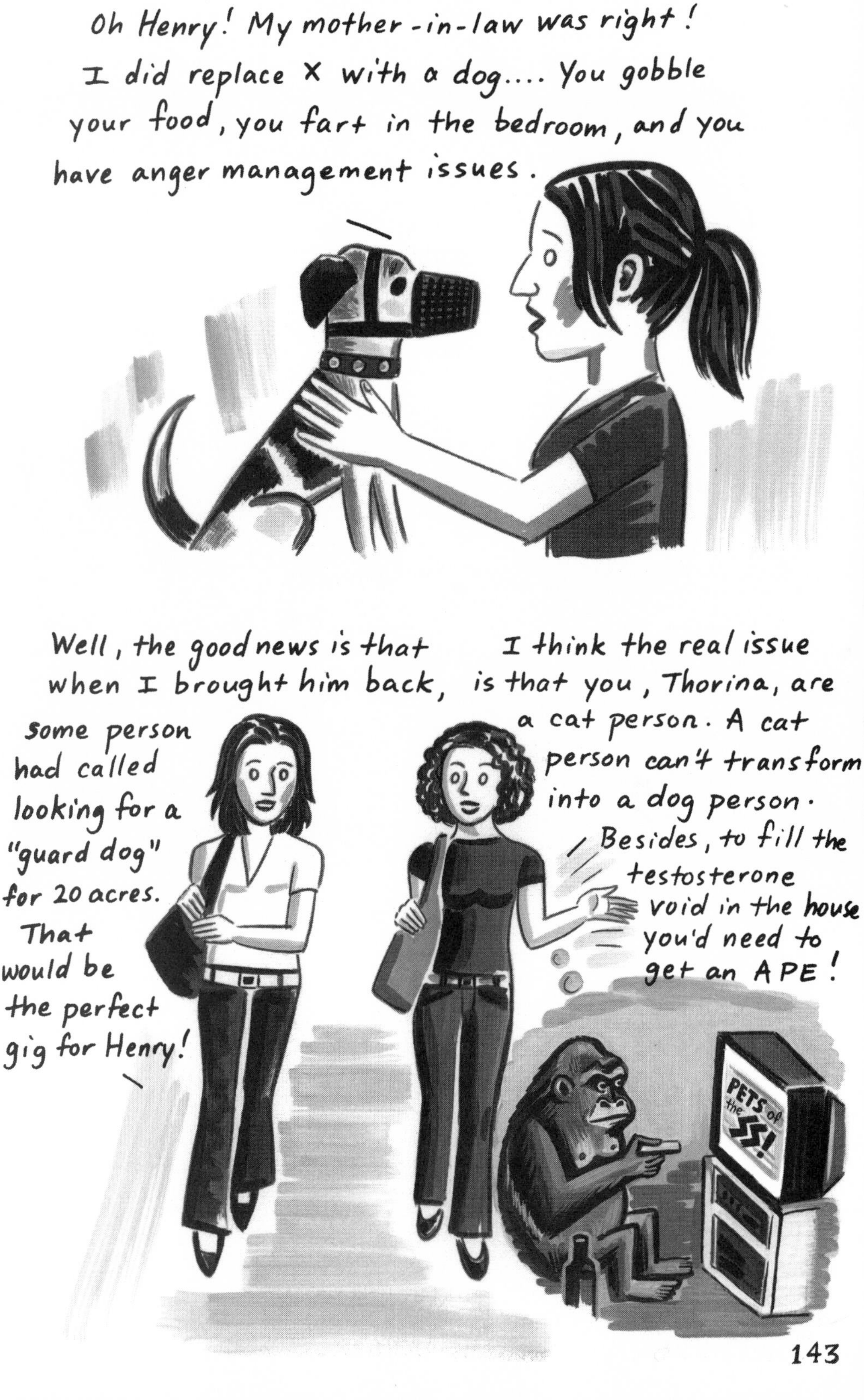
Oh Henry! My mother-in-law was right! I did replace X with a dog.... You gobble your food, you fart in the bedroom, and you have anger management issues.
Well, the good news is that when I brought him back, some person had called looking for a "guard dog" for 20 acres. That would be the perfect gig for Henry!
I think the real issue is that you, Thorina, are a cat person. A cat person can't transform into a dog person. Besides, to fill the testosterone void in the house you'd need to get an APE!
PETS of the SS!

AT THIS POINT IN MY **LIFE**, I'M GAME TO TRY JUST ABOUT ANYTHING TO FEEL BETTER...

REBUILDING MECHANISM #2
"SPIRITUAL HEALING"

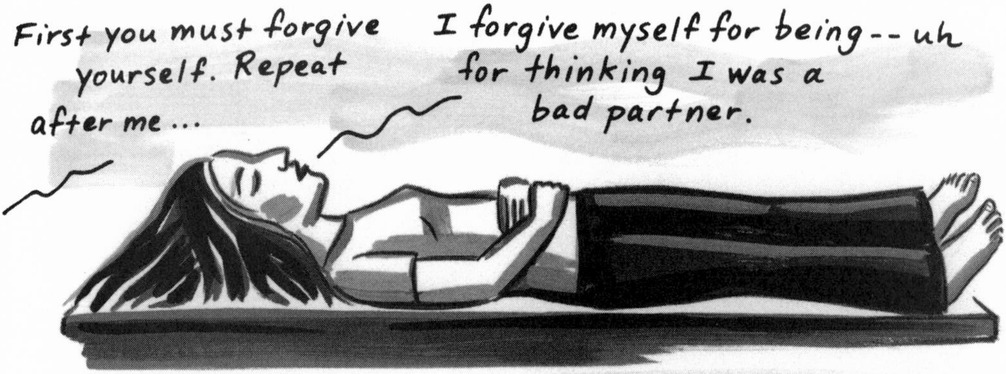
First you must forgive yourself. Repeat after me...
I forgive myself for being-- uh for thinking I was a bad partner.

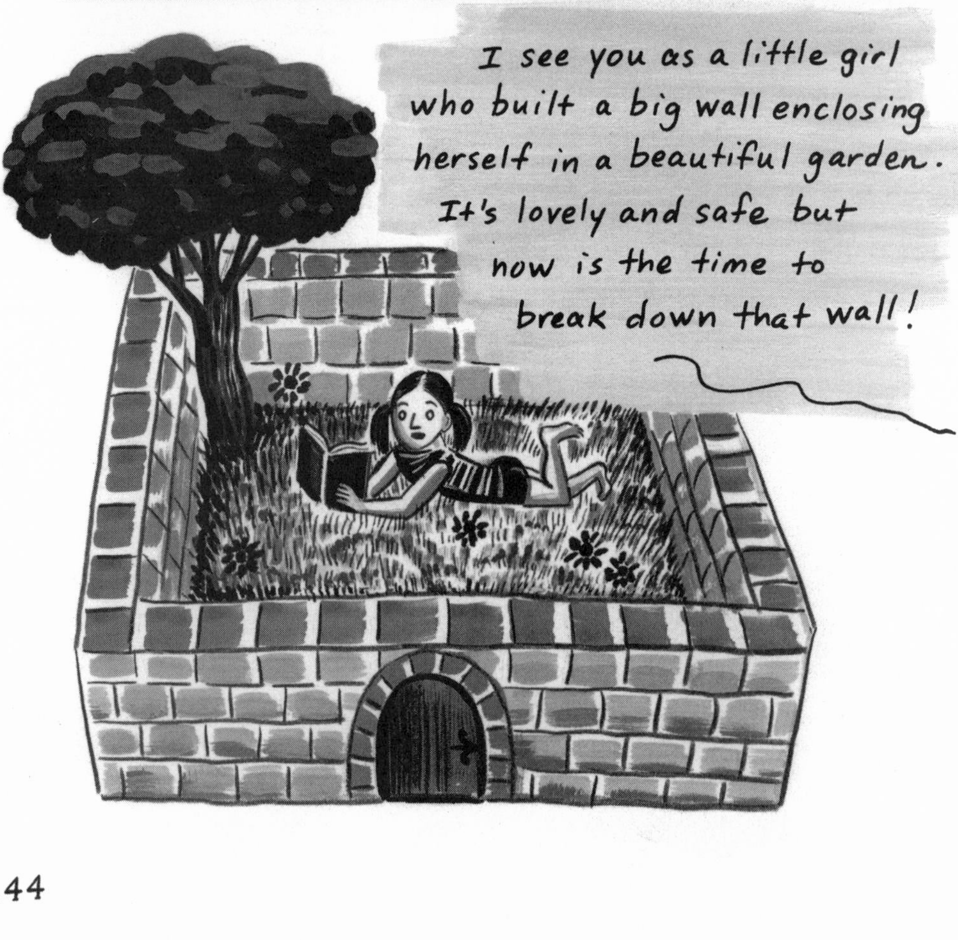
I see you as a little girl who built a big wall enclosing herself in a beautiful garden. It's lovely and safe but now is the time to break down that wall!

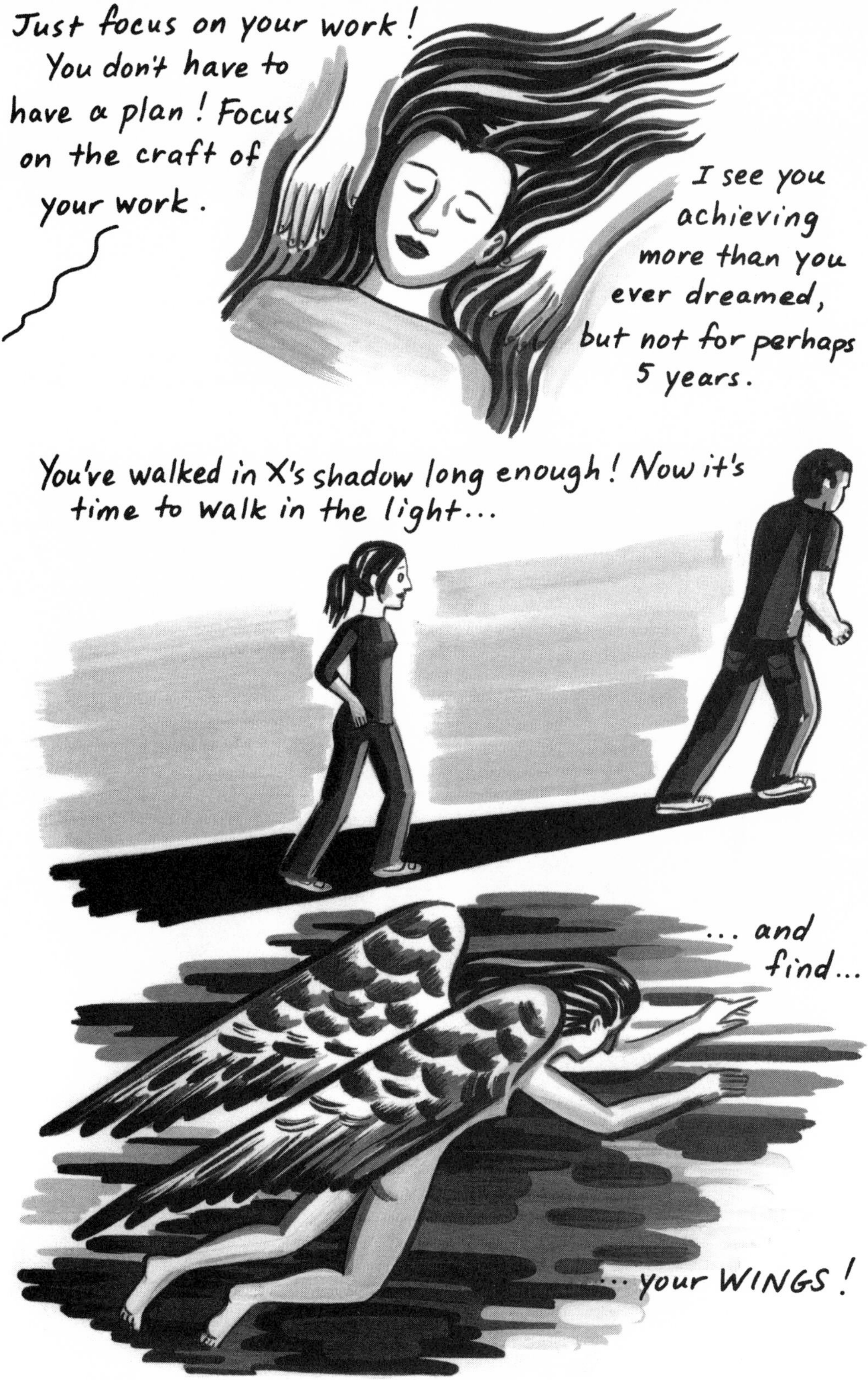
Just focus on your work! You don't have to have a plan! Focus on the craft of your work.
I see you achieving more than you ever dreamed, but not for perhaps 5 years.
You've walked in X's shadow long enough! Now it's time to walk in the light...
... and find...
... your WINGS!

BUT THE COMFORT IS SHORT-LIVED... AND MY ANGST ABOUT BEING ALONE IS AMPLIFIED BY THE INJUSTICE! X DIDN'T HAVE THE GUTS TO BE ALONE FOR EVEN ONE DAY!

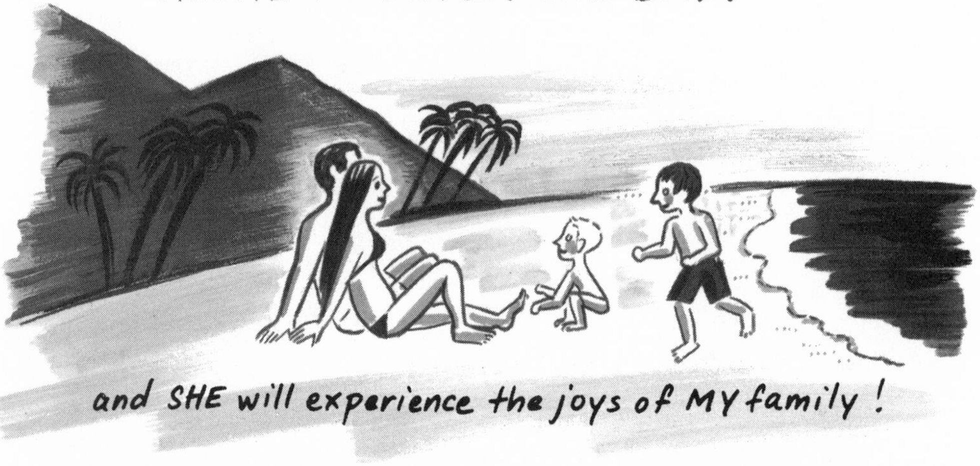
and SHE will experience the joys of MY family!

I LIVE WITH AN UNREQUITED DESIRE FOR

SCHADENFREUDE

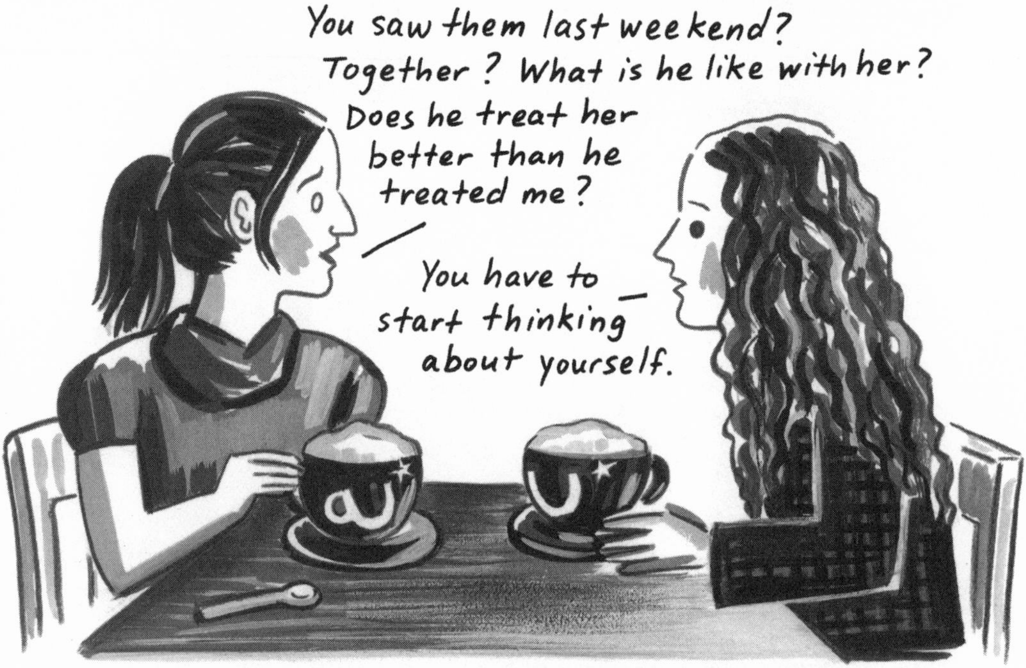
You saw them last weekend? Together? What is he like with her? Does he treat her better than he treated me?
You have to start thinking about yourself.

Words of Wise Women

" The greatest part of our happiness
or misery depends on our dispositions and
not on our circumstances."

Martha Washington

IT'S NOT "HAPPILY EVER AFTER" ON THE
OTHER SIDE OF THE FENCE. MY MARRIED
FRIENDS HAVE FRUSTRATIONS, TOO.

If my husband traveled
LESS I'd go out of my mind.

I feel like you just
excised a tumor and I'm
living with a terminal illness.

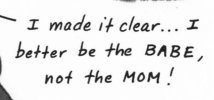

I made it clear... I
better be the BABE,
not the MOM!

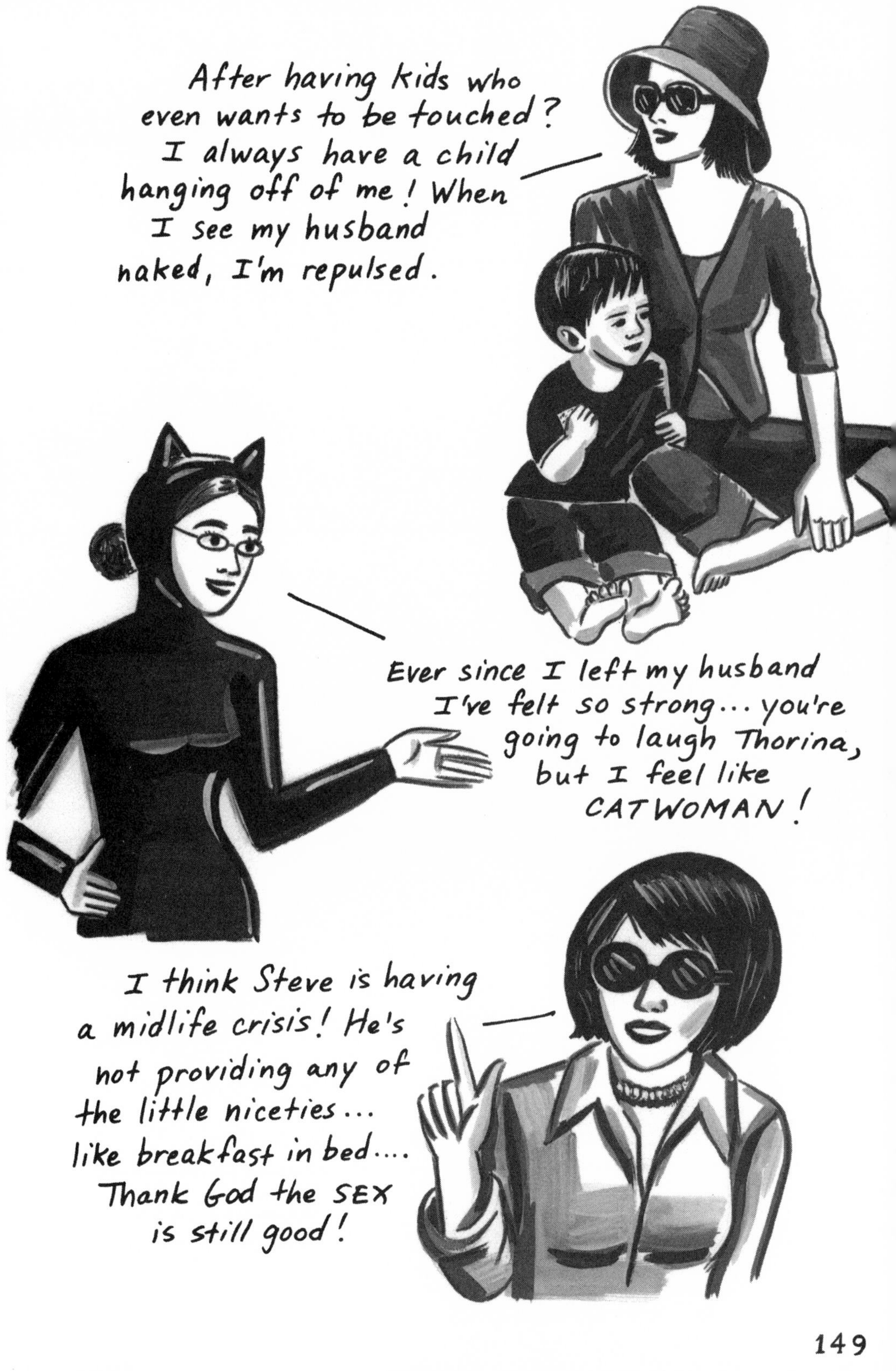
After having kids who even wants to be touched? I always have a child hanging off of me! When I see my husband naked, I'm repulsed.
Ever since I left my husband I've felt so strong... you're going to laugh Thorina, but I feel like CATWOMAN!
I think Steve is having a midlife crisis! He's not providing any of the little niceties... like breakfast in bed.... Thank God the SEX is still good!

AH, SEX! THAT WOULD BE A NICE DISTRACTION!

REBUILDING MECHANISM *3
"Romance"

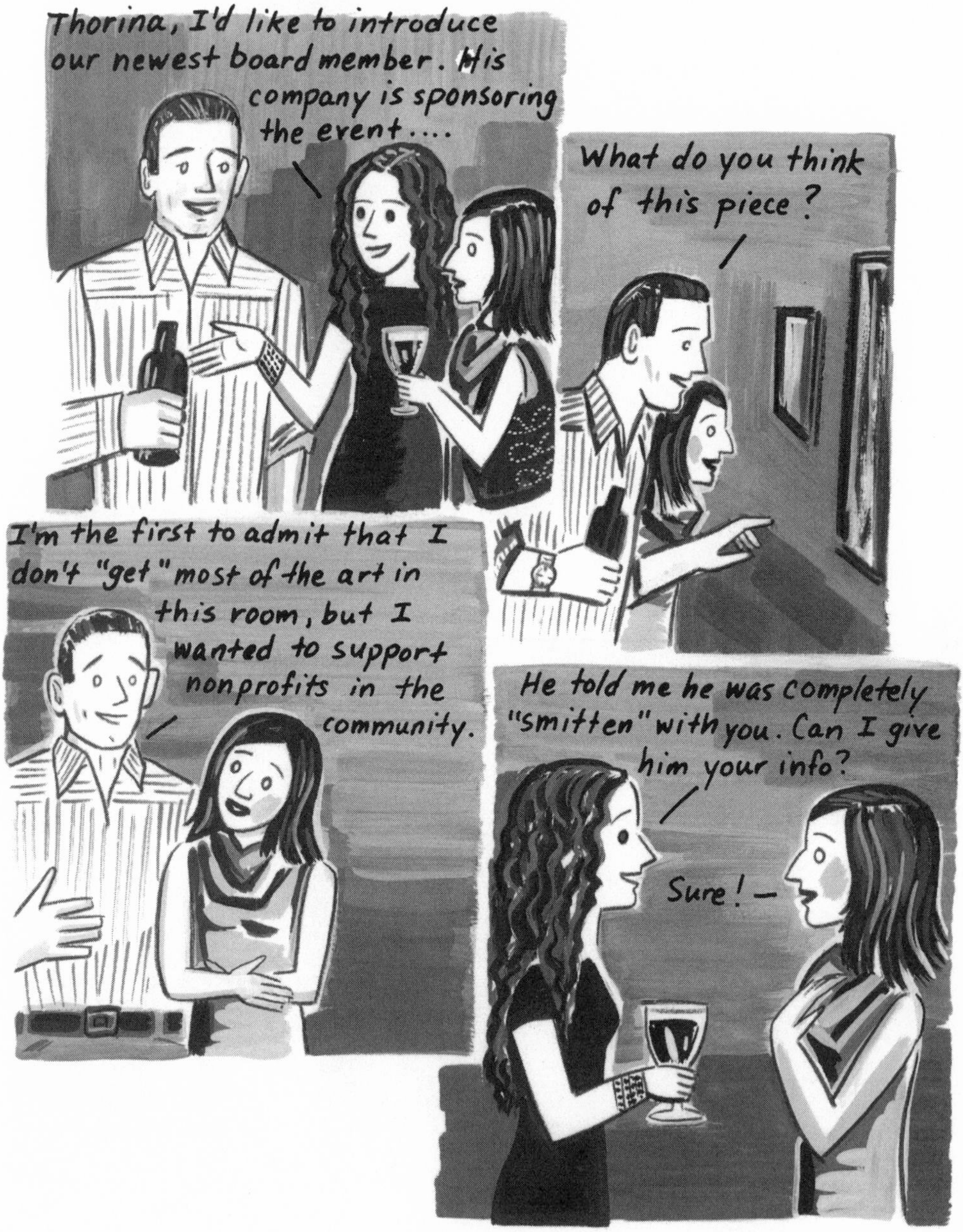
Thorina, I'd like to introduce our newest board member. His company is sponsoring the event....
What do you think of this piece?
I'm the first to admit that I don't "get" most of the art in this room, but I wanted to support nonprofits in the community.
He told me he was completely "smitten" with you. Can I give him your info?
Sure!

THERE IS THE USUAL PROCESSION OF EVENTS THAT LEAD TO THE USUAL DESTINATION....

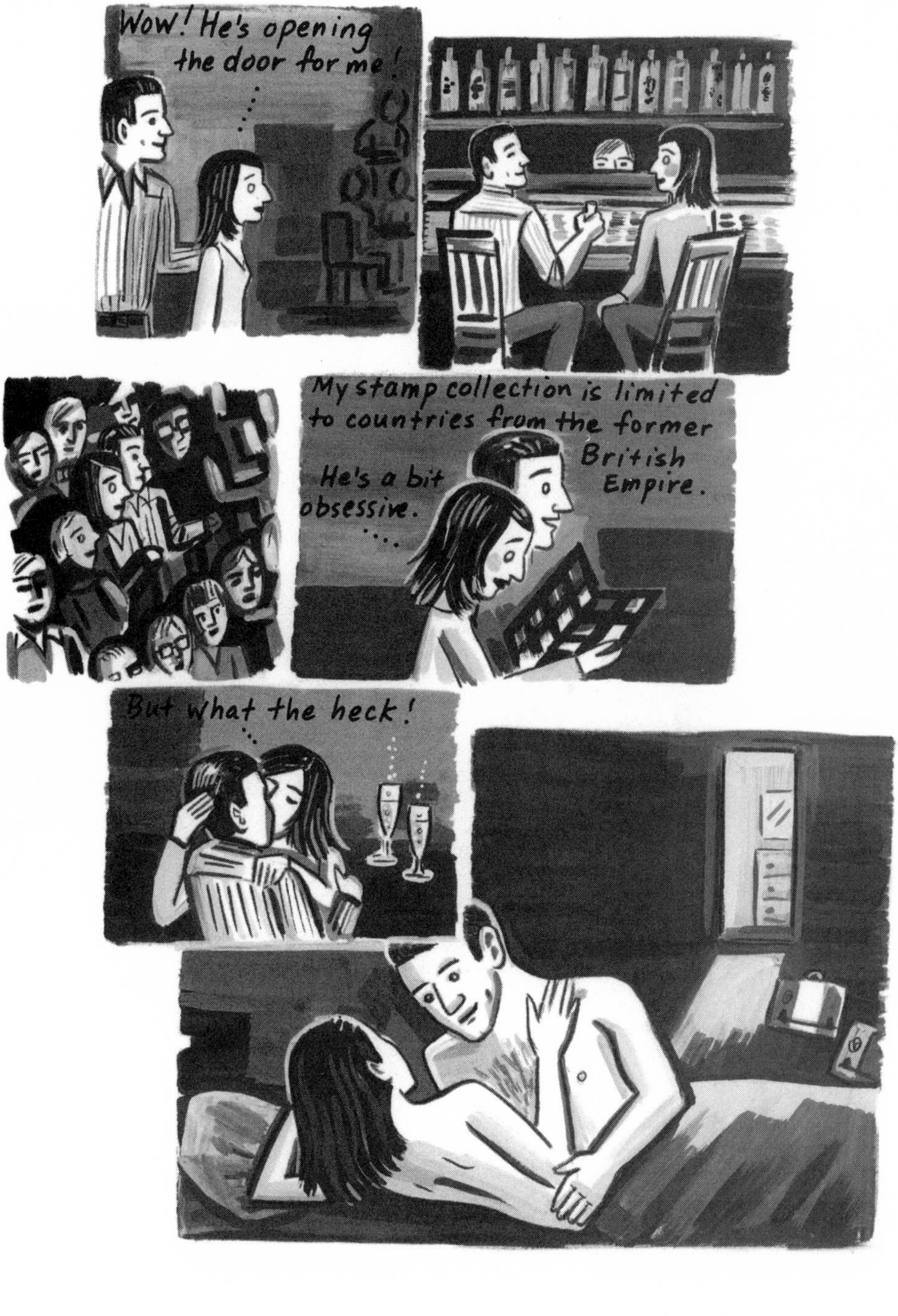
Wow! He's opening the door for me!
My stamp collection is limited to countries from the former British Empire.
He's a bit obsessive.
But what the heck!

I HAD SOME LOVELY TIMES WITH MR. SMITTEN.

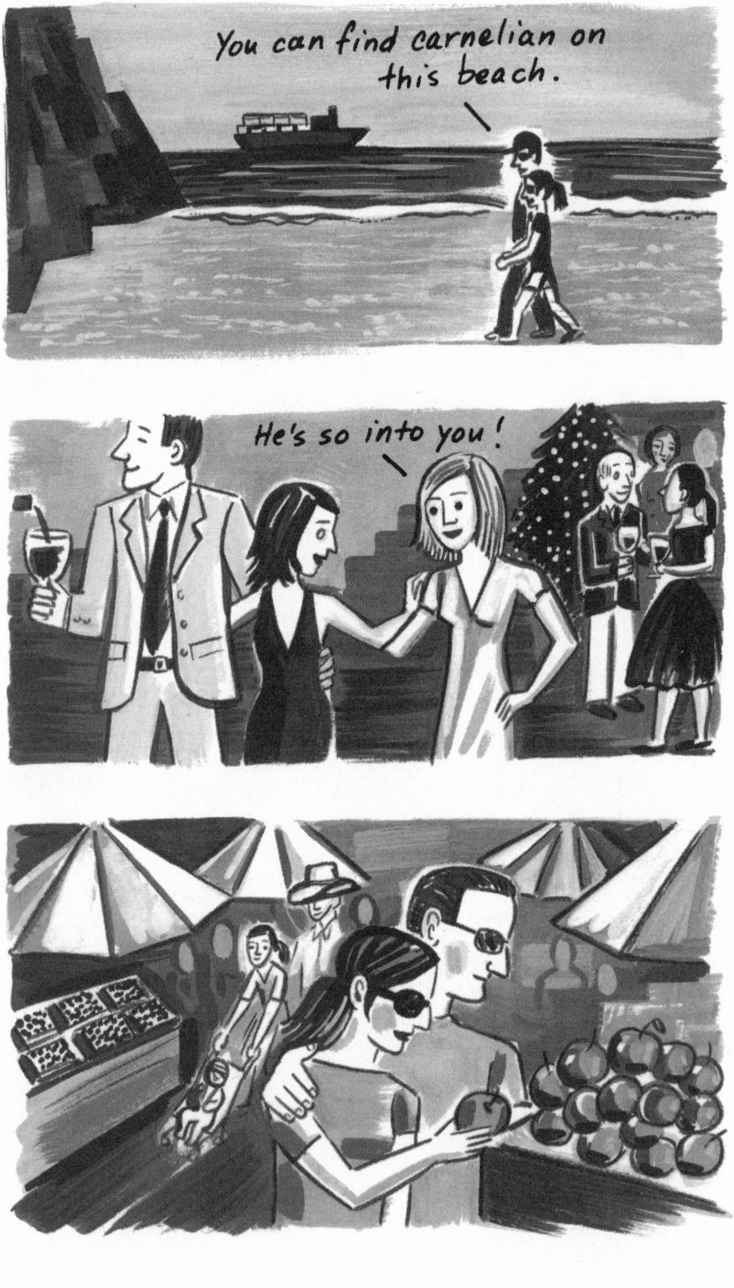
You can find carnelian on this beach.
He's so into you!

BUT OUR RELATIONSHIP ALWAYS TOOK A BACKSEAT TO HIS BUSINESS....

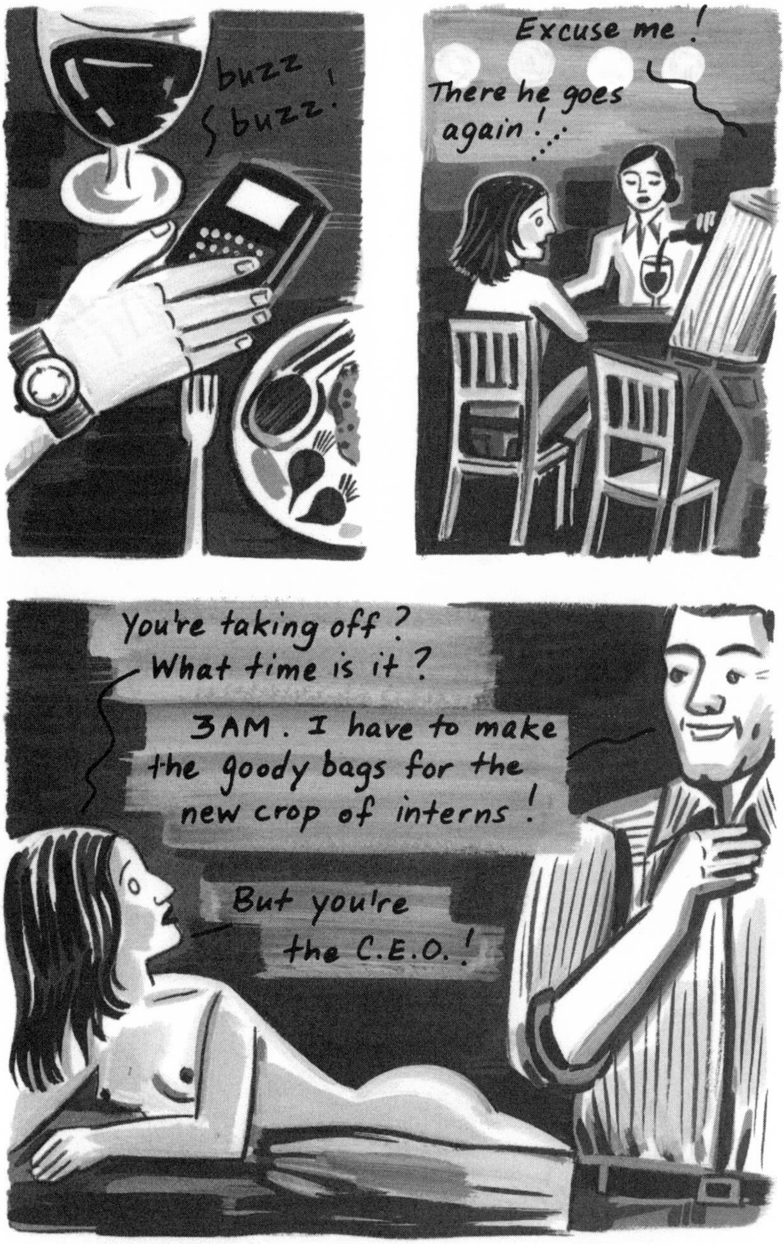
buzz buzz!
Excuse me!
There he goes again!...
You're taking off? What time is it?
3AM. I have to make the goody bags for the new crop of interns!
But you're the C.E.O.!

THINGS JUST TAPERED OFF.... MR. SMITTEN WAS MORE SMITTEN WITH HIS JOB THAN WITH ME.

FEELING SLIGHTLY MIFFED BY MY FIRST EXPERIENCE WITH A STRAIGHT MAN, I LEAP AT THE CHANCE TO VISIT MEXICO WITH SOME DEAR FRIENDS.

REBUILDING MECHANISM #4

"TRAVELS WITH GAY MEN"

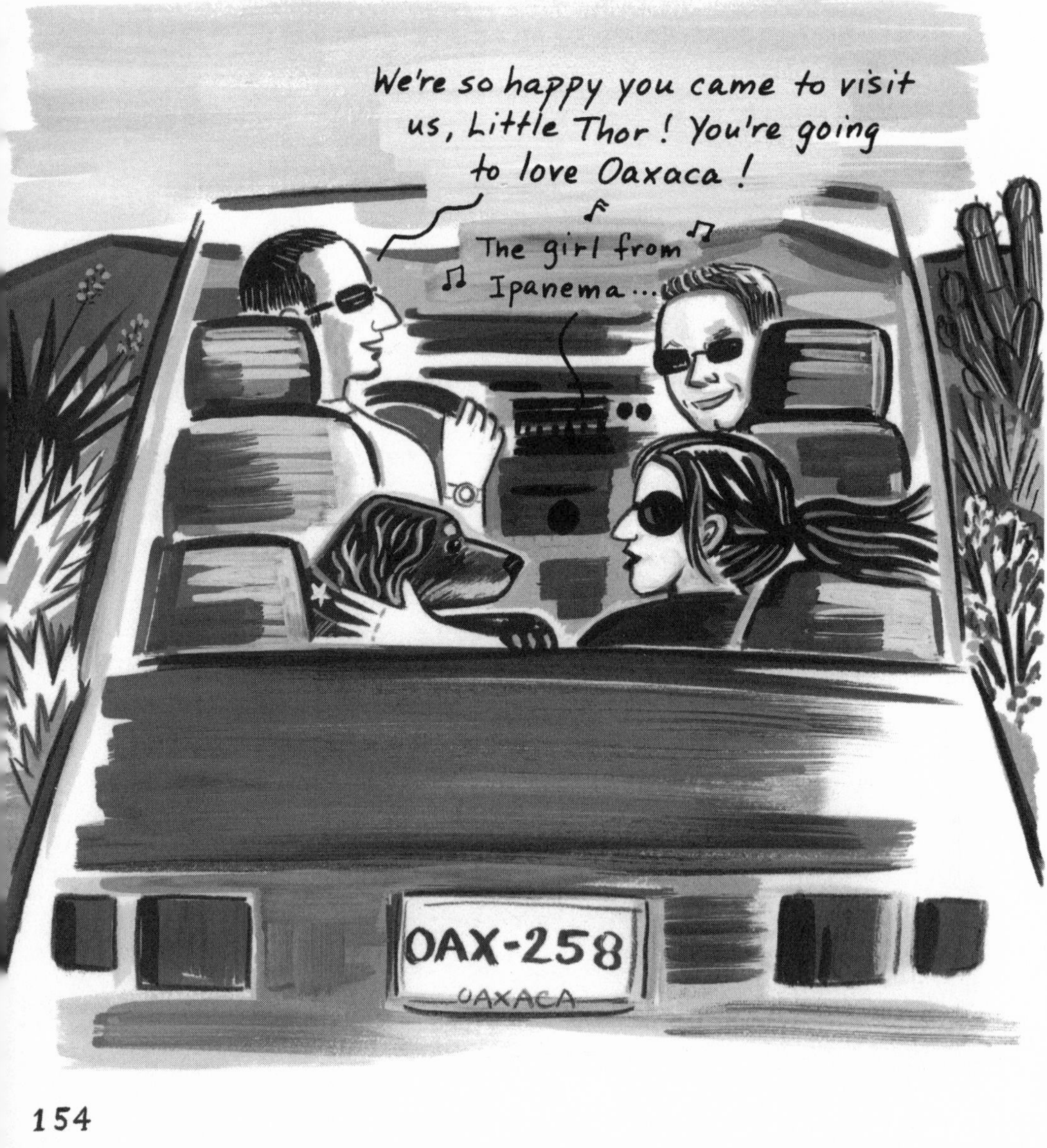

We're so happy you came to visit us, Little Thor! You're going to love Oaxaca!
The girl from Ipanema...
OAX-258
OAXACA

IT'S FORTUNATE THAT MY FRIEND RAÚL ENJOYS PLAYING TOUR GUIDE....

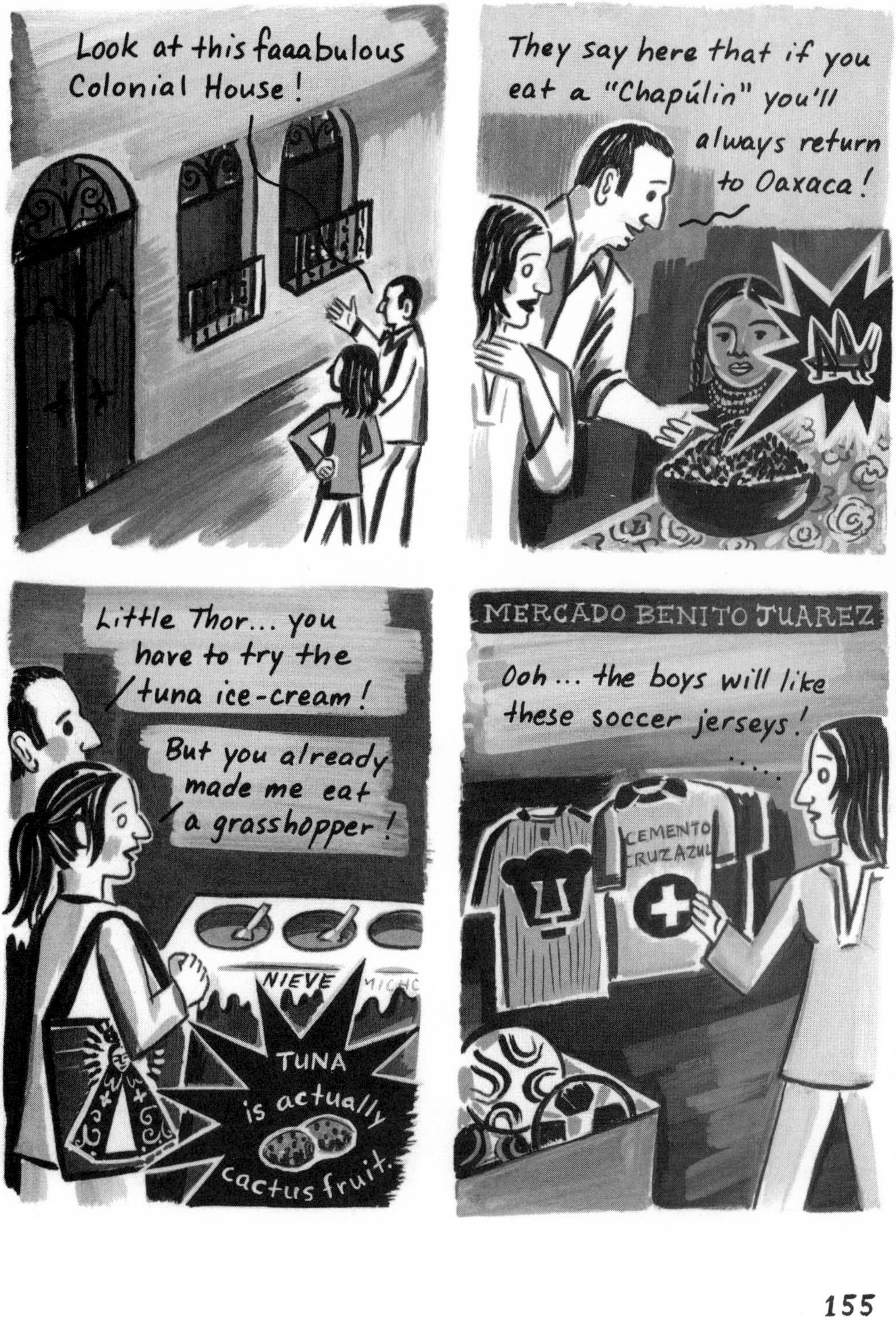
Look at this faaabulous Colonial House!
They say here that if you eat a "Chapúlin" you'll always return to Oaxaca!
Little Thor... you have to try the tuna ice-cream!
But you already made me eat a grasshopper!
NIEVE
TUNA is actually cactus fruit.
MERCADO BENITO JUAREZ
Ooh... the boys will like these soccer jerseys!
CEMENTO

THOUGH MOSTLY WE HUNT FOR REAL ESTATE.

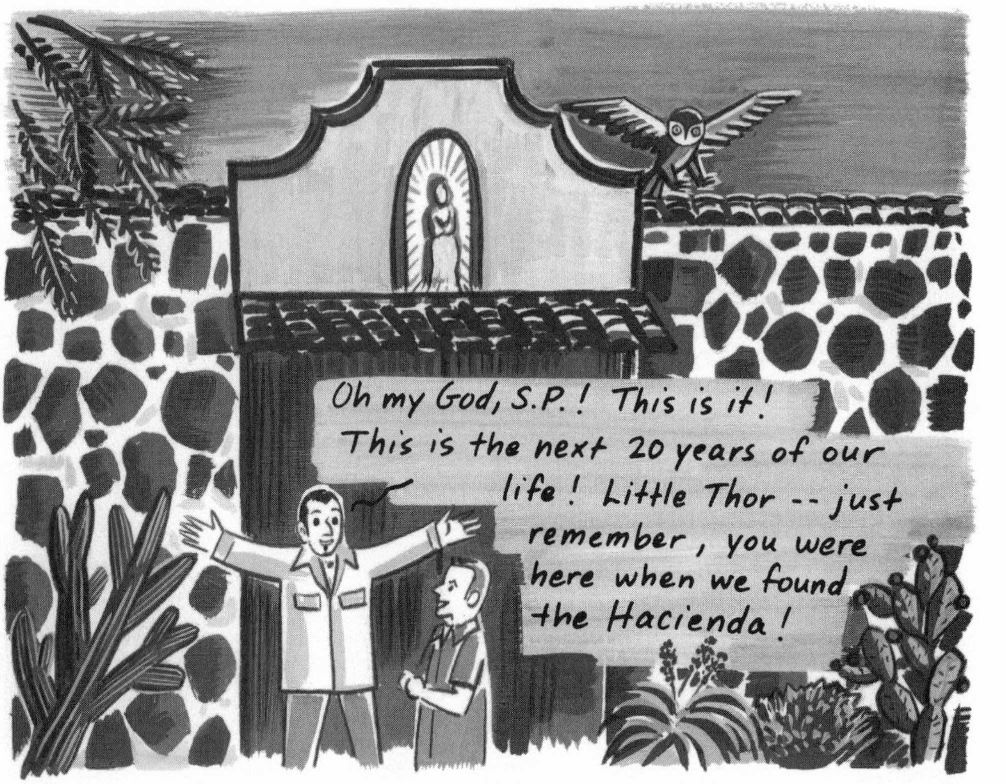
Oh my God, S.P.! This is it! This is the next 20 years of our life! Little Thor -- just remember, you were here when we found the Hacienda!

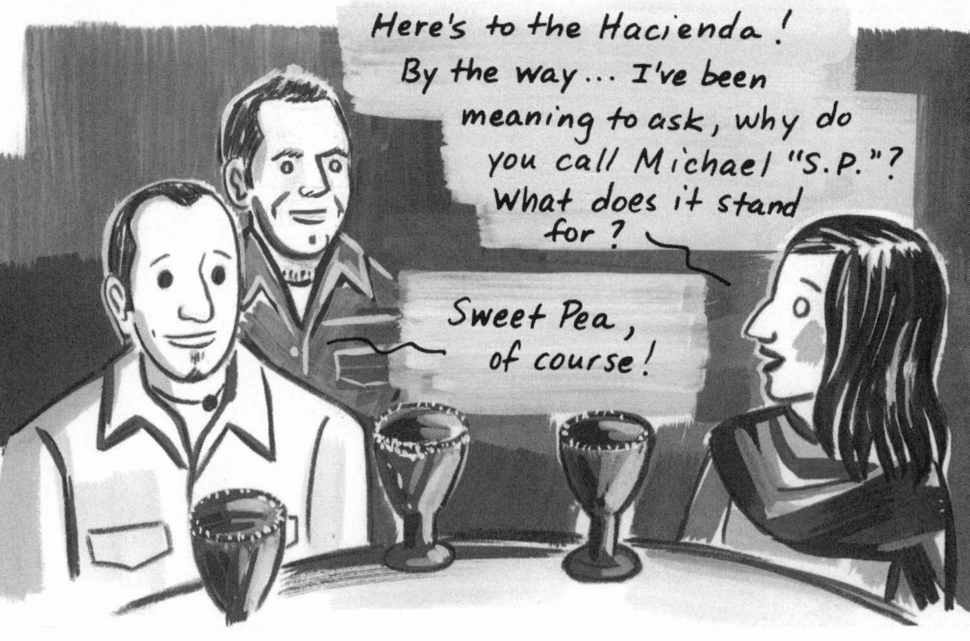
Here's to the Hacienda! By the way... I've been meaning to ask, why do you call Michael "S.P."? What does it stand for?
Sweet Pea, of course!

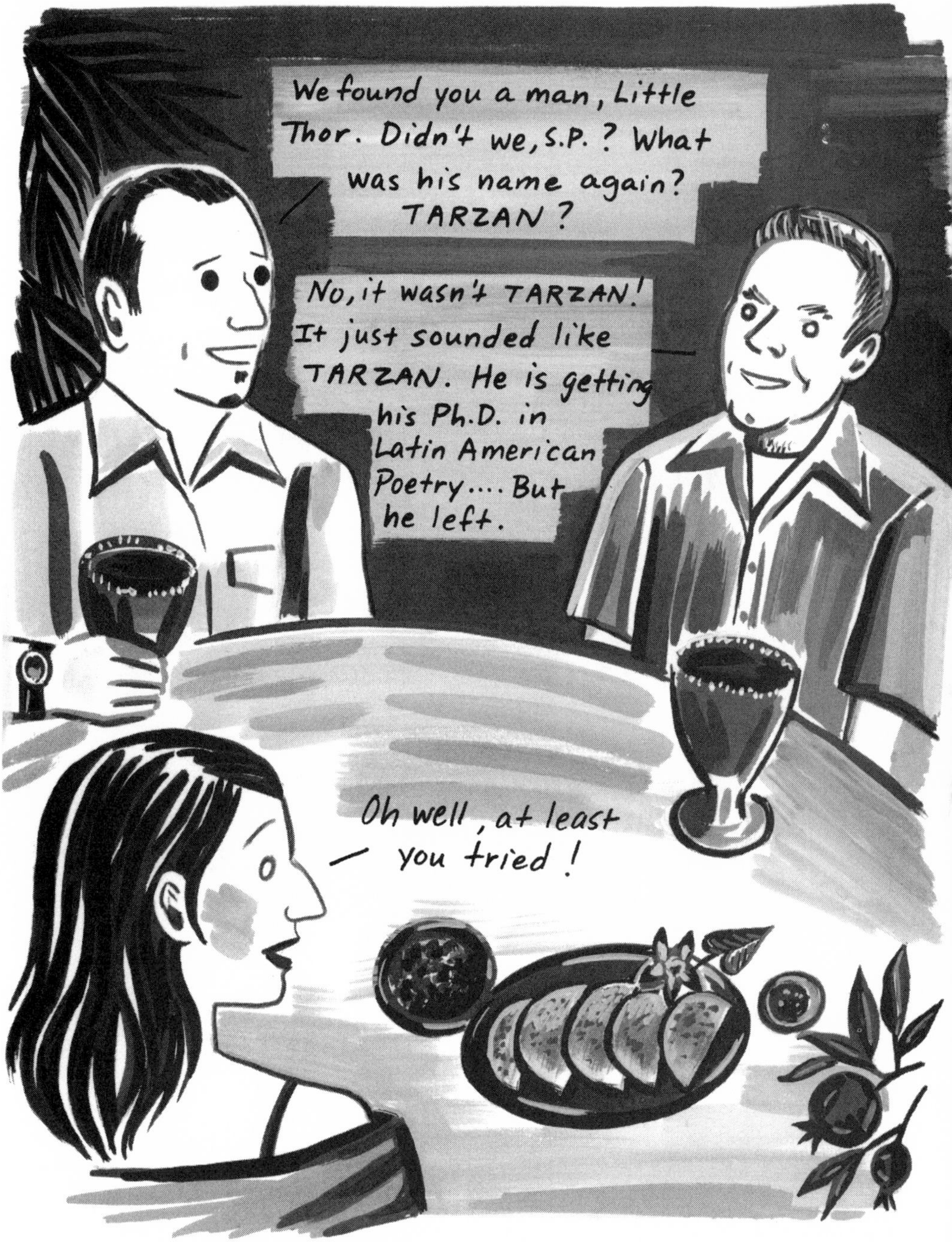
We found you a man, Little Thor. Didn't we, S.P.? What was his name again? TARZAN?
No, it wasn't TARZAN! It just sounded like TARZAN. He is getting his Ph.D. in Latin American Poetry.... But he left.
Oh well, at least you tried!

BUT THERE IS NO ESCAPING REALITY! UPON MY RETURN, THE CONFLICT RESUMES.

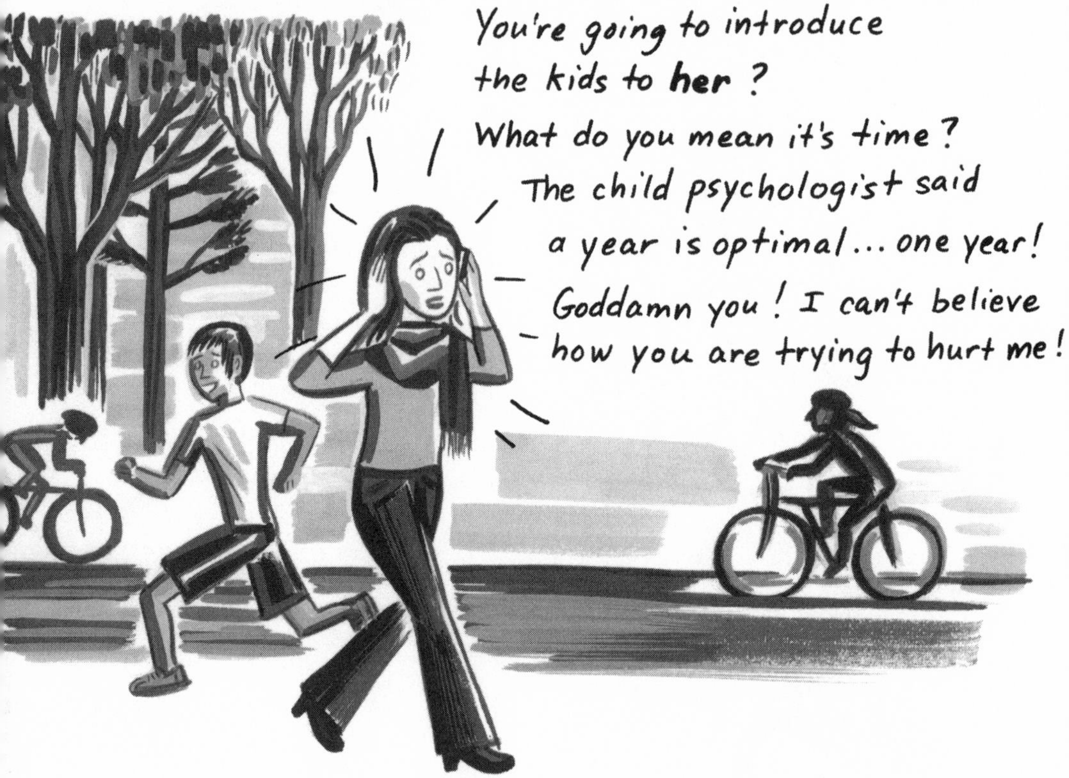
You're going to introduce the kids to **her** ?
What do you mean it's time?
The child psychologist said a year is optimal... one year!
Goddamn you! I can't believe how you are trying to hurt me!

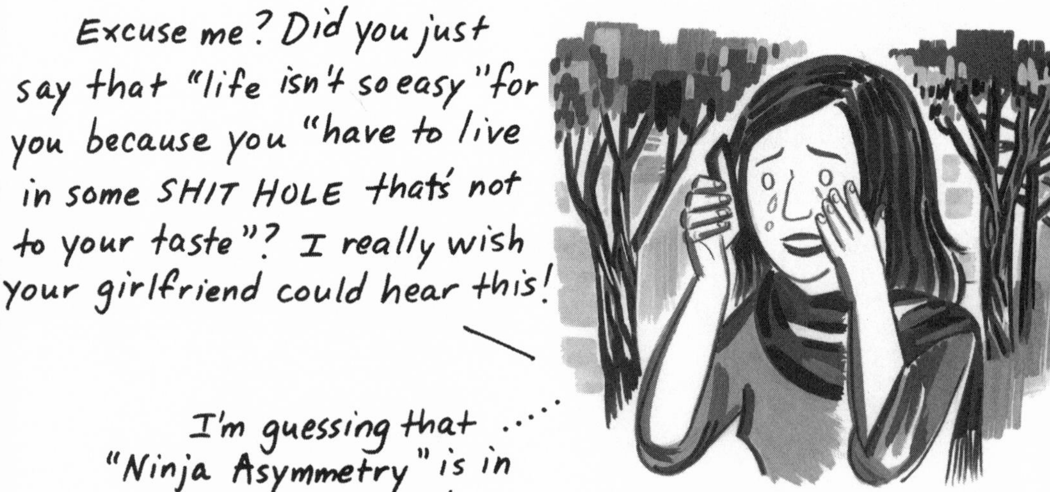
Excuse me? Did you just say that "life isn't so easy" for you because you "have to live in some SHIT HOLE that's not to your taste"? I really wish your girlfriend could hear this!
I'm guessing that ... "Ninja Asymmetry" is in the closet already!

THE MAN HAS NO BOUNDARIES. HE OCCASIONALLY MAKES AN APPEARANCE WHEN HE FEELS THE NEED.

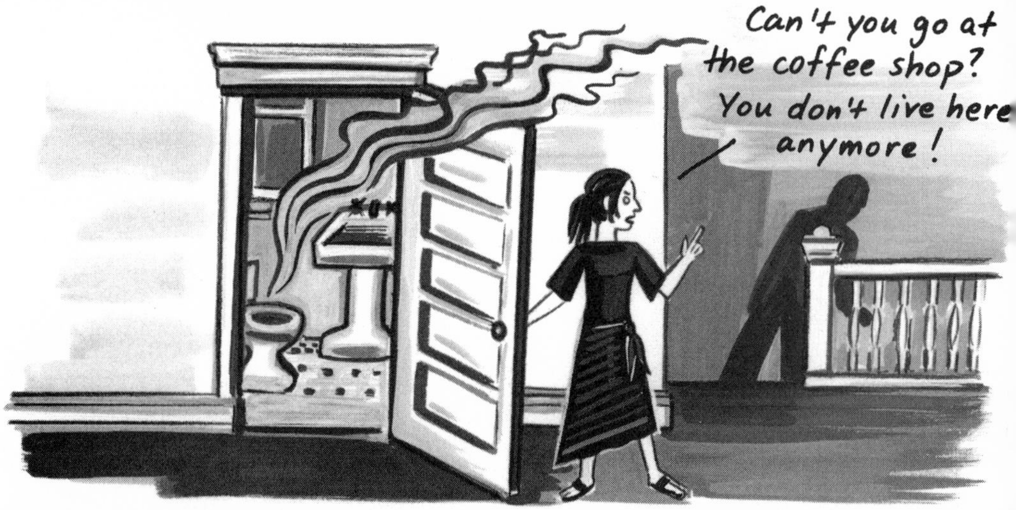

Can't you go at the coffee shop? You don't live here anymore!

AND WHEN MY BOUNDARIES ARE CHALLENGED I RETALIATE BY PUSHING HIS BUTTONS:

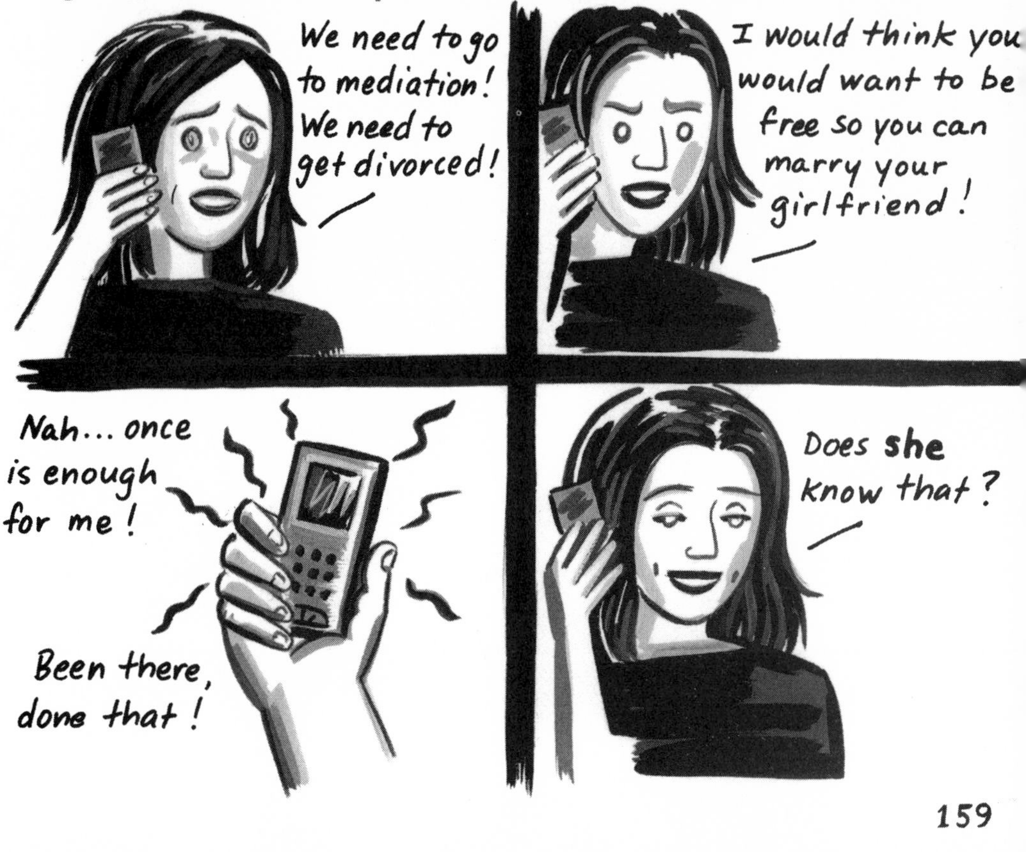

We need to go to mediation! We need to get divorced!
I would think you would want to be free so you can marry your girlfriend!
Nah... once is enough for me!
Been there, done that!
Does **she** know that?

COME TO THINK OF IT, X WAS NEVER CIRCUMSPECT WHEN IT CAME TO OPENING HIS MOUTH. "UNFILTERED" IS THE ADJECTIVE MOST OFTEN APPLIED TO HIM.

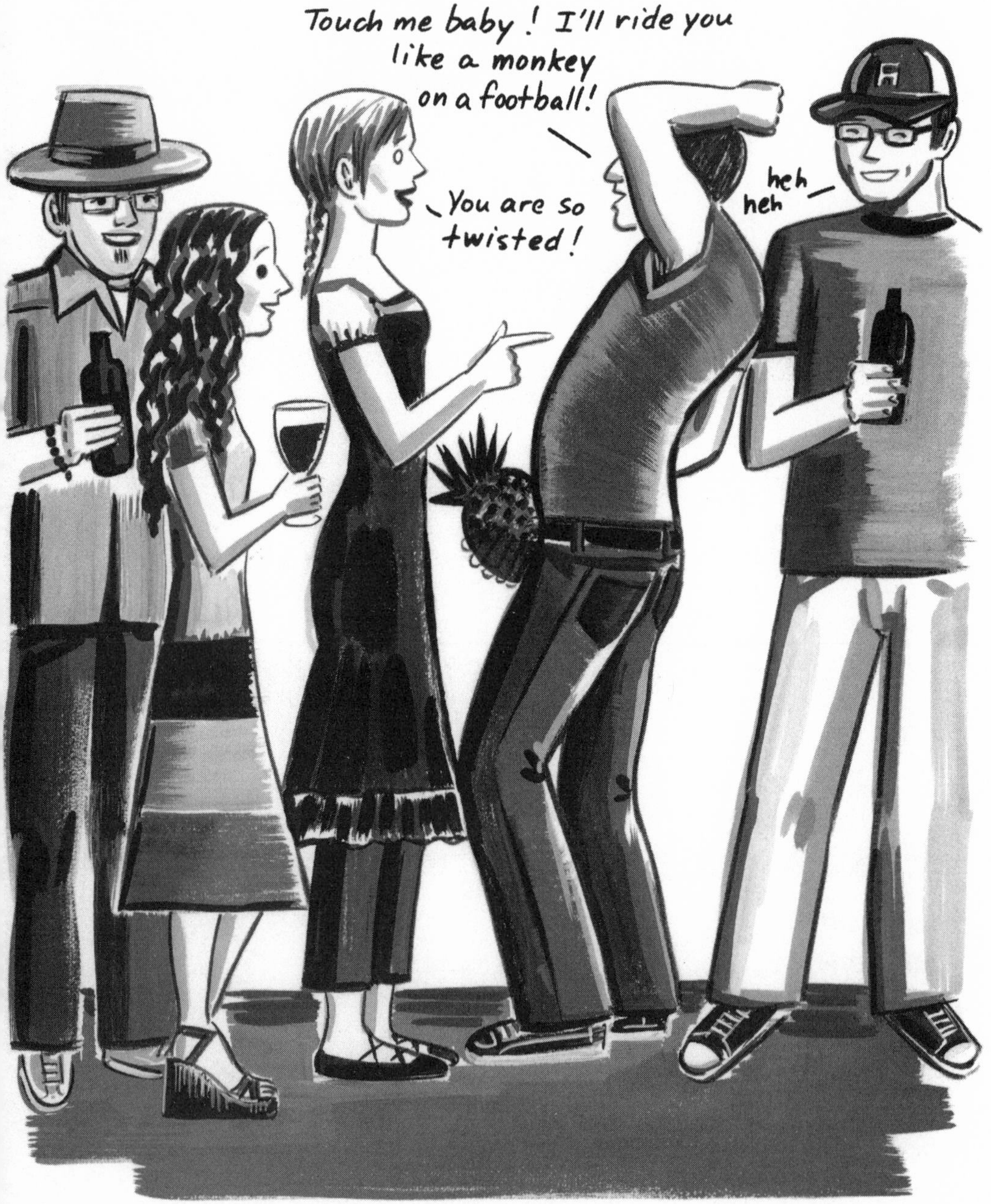

Touch me baby! I'll ride you like a monkey on a football!
You are so twisted!
heh heh

AND THOUGH HE COULD BE THE LIFE OF THE PARTY, HE INVARIABLY OFFENDED, EITHER UNCONSCIOUSLY OR BY DESIGN.

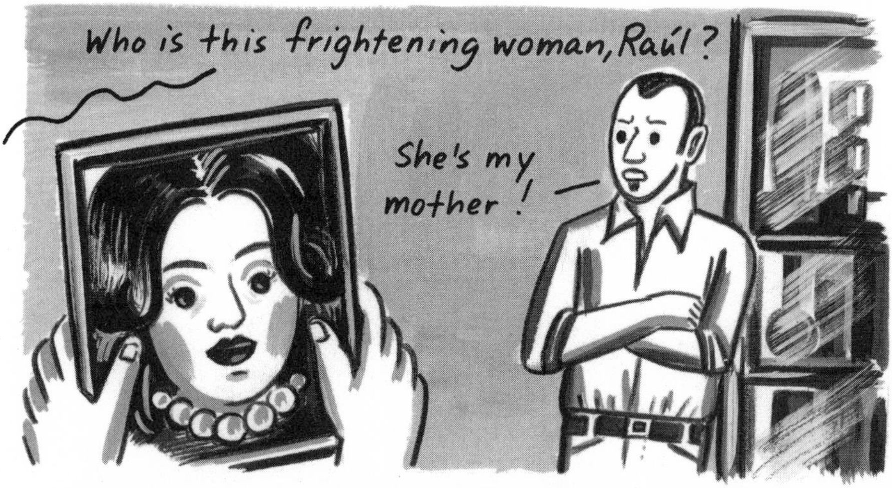
Who is this frightening woman, Raúl?
She's my mother!

IF HE DISLIKED SOMEONE, HE WENT STRAIGHT FOR THE JUGULAR!

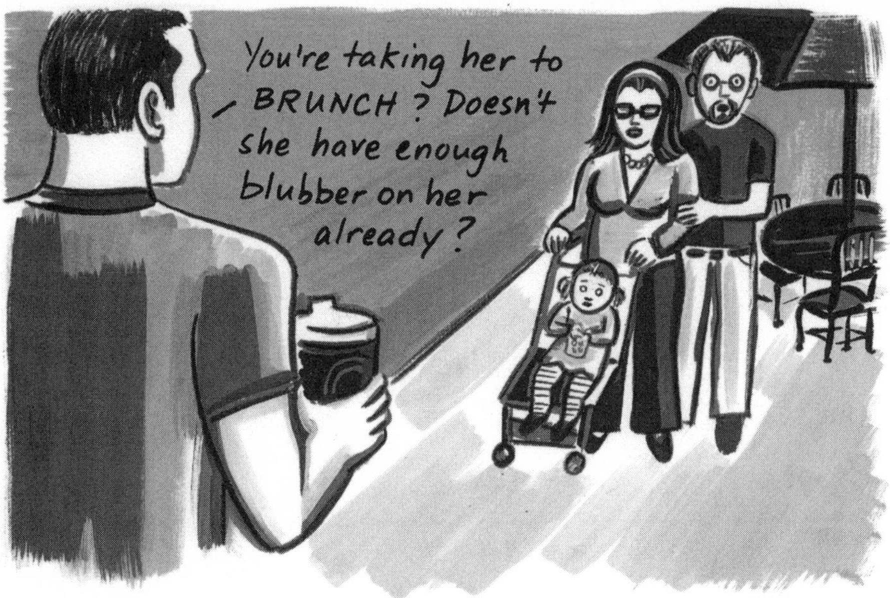
You're taking her to BRUNCH? Doesn't she have enough blubber on her already?

WHICH MEANT I WAS WELL SCHOOLED IN THE ART OF EXCUSE-MAKING,

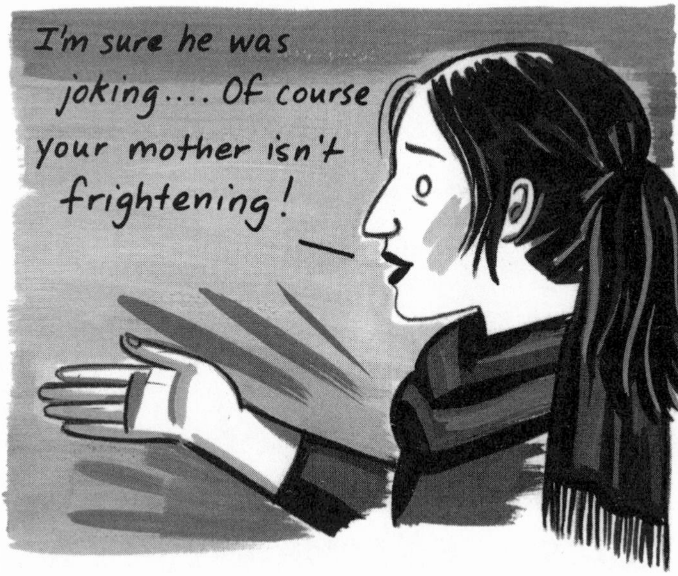
I'm sure he was joking.... Of course your mother isn't frightening!

OR TRYING TO COACH AN UNWILLING PARTICIPANT.

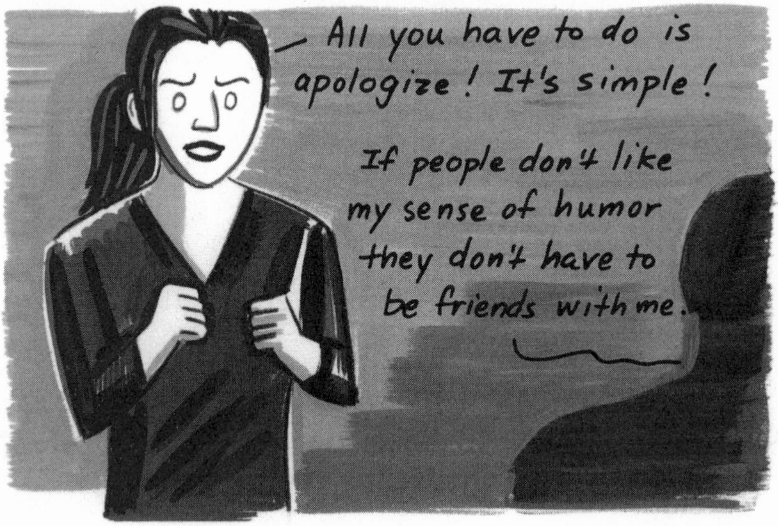
All you have to do is apologize! It's simple!
If people don't like my sense of humor they don't have to be friends with me...

NOW, THERE ARE NO MORE MESSES TO CLEAN UP EXCEPT MY OWN!

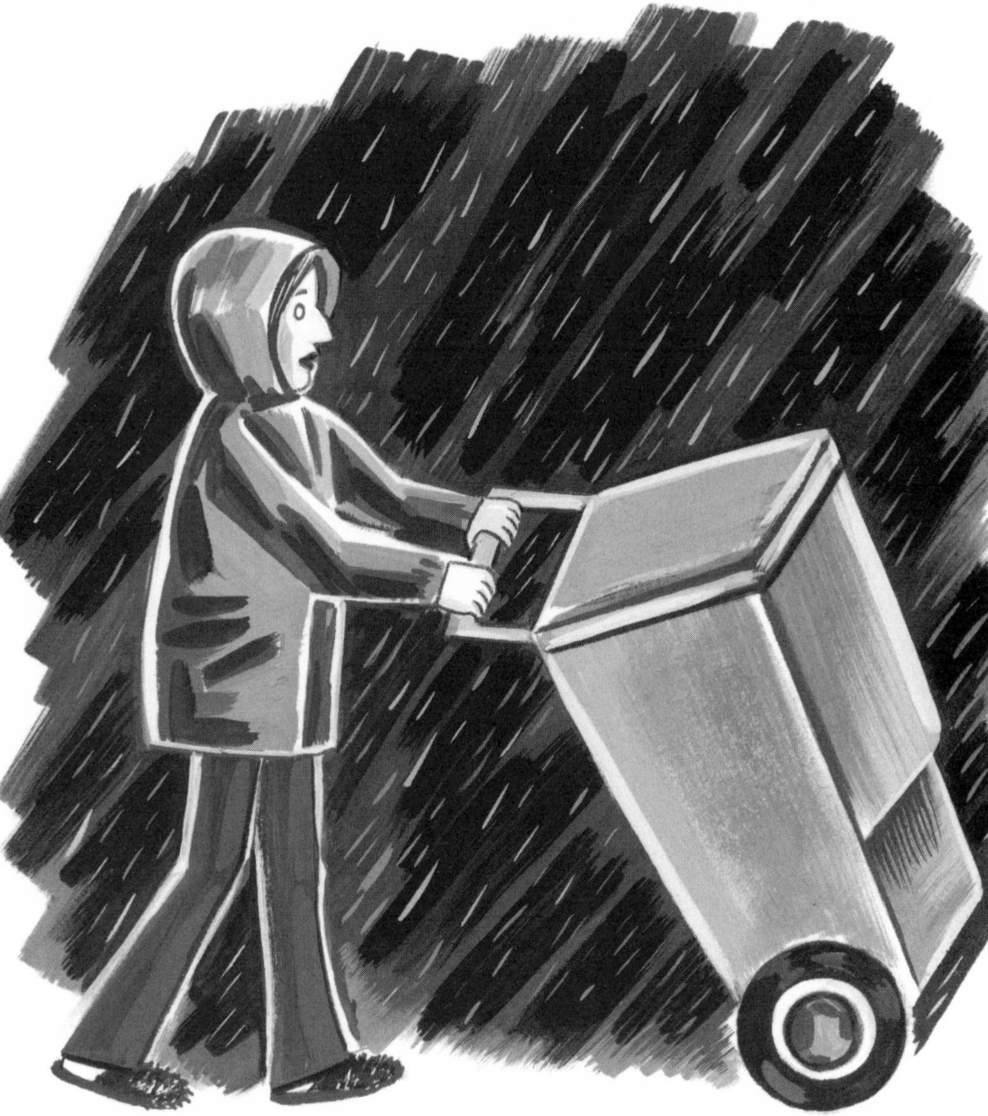

BUT THERE'S A LOT MORE TO BEING A SINGLE WOMAN THAN CHANGING LIGHTBULBS AND TAKING OUT THE TRASH ALL BY YOURSELF.

A SERIES OF MIDWEEK E-MAILS HERALDS A TIME-HONORED INSTITUTION AMONG SINGLE WOMEN....

FRIDAY EVENING GIRLS' NIGHT OUT!

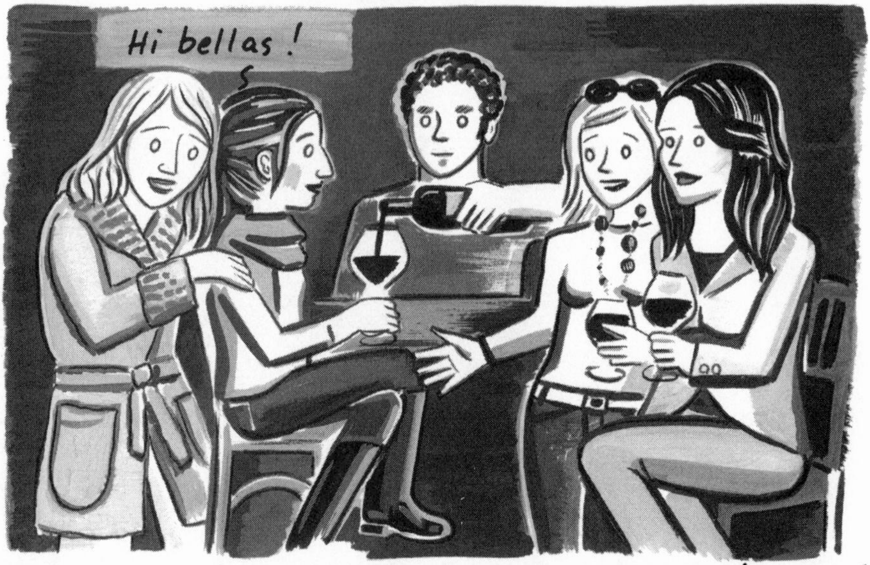
Hi bellas!

It's usually at the same venue where the cute bartender keeps a careful eye on the horizon line of the wineglasses.

MY CONCERN IS THAT, AS YEARS PASS, GIRLS' NIGHT OUT BEGINS TO LOOK MORE LIKE THIS:

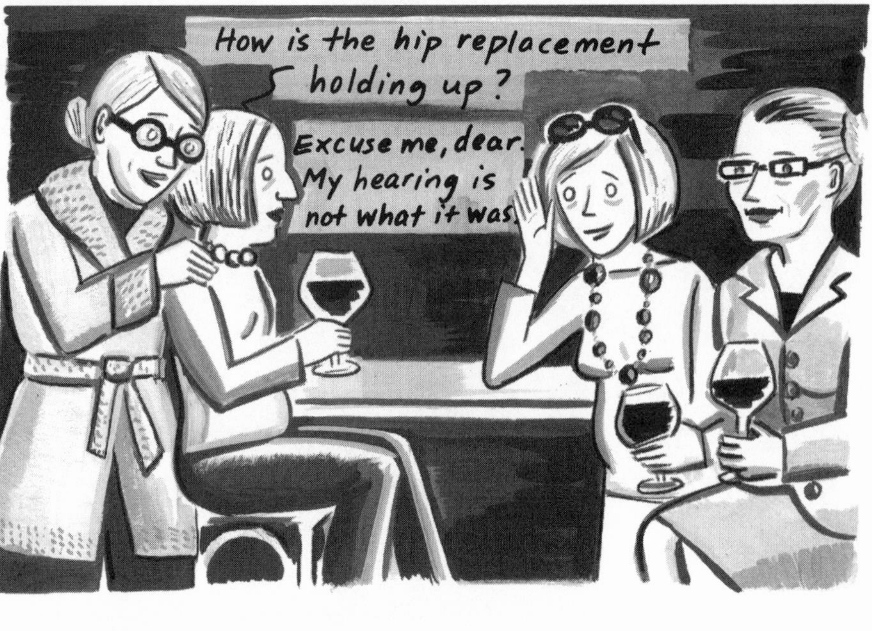
How is the hip replacement holding up?
Excuse me, dear. My hearing is not what it was.

OR WORSE, IT'S JUST ME AND A FEW CHERISHED COMPANIONS AT HOME....

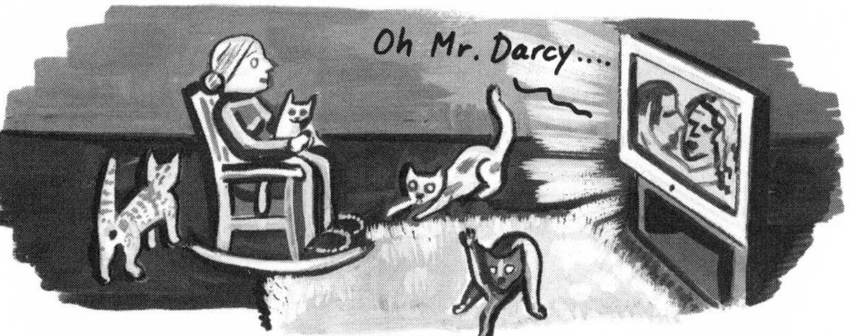
Oh Mr. Darcy....

PERHAPS AS A PRECAUTION I SHOULD ORGANIZE THE "OLD LADY" COMMUNE!

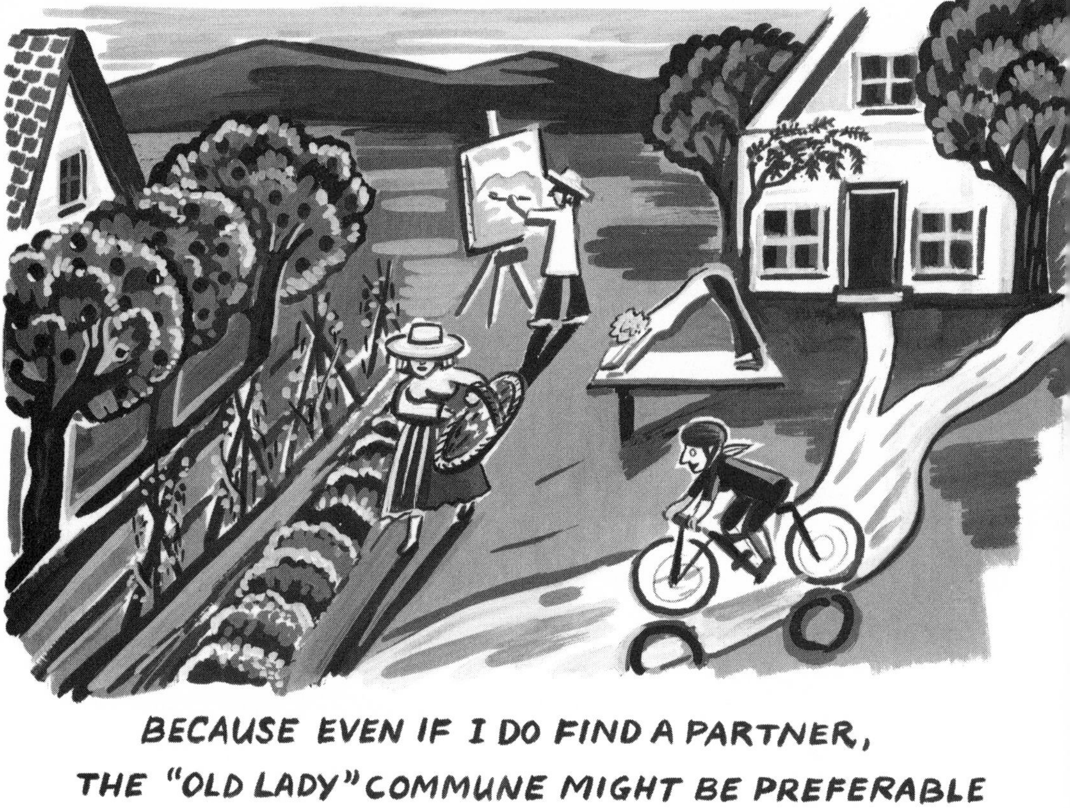

BECAUSE EVEN IF I DO FIND A PARTNER, THE "OLD LADY" COMMUNE MIGHT BE PREFERABLE TO THE SPECTER OF THIS:

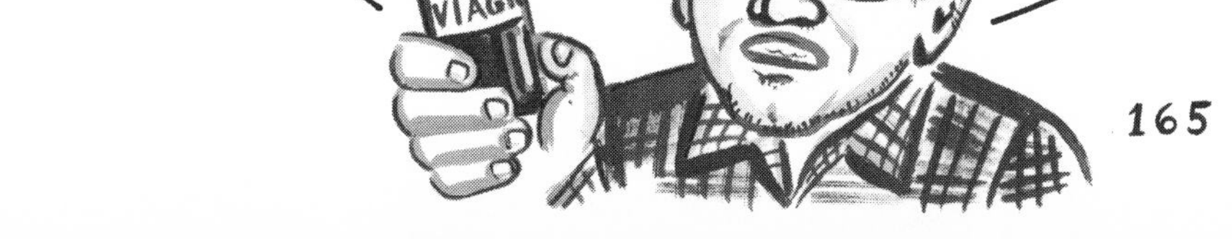
Where are my glasses!
I can't read the label!
VIAGR

WHO KNOWS-- I MIGHT BE ALONE THE REST OF MY LIFE. I'D BETTER TRY TO REIGNITE MY PASSION! I HALFHEARTEDLY ATTEMPT TO PAINT.

REBUILDING MECHANISM ※5 "CREATIVITY"

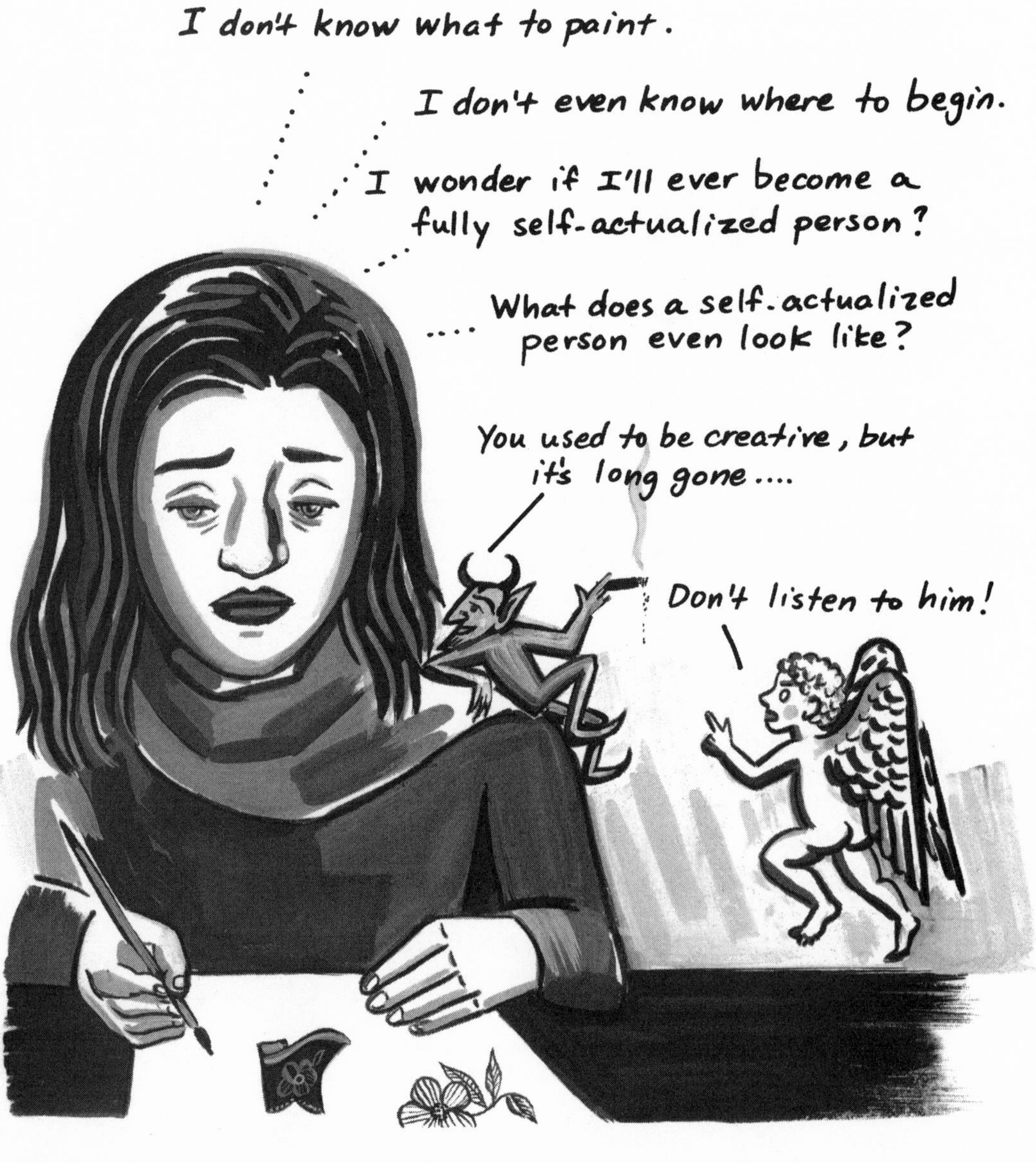

I don't know what to paint.
I don't even know where to begin.
I wonder if I'll ever become a fully self-actualized person?
What does a self-actualized person even look like?
You used to be creative, but it's long gone....
Don't listen to him!

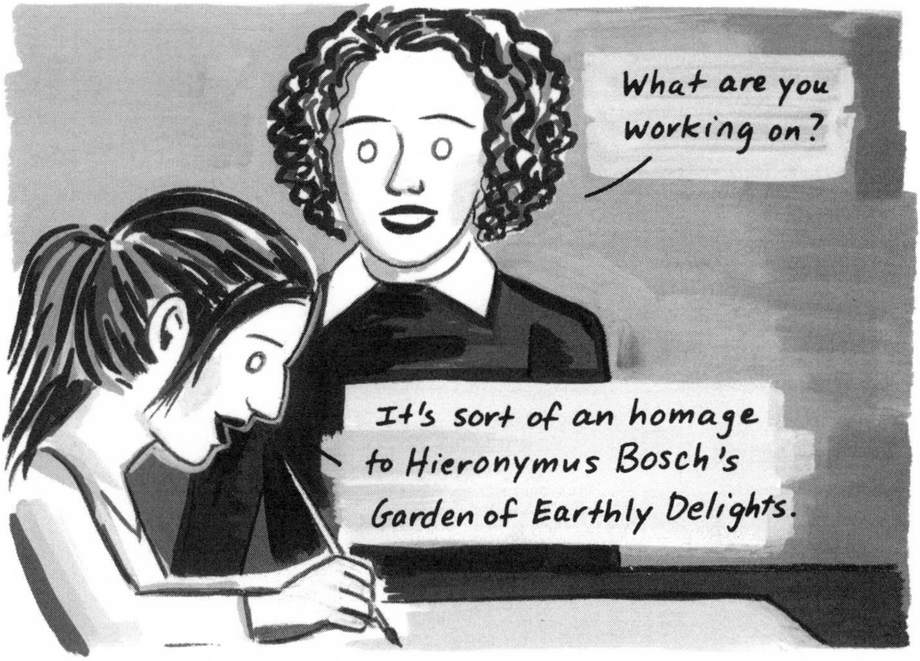
What are you working on?
It's sort of an homage to Hieronymus Bosch's Garden of Earthly Delights.

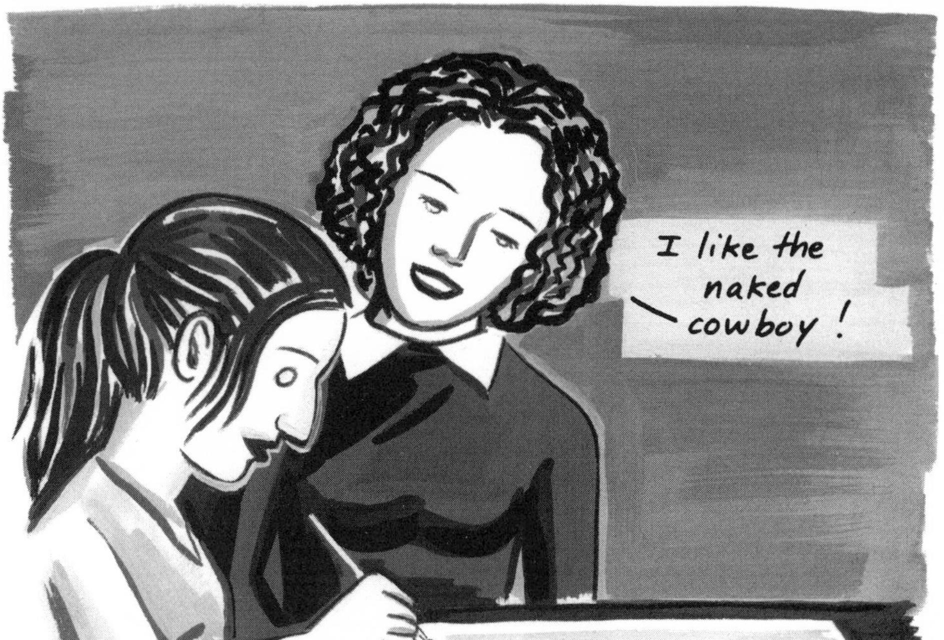
I like the naked cowboy!

WHEN I LEAST EXPECT IT, OPPORTUNITY LANDS IN MY LAP.

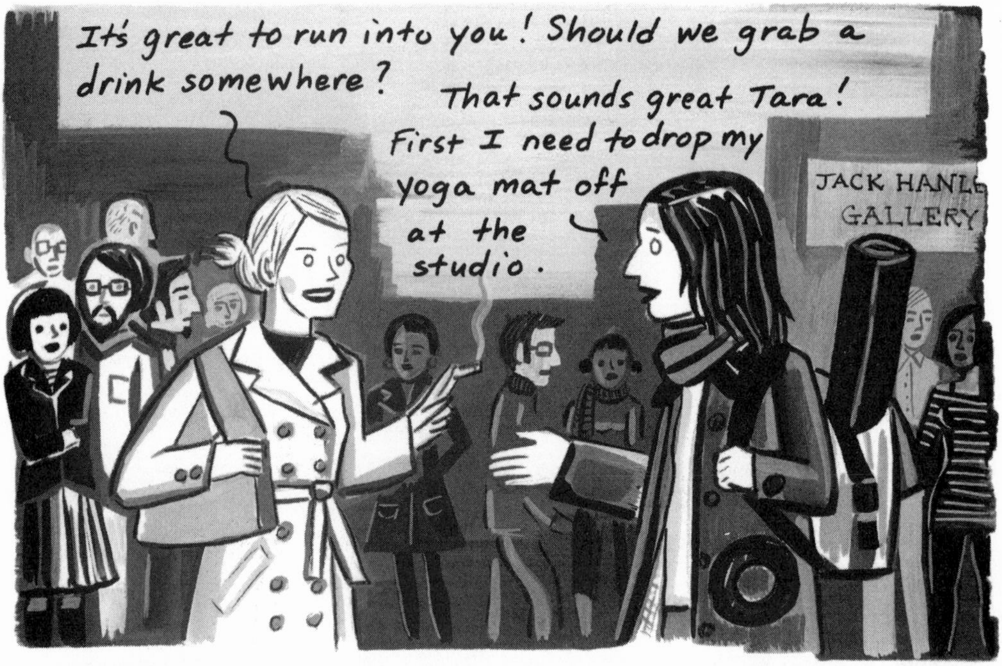
It's great to run into you! Should we grab a drink somewhere?
That sounds great Tara! First I need to drop my yoga mat off at the studio.
JACK HANL
GALLERY

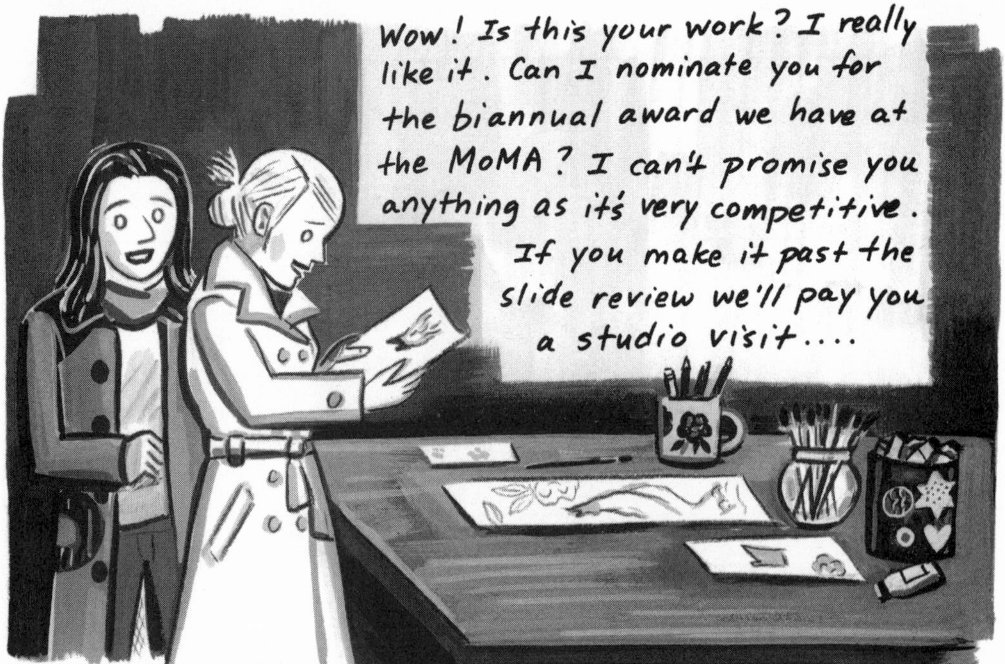
Wow! Is this your work? I really like it. Can I nominate you for the biannual award we have at the MoMA? I can't promise you anything as it's very competitive. If you make it past the slide review we'll pay you a studio visit....

Words of Wise Women

"You gain strength, courage, and confidence in every experience in which you stop to look fear in the face. You are able to say to yourself, I have lived through this horror. I can take the next thing that comes along."

Eleanor Roosevelt

I HAVE ONE MONTH TO GET TWELVE GOOD PAINTINGS MADE! LUCKILY I AM AN ARTIST WHO NEEDS A SERIOUS DEADLINE. IN FACT, I'M RATHER SUSPICIOUS OF ARTISTS WHO FEEL COMPELLED TO "EXPRESS THEMSELVES."

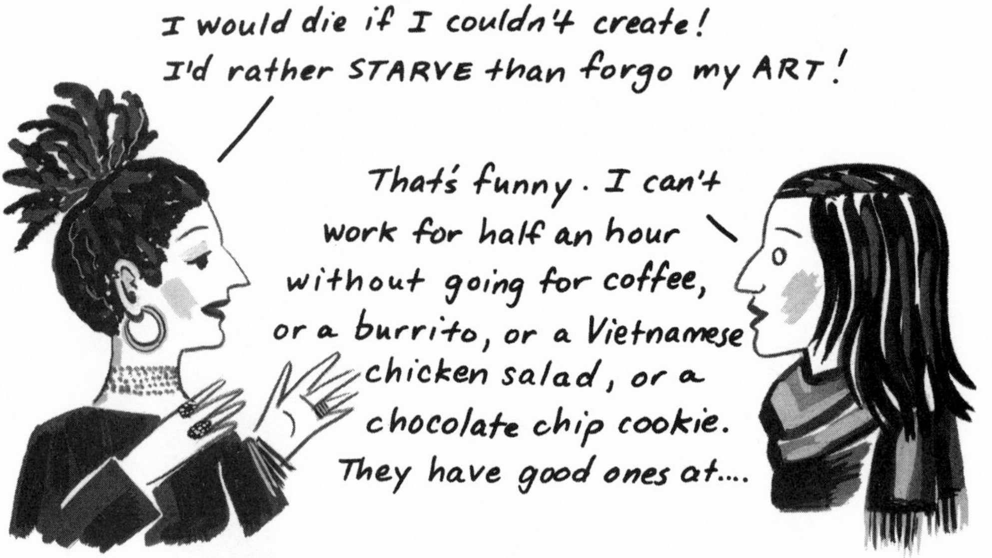
I would die if I couldn't create! I'd rather STARVE than forgo my ART!
That's funny. I can't work for half an hour without going for coffee, or a burrito, or a Vietnamese chicken salad, or a chocolate chip cookie. They have good ones at....

FOR THE FIRST TIME IN YEARS I AM EXCITED ABOUT MY WORK!

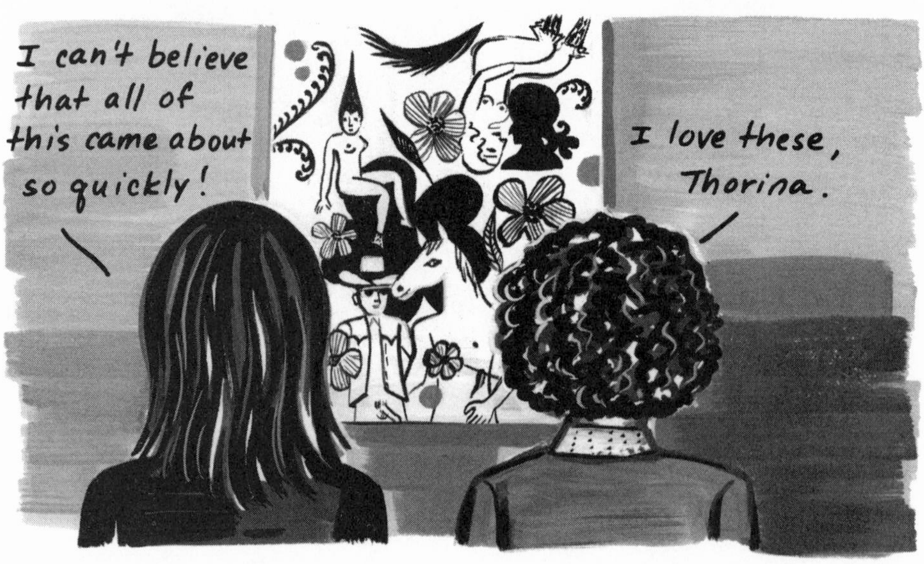
I can't believe that all of this came about so quickly!
I love these, Thorina.

Words of Wise Women

"Just don't give up trying to do what you really want to do. Where there is love and inspiration, I don't think you can go wrong."

Ella Fitzgerald

OF COURSE THERE ARE UPS AND DOWNS.

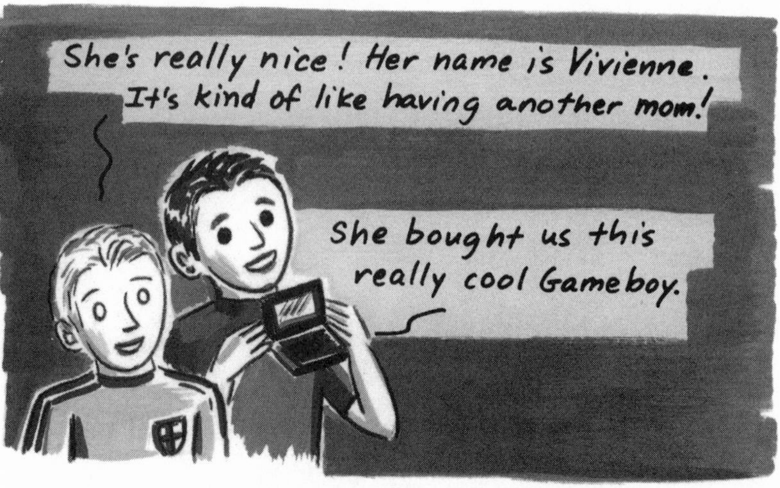
She's really nice! Her name is Vivienne. It's kind of like having another mom!
She bought us this really cool Gameboy.

SOME THINGS STILL HURT, BUT I HAVE TO MAKE THE BEST OF MY NEW LIFE. THERE ARE SO MANY THINGS TO ENJOY!

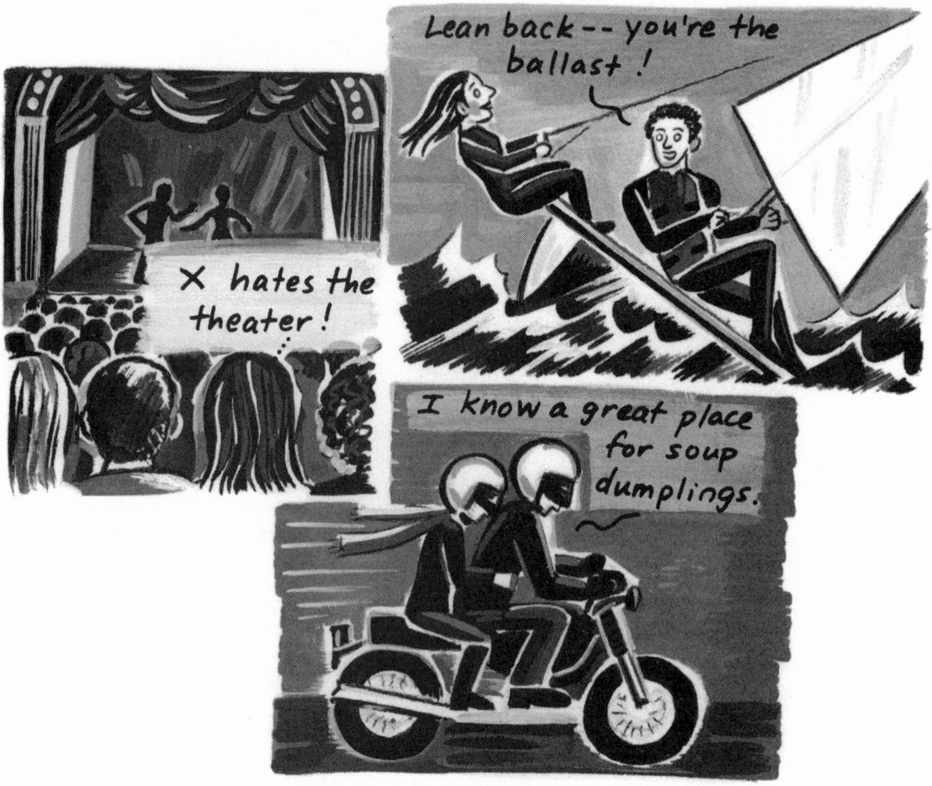
X hates the theater!
Lean back -- you're the ballast!
I know a great place for soup dumplings.

SO WHEN I'M WITH THE KIDS, I AM REFRESHED AND READY TO BE **ON!**

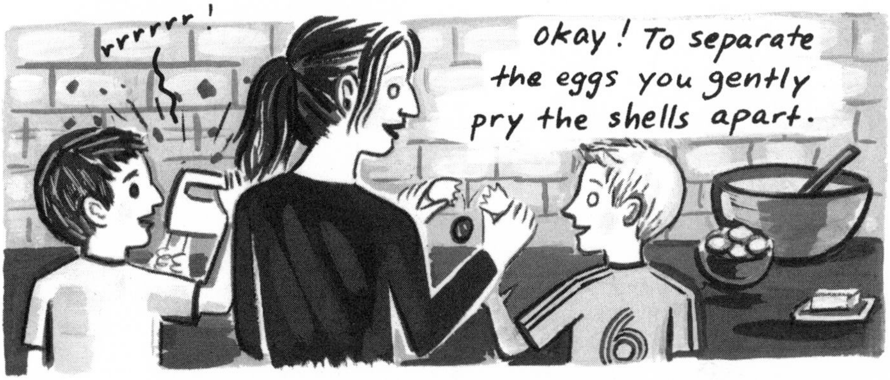
rrrrrr!
Okay! To separate the eggs you gently pry the shells apart.

AND THOUGH I DIDN'T WIN THE AWARD AT THE MoMA, I DID HAVE MY FIRST GALLERY SHOW.

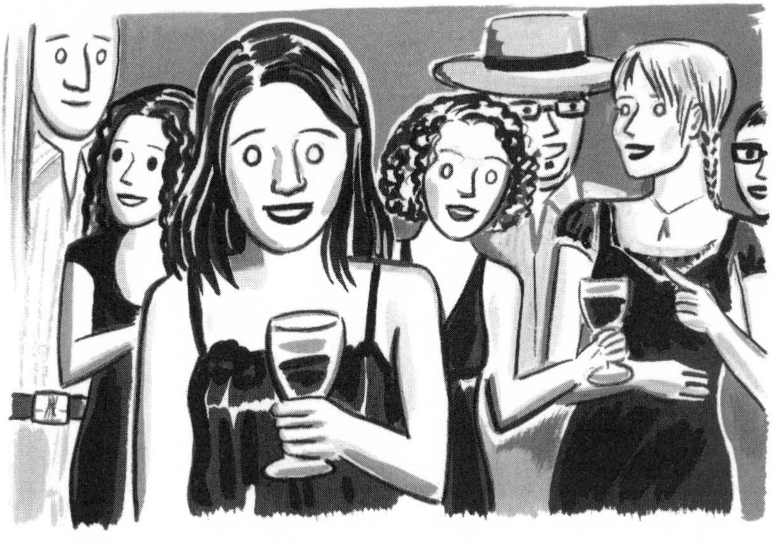

I BEGIN TO DREAM OF POSSIBILITIES....

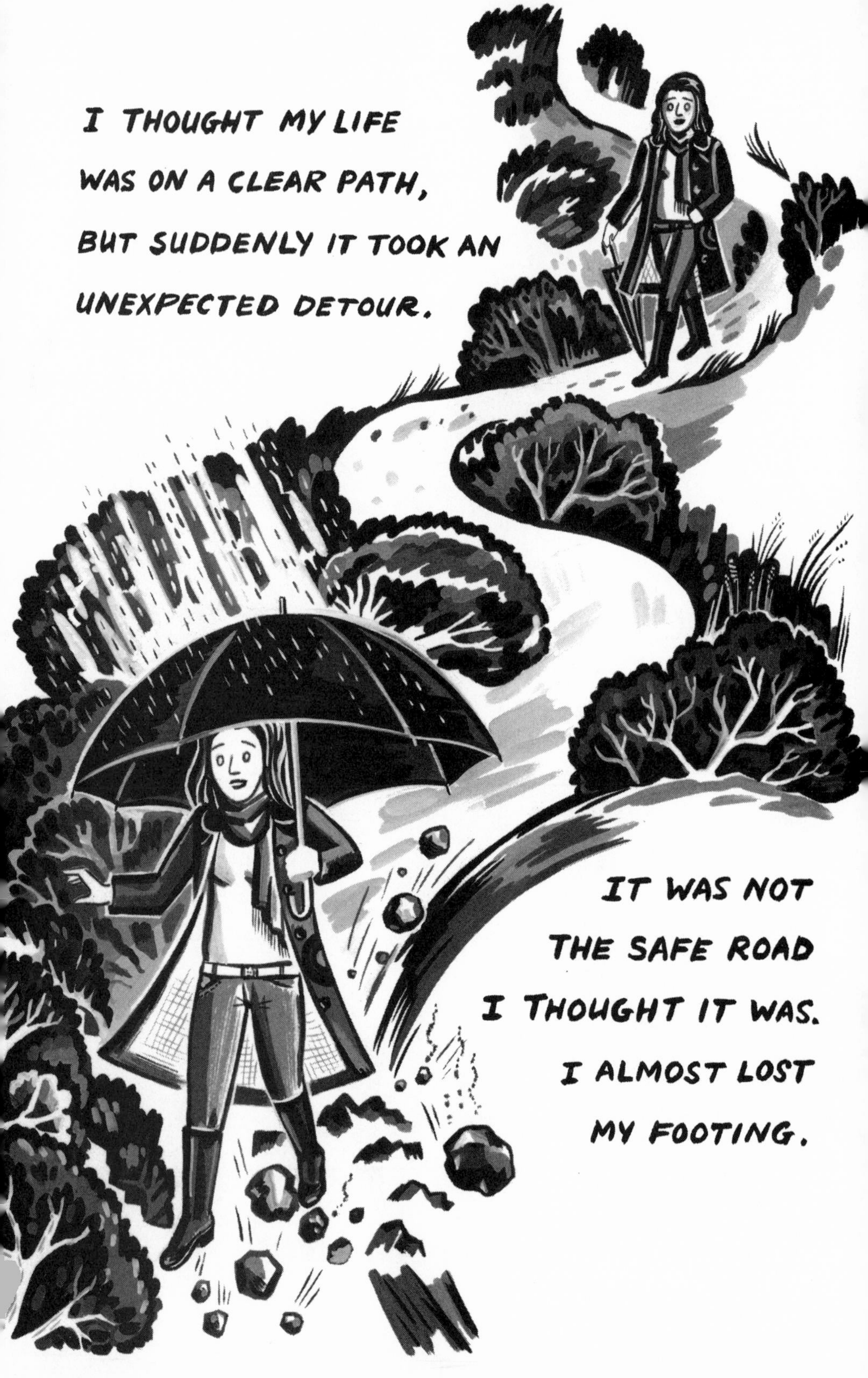
I THOUGHT MY LIFE WAS ON A CLEAR PATH, BUT SUDDENLY IT TOOK AN UNEXPECTED DETOUR.
IT WAS NOT THE SAFE ROAD I THOUGHT IT WAS. I ALMOST LOST MY FOOTING.

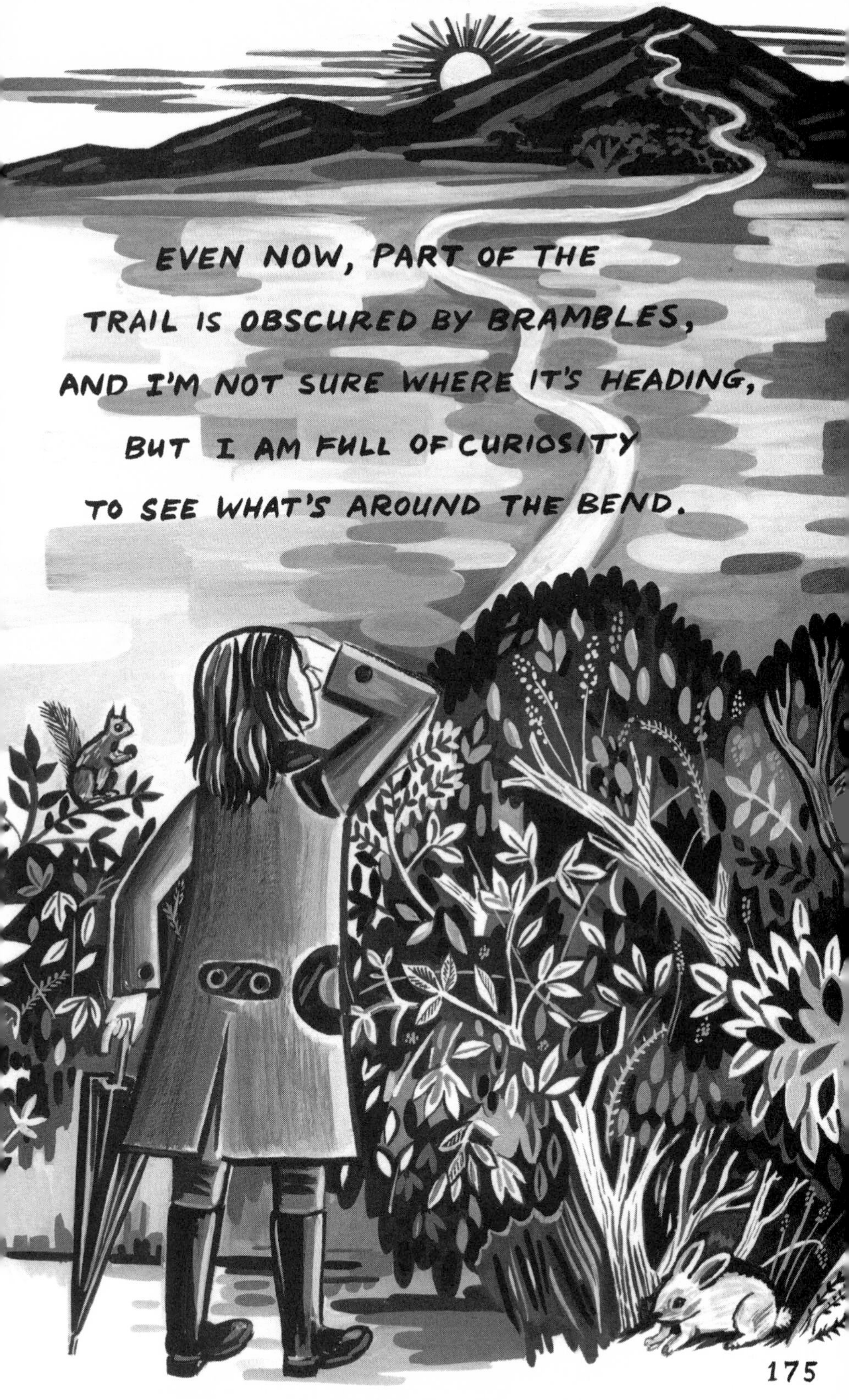
EVEN NOW, PART OF THE
TRAIL IS OBSCURED BY BRAMBLES,
AND I'M NOT SURE WHERE IT'S HEADING,
BUT I AM FULL OF CURIOSITY
TO SEE WHAT'S AROUND THE BEND.